Mosaic 2

Reading

4th Edition

Brenda Wegmann

Miki Knezevic

Marilyn Bernstein

McGraw-Hill Contemporary

McGraw-Hill/Contemporary

A Division of The McGraw·Hill Companies

Mosaic 2 Reading, 4th Edition

Published by McGraw-Hill/Contemporary, a business unit of The McGraw-Hill Companies, Inc.,
1221 Avenue of the Americas, New York, NY 10020. Copyright © 2002, 1996, 1990, 1985 by
The McGraw-Hill Companies, Inc. All rights reserved. No part of this publication may be
reproduced or distributed in any form or by any means, or stored in a database or retrieval
system, without the prior written consent of The McGraw-Hill Companies, Inc., including,
but not limited to, in any network or other electronic storage or transmission, or broadcast
for distance learning.

Some ancillaries, including electronic and print components, may not be available to customers
outside the United States.

This book is printed on recycled, acid-free paper containing 10% postconsumer waste.

3 4 5 6 7 8 9 0 CUS/CUS 0 9 8 7 6 5 4 3

ISBN 0-07-232964-5
ISBN 0-07-118019-2

Editorial director: *Tina B. Carver*
Series editor: *Annie Sullivan*
Developmental editor: *Louis Carrillo*
Director of marketing and sales: *Thomas P. Dare*
Project manager: *Sheila M. Frank*
Coordinator of freelance design: *David W. Hash*
Interior designer: *Michael Warrell, Design Solutions*
Photo research coordinator: *John C. Leland*
Photo researcher: *Amelia Ames Hill Associates/Amy Bethea*
Compositor: *Point West, Inc.*
Typeface: *10.5/12 Times Roman*
Printer:

The credits section for this book begins on page 259 and is considered an extension of
the copyright page.

INTERNATIONAL EDITION ISBN 0-07-118019-2
Copyright © 2002. Exclusive rights by The McGraw-Hill Companies, Inc., for manufacture and
export. This book cannot be re-exported from the country to which it is sold by McGraw-Hill.
The International Edition is not available in North America.

www.mhcontemporary.com/interactionsmosaic

Mosaic 2
Reading

Mosaic 2 Reading

Boost your students' academic success!

Interactions Mosaic, 4th edition is the newly revised five-level, four-skill comprehensive ESL/EFL series designed to prepare students for academic content. The themes are integrated across proficiency levels and the levels are articulated across skill strands. The series combines communicative activities with skill-building exercises to boost students' academic success.

Interactions Mosaic, 4th edition features

- updated content
- five videos of authentic news broadcasts
- expansion opportunities through the Website
- new audio programs for the listening/speaking and reading books
- an appealing fresh design
- user-friendly instructor's manuals with placement tests and chapter quizzes

In This Chapter gives students a preview of the upcoming material.

Chapter 9

Art and Entertainment

IN THIS CHAPTER

North America is a great "melting pot," a place where people from many countries and races have joined to form a new culture. The arts reflect the uniqueness of this culture. Many of its contributions to music have come from people of African descent: jazz, gospel music, rock, the blues. The first selection is from the biography of Duke Ellington. The next two sections explore the striking paintings of Georgia O'Keeffe and the moving poetry of the Chicanos. Finally, a timed reading looks at Jackie Chan, one of the world's best-loved movie stars.

———— 8. By writing specifically for each of his men and letting them play in a natural and relaxed manner, Ellington was able to *probe* the intimate recesses of their minds.

———— 9. While most people follow the ideas of others, every group needs also to have *innovators*.

Read

Do you enjoy listening to jazz? If so, you are not alone, for millions of people throughout the world rate it as their favorite type of music. Jazz began in the United States around the turn of the twentieth century, when it was played informally by African-American bands in New Orleans and other southern cities and towns. In the following selection, you will find out more about this music with the strong rhythmic beat and about the people who create it, especially about one man, Duke Ellington, one of the greatest jazz musicians of all time.

The Man Who Was an Orchestra

Whitney Balliett, jazz critic for *The New Yorker* magazine, has called jazz "the sound of surprise." And it is that expectation of surprise which partly explains the compelling hold of jazz on listeners in just about every country in the world.

5   Most of us lead lives of patterned regularity. Day by day, surprises are relatively few. And except for economic or physical uncertainties, we neither face nor look for significant degrees of risk because the vast majority of us try to attain as much security as is possible.

10   In this sense, jazzmen, of all musicians, are our surrogates for the unpredictable, our models of constant change.

"It's like going out there naked every night," a bass player once said to me. "Any one of us can screw the whole thing up because he had a fight with his wife just before the performance or because he's just not with it that night for any number of reasons. I mean, we're out there

15   improvising. The classical guys have their scores, whether they have them on a music stand or have memorized them. But we have to be creating, or trying to, anticipating each other, transforming our feel-

20   ings into music, taking chances every second. That's why, when jazz musicians are really putting out, it's an exhausting experience. It can be exhilarating, too, but always there's that touch of fear, that feeling

25   of being on a very high wire without a net below."

Introduction to readings builds background knowledge by giving students information on the writer and the source.

Varied genres include formal and informal essays, biographies, speeches, interviews, stories, and poetry.

Photos and illustrations ensure comprehension by supporting the text.

Preliminary activities provide scaffolding to help students understand authentic language.

Skill development prepares students for standardized tests through paraphrasing, summarizing, identifying the theme, formulating an argument, and so on.

20   Mosaic 2   Reading

PART 1   **Into Thin Air**

Before You Read

1   Previewing a Reading. The prefix *pre-* means before, so *previewing* means "viewing (looking) before." It greatly aids comprehension if you look through a selection before reading it. You want to find clues to what the selection is about. Just as it is easier to drive through a neighborhood you know rather than through a strange one, it is easier to read something if you get acquainted with it first. Work by yourself or with a partner and answer these questions:

1. Look at the illustrations. What do they tell you about the subject of the selection? Do they tell you something about who, where, what, why?
2. In English, people talk about disappearing "into thin air." Look at the title. What does it suggest to you? What feelings does it give you?
3. Skim lines 1–44 very fast. Is the reading about an experience that is easy or difficult? Dangerous or safe? Comfortable or demanding?

2   Scanning for More Exact or Colorful Synonyms. In the best-selling book this selection is taken from, the author paints vivid and exciting pictures in the reader's mind. Often he uses words that are more exact, more concise (one short word instead of a whole phrase), or more colorful than ordinary words. For example, look at this sentence:

> *Standing on* the top of the world, one foot in China and the other in Nepal, I cleared the ice from my oxygen mask, *leaned* a shoulder against the wind, and *looked* absently down the vastness of Tibet.

Now, look at the first sentence in the reading. What three synonyms are used instead of the words in italics in the preceding sentence? Notice that the first is more concise and the second and third are more exact and colorful than the words in the preceding sentence.

Scanning for Specific Information

To scan, move your eyes quickly over the reading until you come to the specific piece of information that you want. If you know that it is in the middle or toward the end of the reading, start there. Do not be distracted by other items. Concentrate. When you find what you want, use it. Then go to the next point.

4   **Explaining Key Ideas.** Work with a classmate or in a group to explain the following ideas from the article.

1. the old model of heart disease as a "plumbing problem"
2. the problem of inflammation caused in the blood vessels by the attack of the immune system
3. the CRP test and why it may be important
4. the possible importance of folic acid

Talk It Over

1. In what special ways is the image of the heart used in today's society? Does it have different meanings in different cultures? What does it mean to you?
2. Can you explain these common phrases containing the word *heart*?
    - Let's get to the heart of the matter.
    - Oh, come on, have a heart!
    - It's heartening to hear that news.
    - That broke his heart. I'm afraid he's eating his heart out.
    - Yes, it's time for hearts and flowers.
3. How do you feel about taking medicine in general? Would you consider taking medicine in order to prevent heart disease or some other disease? Why or why not?
4. How do you feel about taking vitamins? Is it a good idea to do this or not? Explain.
5. In your opinion, is there a link between certain types of society or professions and heart attacks? Explain.

Making Connections

From the Internet or the library, find information on one of the following topics and report on it to the class:

1. the best diet for a healthy heart
2. the connection between smoking (or alcohol or coffee) and heart attacks
3. what kinds of exercise are good for your heart
4. the rate of heart attacks in different societies

Groupwork maximizes opportunities for discussion and negotiation.

Talk It Over and **Making Connections** encourage students to evaluate arguments and to do independent research related to the topic of the chapter.

---

5   **Announcing a Discovery.** Work in groups of three or four and play the role of scientists who have just made an important discovery. First decide what your discovery is. (Your teacher may give you some help with this.) Then make up a short speech about it for the public, telling them what it is and why it is important. Your teacher may ask you to "present" your discovery to the class while your classmates play the roles of reporters at a press conference.

Timed Reading

The following selection discusses what many people view as the most recent extension of the human mind: the computer. Is it simply a tool, or can we speak of ait as an intelligent being that "thinks"? Read the selection to find out the author's point of view on this question. Try to finish the reading and comprehension quiz in six minutes. Looking at the quiz first will help you focus on the reading.

Are Computers Alive?

The topic of *thought* is one area of psychology, and many observers have considered this aspect in connection with robots and computers: Some of the old worries about AI (artificial intelligence) were closely linked to the question of whether computers could think. The first massive electronic computers, capable of rapid (if often unreliable) computation and little or no creative activity, were soon dubbed "electronic brains." A reaction to this terminology quickly followed. To put them in their place, computers were called "high-speed idiots," an effort to protect human vanity. In such a climate the possibility of computers actually being alive was rarely considered: It was bad enough that computers might be capable of thought. But not everyone realized the implications of the high-speed idiot tag. It has not been pointed out often enough that even the human idiot is one of the most intelligent life forms on earth. If the early computers were even that intelligent, it was already a remarkable state of affairs.

One consequence of speculation about the possibility of computer thought was that we were forced to examine with new care the idea of thought in general. It soon became clear that we were not sure what we meant by such terms as *thought* and *thinking*. We tend to assume that human beings think, some more than others, though we often call people *thoughtless* or *unthinking*. Dreams cause a problem, partly because they usually happen outside our control. They are obviously some type of mental experience, but are they a type of thinking? And the question of nonhuman life forms adds further problems. Many of us would maintain that some of the higher animals—dogs, cats, apes, and so on—are capable of at least basic thought, but what about fish and insects? It is certainly true that the higher mammals show complex brain activity when tested with the appropriate equipment. If thinking is demonstrated by evident electrical activity in the brain, then many animal species are capable of thought. Once we have formulated clear ideas on what thought is in biological creatures, it will be easier to discuss the question of thought in artifacts. And what is true of thought is also true of the many other mental processes. One of the immense benefits of AI research is that we are being forced to scrutinize, with new rigor, the working of the human mind.

Timed Readings give students specific strategies for improving their reading speed without sacrificing comprehension.

The first book page (left):

170 Mosaic 2 Reading

After You Read

3 **Matching General Ideas and Specific Illustrations.** Like many articles, this one alternates between general and specific ideas. Read the following ideas from the article and decide which of the two columns contains general ideas and which contains specific ideas. Label the columns correctly, and then match each general idea to the specific idea that illustrates it.

A. _____

1. In the field of astronomy, it is easy to list cases in which discoveries were announced in ways calculated to bring credit and personal gain.
2. Some astronomers of the past were modest and did not try to promote their own interests.
3. If you do not follow scientific protocol when announcing your discovery, you will suffer ridicule and criticism from your colleagues.
4. Waiting too long to announce discoveries can also bring criticism.

B. _____

1. Some scientists decided they would "slam Pons and Fleischmann against the wall" because they had called a press conference to announce "cold fusion."
2. In AIDS research, some activists are demanding that new drugs be made available to patients before proof of their efficacy is published in journals.
3. When Galileo discovered the four large moons of Jupiter, he decided to name them after the rich and famous Medici brothers.
4. When William Herschel discovered the planet Uranus in 1781, he did no more to publicize it than mention it to a friend.

4 **Finding Related Words.** Fill in the following chart with words from the article to show the relationships among word families. The first one is done as an example.

Nouns (things)	Nouns (people)	Adjectives	Verbs
1. science	scientist	scientific	X
2. _____		X	discover
3. _____	proponent	proposed	propose
4. _____	X	prior	prioritize
5. _____		astronomical	X
6. _____	public	publicized	_____
7. _____	announcer	announced	_____
8. _____	detective	X	_____
9. _____	revolutionary	revolutionary	_____
10. competition		competitive	compete

Talk It Over

In small groups, discuss the following questions.

1. In your opinion, what are some of the most important discoveries that have been made in rec...

The second book page (right):

Chapter 6 The Mind **101**

After You Read

Study Skills

John Conrad spoke of the importance of having an organized mind for developing one's memory. In this section, two skills will be presented to help you organize materials for study: underlining and marginal glossing.

Underlining

Before underlining, read the material once. Then scan the reading, underlining key words and phrases that relate to main ideas and important statistics or examples that support them. Underline only about 20 to 30 percent of the material. Many students underline with felt pens, often using one color for main concepts and a different color for statistics and examples.

Another effective method is to underline main ideas and circle or draw rectangles around names, terms, or statistics you want to remember. Supporting ideas can be underlined with broken lines. Practice underlining a few different ways until you find a method you like.

Marginal Glossing

Marginal glossing is another way to organize material for study. A marginal gloss is a note in the margin of your book summarizing the material next to it. When you study, these notes stand out and remind you of other points as well. This saves time because you do not reread everything, only the brief notes. You can also try to think of questions that might be asked on a test and write these questions in the margins.

2 **Underlining and Glossing.** Here are the first eight paragraphs from a "Memory for All Seasonings" with underlining and marginal glosses done for the first four paragraphs. Look over the four paragraphs that have been marked. Then finish the remaining paragraphs by underlining and glossing them yourself. Afterward, compare your work with your classmates. You should find that the first part of the comprehension quiz is quite easy after this preparation.

Peter Polson, from University Colo. Psy. Dept., saw a waiter at Bananas Restaurant with an amazing memory. The waiter was John Con...

One evening two years ago, (Peter Polson,) a member of the <u>psychology department</u> at the <u>University of Colorado</u>, took his son and daughter to dinner at <u>Bananas</u>, a fashionable <u>restaurant</u> in Boulder. When the <u>waiter</u> took their orders, Polson noticed that the young man <u>didn't write anything down</u>. He just listened, made small talk, told them that his name was (John Conrad,) and left. Polson didn't think this was exceptional: There were, after all, only three ...

Promotional text:

Vocabulary and language-learning strategies for synonyms, antonyms, context clues, and word families give students comprehension and self-assessment tools.

Study Skills, such as underlining, marginal glosses, and study maps, help students cope with heavy reading assignments.

Don't forget to check out the new ***Interactions Mosaic*** Website at www.mhcontemporary.com/interactionsmosaic.

- Traditional practice and interactive activities
- Links to student and teacher resources
- Cultural activities
- Focus on Testing
- Activities from the Website are also provided on CD-ROM

Chapter	Readings	Vocabulary Development	Reading Skills
1 **Language and Learning** **Page 1**	■ *Native Americans,* Jamake Highwater ■ *English as a Universal Language,* Patricia Aburdene, John Naisbitt	■ Using context clues ■ Identifying exact verbs	■ Completing a summary ■ Skimming for main idea ■ Scanning for statistics
2 **Danger and Daring** **Page 19**	■ *Into Thin Air,* John Krakauer ■ *The World We Lost,* Farley Mowat	■ Identifying expressive synonyms ■ Using context clues	■ Previewing ■ Making inferences
3 **Sex and Gender** **Page 37**	■ *For Better or Worse, Arranged Marriages Still Thrive in Japan,* Urban C. Lehner ■ *Finding Real Love,* Cary Barbor	■ Identifying expressive synonyms	■ Distinguishing the general from the specific ■ Finding support for general ideas ■ Previewing for organization ■ Identifying causes
4 **Mysteries Past and Present** **Page 53**	■ *The Lady or the Tiger?,* Frank Stockton ■ *It All Started with Dragon Bones,* Raymond Chang, Margaret Scrogin Chang	■ Using context and structure clues ■ Scanning for synonyms	■ Scanning for narrative elements ■ Identifying support for hypotheses ■ Identifying the theme ■ Summarizing an article
5 **Transitions** **Page 75**	■ *Conversations in Malaysia,* V.S. Naipaul ■ *Grisha Has Arrived,* Tanya Filanovsky	■ Recognizing dialectal differences ■ Selecting appropriate adjectives	■ Understanding interview structure ■ Finding support for main idea ■ Scanning for information ■ Predicting narrative events ■ Summarizing a narrative
6 **The Mind** **Page 95**	■ *A Memory for All Seasonings,* Stephen Singular ■ *The Tell-Tale Heart,* Edgar Allan Poe	■ Using context clues	■ Anticipating the reading ■ Underlining and glossing ■ Recalling information ■ Finding support for/against a hypothesis ■ Summarizing points of view ■ Identifying story elements
7 **Working** **Page 121**	■ *The San Francisco Sculptor Who Created Nicolas Cage's "Dreadful Dragon,"* Kristine M. Carber ■ *A Lifetime of Learning to Manage Effectively,* Ralph Z. Sorenson ■ *Barriers Fall for Women at Work,* Lisa Genasci	■ Scanning for specific terms ■ Inferring meaning ■ Finding related nouns and verbs	■ Skimming for main idea ■ Recalling information ■ Justifying inferences ■ Highlighting and glossing ■ Distinguishing between general and specific

Language	Critical Thinking Skills/Culture	Focus on Testing	Video Topics
■ Understanding animal-associated expressions ■ Understanding acronyms and abbreviations	■ Universal languages ■ Influence of English on other languages	■ Analyzing summary statements	■ The School of Success
■ Understanding everyday phrases	■ Problem solving	■ Summarizing a narrative	■ Extreme Sports
■ Understanding idioms and expressions ■ Reading rhymes in poetry	■ Arranged marriages ■ Communication between men and women	■ Improving your chances on multiple-choice exams	■ Seeking Love
■ Forming an argument ■ Solving riddles	■ Truth of legends ■ Fire walking	■ Improving your chances on True/False exams	■ Abduction by Aliens
■ Conducting an interview	■ Family feeling vs. material success ■ Refugees	■ Avoiding "traps" in standardized vocabulary tests	■ College Graduation
■ Using a study map	■ Analyzing "The Tell-Tale Heart" ■ Mental illness	■ Reading for speed	■ Social Phobia
■ Understanding idiomatic phrases	■ Ideal work ■ Home offices	■ Understanding a chart "The Worst Recruiters Have Seen"	■ Telecommuting

Language	Critical Thinking Skills/Culture	Focus on Testing	Video Topics
■ Refuting false arguments	■ Cloning ■ Genetic screening ■ Scientific careers ■ New political division of Canada	■ Speaking in front of people ■ "Are Computers Alive?"	■ Advances in Medicine
■ Expressing reactions to music ■ Paraphrasing complex ideas ■ Writing a comparison	■ Evaluating art ■ Body decoration	■ Preparing for exams with study maps ■ "Jackie Can!"	■ Women in Jazz
■ Identifying modern usage	■ Greek and Roman mythology ■ Public and private apologies ■ Amnesty	■ Poetry interpretation replaces Focus on Testing in this chapter.	■ A Strike
■ Stating an opinion	■ Traditional medicine ■ Organ transplants	■ "Education Doesn't Happen Only in Schools"	■ Stealth Surgery
■ Writing a news story	■ Astrology and fortune telling ■ The Kremani prophecies	■ Writing an extemporaneous essay ■ "The Affectionate Machine"	■ Concept Cars

Chapter 1

Language and Learning

IN THIS CHAPTER

The author of the first selection describes his early encounters with learning English, the language that finally helped him to overcome his feelings of being an outsider in the dominant culture. The second reading talks about the role of English in today's world.

Native Americans

Before You Read

1   **Getting Meaning from Context.** Try to guess the meanings of unfamiliar words as you read. One way of understanding a new word is to break it into smaller words, prefixes, and suffixes. Another way is to look for a synonym or explanation near the word. Practice these skills by writing your own definitions for the italicized words in the following sentences taken from the first reading selection. Use the hints to help you.

1.   We are born into a cultural *preconception* that we call reality and that we never question. (Do you know the meaning of the prefix *pre-* and the word *concept*?)
     preconception: _____

2.   We essentially know the world in terms of that cultural package or preconception, and we are so unaware of it that the most liberal of us go through life with a kind of *ethnocentricity*. (The word *ethnic* means "belonging to a particular culture or group." What do you think *centr-* means?)
     ethnocentricity: _____

3.   I grew up in a place that was called a *wilderness*, but I could never understand how that amazing ecological park could be called "*wilderness*," something wild that needs to be harnessed. (What part of the sentence explains the meaning of *wilderness*?)
     wilderness: _____

4.   Nature is some sort of foe, some sort of *adversary*, in the dominant culture's mentality. (Because of the repetition of the words *some sort of*, you can see that there is another word that is very close in meaning to *adversary*. What word is this?)
     adversary: _____

2   **Making Good Guesses.** If you cannot break a word apart or find a nearby synonym or explanation, you simply have to guess a likely meaning to fit the context. Choose the best word to substitute for each italicized word in the following sentences from the selection.

1.   The bird had a very particular *significance* to me because I desperately wanted to be able to fly too.
     a.   beauty
     b.   meaning
     c.   appearance
     d.   name

2.   When I was ten years old, my life changed *drastically*. I found myself adopted forcefully and against my parents' will.
     a.   slowly
     b.   happily
     c.   easily
     d.   violently

3. …they were considered *inadequate* parents because they could not make enough money to support me.
   a. unintelligent
   b. wealthy
   c. not suitable
   d. not interesting

4. …I was even more confused when I found out that the meaning of the verb "to duck" came from the bird and not *vice versa*.
   a. the other way around
   b. from something else
   c. with many meanings
   d. written in a different way

5. …we are so unaware of it that the most liberal of us go through life with a kind of ethnocentricity that automatically *rules out* all other ways of seeing the world.
   a. eliminates
   b. emphasizes
   c. includes
   d. improves

6. …I could never understand how that amazing ecological park could be called "wilderness," something wild that needs to be *harnessed*.
   a. changed
   b. set free
   c. controlled
   d. appreciated

7. I grew up in a culture that considers us *literally* a part of the entire process that is called nature, to such an extent that when Black Elk called himself the brother of the bear, he was quite serious.
   a. in an imaginative way
   b. in reality
   c. intellectually
   d. poetically

8. You can imagine my *distress* when I was ten years old to find out that synonyms for the word *earth—dirt* and *soil*—were used to describe uncleanliness on the one hand and *obscenity* on the other.
   distress:
   a. fear
   b. joy
   c. suffering
   d. laughter

   obscenity:
   a. correct speech and manners
   b. offensive language and actions
   c. religious customs
   d. objects considered beautiful

9. I could not possibly understand how something that could be dirty could have any kind of negative *connotations*.
    a. sounds connected to a word
    b. ideas associated with a word
    c. ways of spelling
    d. ways of writing

Read

Many people who live in English-speaking countries do not speak English as their first language. This group includes most immigrants and, in the United States, many Native Americans (sometimes referred to as "Indians"). The author of the following selection, Jamake Highwater, is a Native American and a well-known author who writes in English. He speaks of the terrible shock that certain English words caused him when he first learned them at school. As you read, notice Highwater's attitudes toward the two languages and the two cultures that have formed him.

Native Americans

When I was about five years old, I used to watch a bird in the skies of southern Alberta from the Blackfeet Blood Reserve in northern Montana where I was born. I loved this bird; I would watch him for hours. He would glide effortlessly in that gigantic sky, or he would come down and light on the water and float there very majestically. Sometimes when I watched him he would creep into the grasses and waddle around not very gracefully. We called him *meksikatsi*, which in the Blackfeet language means "pink-colored feet"; *meksikatsi* and I became very good friends.

The bird had a very particular significance to me because I desperately wanted to be able to fly too. I felt very much as if I was the kind of person who had been born into a world where flight was impossible, and most of the things that I dreamed about or read about would not be possible for me but would be possible only for other people.

When I was ten years old, my life changed drastically. I found myself adopted forcefully and against my parents' will; they were considered inadequate parents because they could not make enough money to support me, so I found myself in that terrible position that 60 percent of Native Americans find themselves in: living in a city that they do not understand at all, not in another culture but between two cultures.

A teacher of the English language told me that *meksikatsi* was not called *meksikatsi*, even though that is what my people had called that bird for thousands of years. *Meksikatsi*, he said, was really "duck." I was very disappointed with English. I could not understand it. First of all, the bird didn't look like "duck," and when it made a noise it didn't sound like "duck," and I was even more confused when I found out that the meaning of the verb "to duck" came from the bird and not vice versa.

This was the beginning of a very complex lesson for me that doesn't just happen to black, Chicano, Jewish, and Indian children but to all children. We

are born into a cultural preconception that we call reality and that we never
question. We essentially know the world in terms of that cultural package or
preconception, and we are so unaware of it that the most liberal of us go
through life with a kind of ethnocentricity that automatically rules out all other
ways of seeing the world.

As I came to understand English better, I understood that it made a great
deal of sense, but I never forgot that *meksikatsi* made a different kind of
sense. I realized that languages are not just different words for the same
things but totally different concepts, totally different ways of experiencing and
looking at the world.

As artists have always known, reality depends entirely on how you see
things. I grew up in a place that was called a wilderness, but I could never
understand how that amazing ecological park could be called "wilderness,"
something wild that needs to be harnessed. Nature is some sort of foe, some
sort of adversary, in the dominant culture's mentality. We are not part of nature in this society; we are created above it, outside of it, and feel that we must
dominate and change it before we can be comfortable and safe within it. I
grew up in a culture that considers us literally a part of the entire process that
is called nature, to such an extent that when Black Elk called himself the brother of the bear, he was quite serious. In other words, Indians did not need Darwin to find out that they were part of nature.

I saw my first wilderness, as I recall, one August day when I got off a
Greyhound bus in a city called New York. Now that struck me as being fairly
wild and pretty much out of hand. But I did not understand how the term could
be applied to the place where I was from.

Gradually, through the help of some very unusual teachers, I was able to
find my way into two cultures rather than remain helplessly between two cultures. The earth is such an important symbol to most primal people that when

we use European languages we tend to capitalize the *E* in much the same way that the word *God* is capitalized by people in the dominant culture. You can imagine my distress when I was ten years old to find out that synonyms for the word *earth*—*dirt* and *soil*—were used to describe uncleanliness on the one hand and obscenity on the other. I could not possibly understand how something that could be dirty could have any kind of negative connotations. It would be like saying the person is godly, so don't go near him, and I could not grasp how these ideas made their way into the English language.

60

Jamake Highwater

After You Read

3   **Completing a Summary.** Complete the following summary of "Native Americans" by filling in the blanks with key words from the selection.

An Indian Boy Meets the English Language

When Jamake Highwater was ten years old, he had to move from the _____ to a _____. At school a teacher told him that the *meksikatsi* he loved was really called a _____. He had grown up in a culture that considered people as part of _____. He thought that he saw his first "wilderness" when he went to _____. At first he felt he was between two cultures, but he became part of both of them with the help of some unusual _____. He finally got over his shock at finding out that in English synonyms for the word _____ had negative _____: they were used to describe _____ on the one hand and _____ on the other.

Talk It Over

In small groups, discuss the following questions.

1. Why did the duck have a special significance for Jamake Highwater when he was very young?
2. What drastic change occurred when he was ten years old? Why did he describe himself then as "between two cultures"?
3. Why didn't the author like the word *duck*? What are some English words that have surprised or displeased you? Explain.
4. According to Highwater, where was the wilderness? Explain.
5. Do you know who Charles Darwin is? (If not, how can you find out?) Why does the author say that the Indians did not need Darwin?
6. Why did it bother the author that in English obscene words and jokes are often referred to as "dirty" words and jokes? In some cultures, obscene jokes are referred to as "green stories." Is there any color associated with them in your culture? How are they referred to?
7. How did the author's attitude toward English change?

4 **Finding Verbs with Precise Meanings.** It is obvious that Jamake Highwater has mastered his second language well. Reread his description of the *meksikatsi* bird in the first paragraph and find the verbs that he used instead of the more ordinary ones given in the sentences that follow.

1. The bird would *fly* in the sky (without moving his wings): _____
2. Then he would come down and *land* on the water (gently and without making a splash): _____
3. Afterward the bird would *come* (slowly and carefully) into the grasses: _____
4. There he would *walk around* (swaying from side to side) not very gracefully: _____

5 There are many expressions in English that use animal names or words associated with animals to convey special meanings. Like Jamake Highwater, people from other cultures may be confused or even offended by animal-associated language in English. For example, the English expression "clumsy as an elephant" surprises people from India. They know elephants quite well and claim that they are among the most graceful of all animals. This caused some embarrassment for the Indian gentleman who once told an American lady that she "walked like an elephant." He couldn't understand why she got angry!

For some expressions, the animal association is very clear—for example, to be *slow as a turtle* (turtles move slowly), but for others it is not so clear. Can you clarify the following by explaining the meaning?

1. duck the issue _____
2. have a whale of a good time _____
3. be hungry as a bear _____
4. be sly as a fox _____

6 Read the following sentences and guess the meanings of the italicized words. Try to explain what animal and what behavior or quality are associated with each one.

1. He *wolfed* down his dinner with his eye on the clock.
   wolf: to eat very fast as a wolf supposedly does

2. The people *craned* their necks to see the famous actor.

3. She worked at the task with *dogged* determination.

4. A sparkling river *snaked* through the lush green valley below.

5. The teacher got angry because the students were *horsing* around.

6. That professor has an *elephantine* memory.

7. The new boy was a *bully* who liked to scare the other children.

8. She *fished* around in her purse until she found her glasses.

9. After winning the Nobel Prize, the scientist was *lionized* by the crowd of reporters.

Making Connections

One of the most useful features of the Internet is its ability to help you find information about almost anything or anyone. One of the best ways to do so is to use a search engine. There are many excellent search engines such as Ask Jeeves, AltaVista, Yahoo, and Lycos. Use a search engine to find out information about Jamake Highwater. Then share and compare the information with a partner.

If you do not have a "bookmark" or "favorites" entry for a search engine, try typing *www.* followed by the name of the search engine—for example, *www.altavista.com*— in the address or location box at the top of your Internet Webpage. Then press "Enter."

PART 2	# English as a Universal Language

Before You Read

1   **Getting the Meaning from Context.** Choose the best meaning for the italicized words in the following sentences taken from the next reading selection. Guess the meaning of new words by breaking them apart—into smaller words or into prefixes and suffixes—or by using clues from the context.

1. English...has semiofficial *status* in many countries.
    a. difficulty
    b. rank
    c. statement
    d. enjoyment

2. There may be as many people speaking the various *dialects* of Chinese.
    a. words
    b. dialogs
    c. lists of rules
    d. ways of speaking

3. English is certainly more *widespread* geographically.
    a. restricted
    b. extended
    c. regional
    d. popular

4. By the year 2000, that figure is likely to *exceed* 1.5 billion.
    a. be more than
    b. be less than
    c. equal
    d. approach

5. English is not replacing other languages; it is *supplementing* them.
    a. proving its superiority over
    b. taking the place of
    c. being used in addition to
    d. being used exclusively by

6. English *prevails* in transportation and the media.
    a. exists
    b. preserves
    c. continues
    d. predominates

7. *Maritime* traffic uses flag and light signals, but vessels may at times communicate verbally.
    a. sea
    b. air
    c. ground
    d. rail

8. It is a foreign *tongue* for all six member nations.
    a. challenge
    b. body
    c. trade
    d. language

2   Skimming for Main Ideas. Skimming is a useful way to get an overview of a reading selection. It is different from scanning. You scan for specific facts or details. You skim for general ideas. To skim, move your eyes quickly through the whole reading. Do not stop for details or worry about words you don't understand. Keep going like a fast-moving train from beginning to end. Afterward you will have a general idea of the contents. Then you can read the selection again with better comprehension.

Take two minutes and skim the next selection. Then look at the following list of ideas. Put a check in front of the ideas that are discussed in the reading.

_____ How English is taught in different countries
_____ Where English is taught
_____ The use of English among young people
_____ The use of English in literature and poetry
_____ The use of English in business, science, and diplomacy
_____ Comparisons of the use of English and the use of some other languages

Read

Is English truly a universal language, or will it be at some time in the near future? The following selection from the book *Megatrends 2000* presents one opinion on this subject and supports it with numerous details and statistics. Read to see if you agree with the author's opinion.

English as a Universal Language

English is becoming the world's first truly universal language. It is the native language of some 400 million people in twelve countries. That is a lot fewer than the 885 million people or so who speak Mandarin Chinese. But another 400 million speak English as a second language. And several hundred mil-
5   lion more have some knowledge of English, which has official or semiofficial status in some sixty countries. Although there *may* be as many people speaking the various dialects of Chinese as there are English speakers, English is

certainly more widespread geographically, more genuinely universal than Chinese. And its usage is growing at an extraordinary pace.

Today there are about 1 billion English speakers in the world, and the number is growing. The world's most taught language, English is not replacing other languages; it is supplementing them:

- Two hundred and fifty million Chinese—more than the entire population of the United States—study English.
- In eighty-nine countries, English is either a common second language or widely studied.
- In Hong Kong, nine of every ten secondary school students study English.
- In France, state-run secondary schools require students to study four years of English or German; most—at least 85 percent—choose English.
- In Japan, secondary students are required to take six years of English before graduation.

Media and Transportation

English prevails in transportation and the media. The travel and communication language of the international airwaves is English. Pilots and air traffic controllers speak English at all international airports. Maritime traffic uses flag and light signals, but "if vessels needed to communicate verbally, they would find a common language, which would probably be English," says the U.S. Coast Guard's Werner Siems.

Five of the largest broadcasters—CBS, NBC, ABC, the BBC, and the CBC—reach a potential audience of about 300 million people through English broadcast. It is also the language of satellite TV.

The Information Age

35 The language of the information age is English. Computers talk to each other in English.

More than 80 percent of all the information stored in the more than 100 million computers around the world is in English.

Eighty-five percent of international telephone conversations are con-
40 ducted in English, as are three-fourths of the world's mail, telexes, and ca-
bles. Computer program instructions and the software itself are often supplied only in English.

German was once the language of science. Today more than 80 percent of all scientific papers are published first in English. Over half the world's tech-
45 nical and scientific periodicals are in English, which is also the language of medicine, electronics, and space technology.

International Business

English is the language of international business.

When a Japanese businessman strikes a deal anywhere in Europe, the
50 chances are overwhelming that the negotiations were conducted in English.

Manufactured goods indicate their country of origin in English: "Made in Germany," not *Fabriziert in Deutschland*. It is the language of choice in multinational corporations. Datsun and Nissan write international memorandums in English. As early as 1985, 80 percent of the Japanese Mitsui and Compa-
55 ny's employees could speak, read, and write English. Toyota provides in-
service English courses. English classes are held in Saudi Arabia for the ARAMCO workers and on three continents for Chase Manhattan Bank staff.

Diplomacy

English is replacing the dominant European languages of centuries past. Eng-
60 lish has replaced French as the language of diplomacy; it is the official lan-
guage of international aid organizations such as Oxfam and Save the Children as well as of UNESCO, NATO, and the UN.

Lingua Franca

English serves as a common tongue in countries where people speak many
65 different languages. In India, nearly 200 different languages are spoken; only 30 percent speak the official language, Hindi. When Rajiv Gandhi addressed the nation after his mother's assassination, he spoke in English. The European

Free Trade Association works only in English even though it is a foreign tongue
for all six member countries.

70   *Official Language*
English is the official or semiofficial language of twenty African countries, including Sierra Leone, Ghana, Nigeria, Liberia, and South Africa. Students are
instructed in English at Makerere University in Uganda, the University of Nairo-
bi in Kenya, and the University of Dar es Salaam in Tanzania.

75   English is the ecumenical language of the World Council of Churches,
and the official language of the Olympics and the Miss Universe competition.

Youth Culture
English is the language of international youth culture. Young people world-
wide listen to and sing popular songs in English often without fully under-
80   standing the lyrics. "Break dance," "rap music," "bodybuilding," "windsurfing,"
and "computer hacking" are invading the slang of German youth.

Patricia Aburdene, John Naisbitt

After You Read

3 **Scanning for Supporting Statistics.** The selection supports its ideas with many and
varied statistics. Scan for the following information and write it in the blanks.

1. the number of English speakers in the world at the time the article was written:
    1 billion English

2. the number of Chinese studying English: *two hundred and fifty millions*

3. the approximate number of computers in the world: *100 million computers*

4. the percentage of scientific papers published first in English: *more than 80%*

5. the number of different languages spoken in India: *200 are spoken*

6. the number of African countries in which English has official or semiofficial status:
    20

Talk It Over

In small groups, discuss the following questions.

1. Why does the author feel that English is more universal than Chinese?
2. Where is English used as a common second language? *89*
3. In your opinion, why do people in many parts of the world study English? Why
    are you studying English?
4. In what situations can you imagine that a knowledge of English could mean the
    difference between life and death?
5. How has technology helped to make English popular?
6. Can you explain the meaning of *lingua franca* (used as one of the subheads) in the
    selection? Is English a *lingua franca* or not? Why?
7. What English terms or phrases are common in your culture?

Focus on Testing

Analyzing Summary Statements

On reading comprehension tests, you may be given several statements and asked to select the one that best summarizes a selection. In order to do this, first read the statements and see if any of them does not match the information in the reading. If so, eliminate it. Next, look at the other statements and decide which one best expresses the main idea of the reading selection. This statement must be a better summary than a statement that gives a secondary idea or summarizes only some parts of the selection. If there are subheads in the selection, they can help to remind you of the important ideas that should be included in a summary statement.

Circle the letter of the statement below that best summarizes "English as a Universal Language." Then explain your answer.

a.   English is replacing the dominant European languages of the past, and serves as a common means of communication in India and Africa and for scientists all over the world.

b.   English is the most important language in the world for transportation, information, business, diplomacy, trade, and communication among the young.

c.   English is the predominant language in the world because it is spoken by many more people than any other language and is used in most multinational companies.

Some TOEFL Information

Over 2300 colleges and universities in the United States and Canada require students who do not speak English as their first language to take the TOEFL (Test of English as a Foreign Language). Many "practice tests" are commercially available to help you prepare for the TOEFL. These are available in bookstores and from the Internet. In addition, there is a lot of information on the Internet about the TOEFL, including the official Website—*www.toefl.org*.

4 **Understanding Acronyms and Abbreviations.** Acronyms are words formed from the first letters of a phrase, such as LASER, which stands for **l**ightwave **a**mplification by **s**timulated **e**mission of **r**adiation or SCUBA—**s**elf-**c**ontained **u**nderwater **b**reathing apparatus. Abbreviations are letters that stand for names and phrases, such as UN—United Nations—or they are the first letters of a word such as *Inc.* for "Incorporated." Can you identify what the following acronyms and abbreviations stand for? If you don't know, ask a classmate or look in a dictionary. Write the information in the blanks. The first five items were used in the previous reading selection.

1. ABC _____
2. BBC _____
3. CBC _____
4. UNESCO _____
5. NATO _____
6. NAFTA _____
7. etc. _____
8. RADAR _____
9. INTERPOL _____
10. ASAP _____
11. CD _____
12. DVD _____
13. ESL _____
14. TOEFL _____

5 **Reacting to an Opinion.** In a small group, tell what you think about the following opinion. Do you agree with it or not? Explain. Compare the opinions of your group with those of other groups.

"This article expresses a very one-sided and nationalistic view in favor of the English language. There are many important languages in the world today. The author admits that French used to be the language of diplomacy and German used to be the language of science. Now it is the turn of English to be important in these two spheres, but it may be different in the future. No one can predict the future. Language reflects culture, and there are many varied cultures on our planet. No one language can claim to be universal."

6 **Reading a Shaded Map.** Look at the map of the world on page 16, read its legend, and answer the following questions.

1. What do the shaded parts of the map indicate?
2. What is the difference between the two types of shading?
3. Looking at the map, tell on what continents English is spoken (in some countries) as the mother tongue.
4. On what continents is English spoken as a second language?
5. Which of these two groups is larger? Which is more important for the status of English as a *global* language?

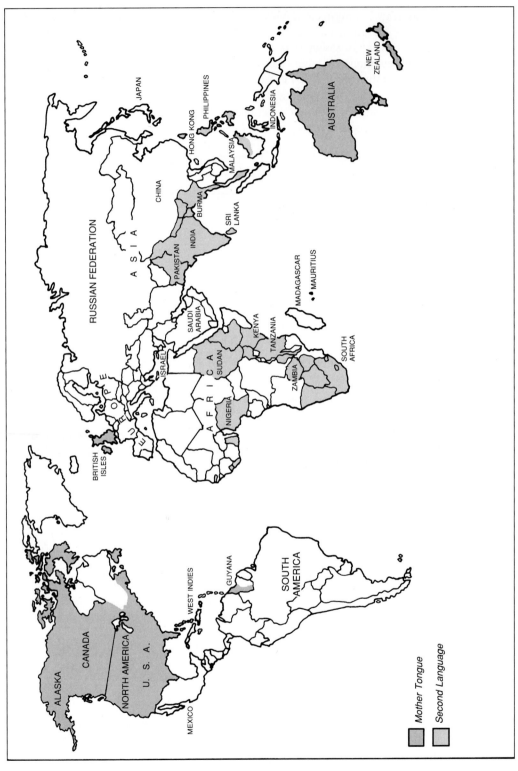

English today is spoken as a mother tongue by about 400 million people (see map), and at least 400 million more who use it as a second language in societies—Africa, for instance—with dozens of competing languages. People in many European countries learn English as a second language. It is also the language of international business and politics, transcending ideological and religious divisions. In total, there are probably more than a billion speakers of English, at least a quarter of the world's population.

Talk It Over

Famous Quotations on Education

Which of the following quotations relates most directly to your own personal ideas about education? Why? Share your ideas with your classmates.

Knowledge is power.
—Francis Bacon, 1561–1626

Education is a thing of which only the few are capable. Teach as you will, only a small percentage will profit by your most zealous energy.
—George Gissing, 1857–1903

We do not know what education could do for us, because we have never tried it.
—Robert Maynard Hutchins, 1899–1977

'Tis Education forms the common mind:
Just as the twig is bent the tree's inclined.
—Alexander Pope, 1688–1744

There are two ways of spreading light: to be the candle or the mirror that reflects it.
—Edith Wharton, 1862–1937

Experience is the best teacher.
—traditional proverb

What Do You Think?

Attack on English

In 1994, the French Cultural Minister promoted a law requiring that 3000 English words widely used in France be replaced by newly created French equivalents. He felt the French were losing an important part of their culture by using English words. This would mean changing "prime time" to *heure de grande écoute*, or calling a "corner" kick in soccer a *jet de coin*. Although government officials will have to follow the new laws, the French Constitutional Congress ruled that the law violates the "freedom of expression" of the general public. Do you think the minister was right in trying to keep foreign words out of the French language? Does your language include words of English origin? What are some examples? What words do you know in English that come from other languages?

Video Activities: The School for Success

Before You Watch.   Discuss these questions in small groups.

1. Which of these things do you think are most important for students'
    academic success? Why?
    a. their school   b. their home life   c. their parents
2. What can parents do to help their children be more successful in school?

Watch.   Answer these questions in small groups.
1. What is the name of the school featured in the video?_____
2. Who takes classes at this school?_____
3. Which of these things does George Frasier think causes failure in schools?
    a. Children watch too much television.
    b. Schools don't have enough money.
    c. Parents are not paying enough attention to their children.
4. Circle the things that George Frasier says that parents must give their children.
    a. love   d. support
    b. attention   e. values
    c. discipline

Watch Again.   Listen for these words and say what they mean.
1. *Link* means the same as _____.
    a. connect   b. establish   c. separate
2. *Maintain* means the same as _____.
    a. begin   b. finish   c. continue
3. *Nurturing* means _____.
    a. talking to   b. taking care of   c. leaning on
4. *Structured* means _____.
    a. having rules   b. being free   c. safe

After You Watch.   Find an article about education. First skim the article to get
the general idea. Write one sentence about what you think the general idea is. Then
read the article. How accurate was your guess about the general idea when you
skimmed?

Chapter 2

Danger and Daring

Why take risks? Why face danger and death when you could stay home in safety and comfort? Throughout history, there have been many who dared: explorers, mountain climbers, travelers, soldiers, religious leaders. The first selection is an excerpt from a book about the tragic and terrifying events that occurred a few years ago on the slopes of the highest mountain in the world. The second selection is the true account of a Canadian naturalist and writer who lived among wild animals and made an important discovery—about himself.

Into Thin Air

Before You Read

1   **Previewing a Reading.** The prefix *pre-* means before, so *previewing* means "viewing (looking) before." It greatly aids comprehension if you look through a selection before reading it. You want to find clues to what the selection is about. Just as it is easier to drive through a neighborhood you know rather than through a strange one, it is easier to read something if you get acquainted with it first. Work by yourself or with a partner and answer these questions:

1. Look at the illustrations. What do they tell you about the subject of the selection? Do they tell you something about who, where, what, why?

2. In English, people talk about disappearing "into thin air." Look at the title. What does it suggest to you? What feelings does it give you?

3. Skim lines 1–44 very fast. Is the reading about an experience that is easy or difficult? Dangerous or safe? Comfortable or demanding?

2   **Scanning for More Exact or Colorful Synonyms.** In the best-selling book this selection is taken from, the author paints vivid and exciting pictures in the reader's mind. Often he uses words that are more exact, more concise (one short word instead of a whole phrase), or more colorful than ordinary words. For example, look at this sentence:

> *Standing on* the top of the world, one foot in China and the other in Nepal, I cleared the ice from my oxygen mask, *leaned* a shoulder against the wind, and *looked* absently down the vastness of Tibet.

Now, look at the first sentence in the reading. What three synonyms are used instead of the words in italics in the preceding sentence? Notice that the first is more concise and the second and third are more exact and colorful than the words in the preceding sentence.

Scanning for Specific Information

To scan, move your eyes quickly over the reading until you come to the specific piece of information that you want. If you know that it is in the middle or toward the end of the reading, start there. Do not be distracted by other items. Concentrate. When you find what you want, use it. Then go to the next point.

Scan the reading for the more exact, concise, or colorful synonyms. The phrases are listed in the order of their appearance.

1. I understood on some dim, detached level that the sweep of earth beneath my feet was a (wonderful) ___spectacular___ sight.
2. I'd (thought) _____ about this moment, and the release of emotion that would accompany it for many months....
3. But now that I was finally here, actually standing on the (peak) _____ of Mount Everest....
4. Weeks of violent coughing had left me with two separated ribs that made ordinary breathing (a painful) _____ trial.
5. I (took) _____ four quick photos....
6. ...after surgeons had (cut off) _____ the gangrenous right hand of my teammate....
7. ...why, if the weather had begun to (get worse) _____ , had climbers on the upper mountain not (paid attention to) _____ the signs?
8. Why did veteran Himalayan guides keep moving upward, ushering a (group) _____ of relatively inexperienced amateurs.... (This is a picturesque word because it usuallly refers to a group of geese.)
9. Moving at the snail's pace that is the norm above 26,000 feet, (the crowd) _____ labored up the Hillary Step.
10. As I exchanged (commonplace) congratulations with the climbers filing past,...
11. ...it began to snow lightly and (the ability to see) _____ went to hell.
12. ...my (friends) _____ (took their time) _____ to memorialize their arrival at the apex of the planet....

Read

The peak of Mt. Everest, which lies between China and Tibet, is the highest place on earth, 29, 028 feet above sea level, and many have tried to reach it. Some have achieved this goal, especially in recent decades when it has become possible to carry oxygen tanks that facilitate breathing at high altitude. Some have died in the attempt. Others have returned from their expeditions with permanent physical injuries or psychological damage due to having witnessed the death or injury of other climbers.

Almost all of the climbers, no matter what country they come from, use natives called Sherpas to carry their equipment and aid them in the difficult and dangerous journey to the summit. The Sherpas know this mountain well and consider it sacred. They earn their living carrying heavy loads and serving as guides.

• Why do you think so many people try to climb Mt. Everest?
• If you had the money and opportunity, would you like to do it? Why or why not?

The following selection is from the true narrative book *Into Thin Air* by John Krakauer. This book has been called "the definitive account of the deadliest season in the history of Everest." The selection begins at the moment that Krakauer arrives at the peak of the mountain in the early afternoon of May 10, 1996.

Into Thin Air

Straddling the top of the world, one foot in China and the other in Nepal, I cleared the ice from my oxygen mask, hunched a shoulder against the wind, and stared absently down the vastness of Tibet. I understood on some dim, detached level that the sweep of earth beneath my feet was a spectacular
5 sight. I'd fantasized about this moment, and the release of emotion that would accompany it for many months. But now that I was finally here, actually standing on the summit of Mount Everest, I just couldn't summon the energy to care. It was early in the afternoon of May 10, 1996. I hadn't slept in fifty-seven hours. The only food I'd been able to force down over the preceding three days was
10 a bowl of ramen soup and a handful of peanut M&Ms. Weeks of violent coughing had left me with two separated ribs that made ordinary breathing an excruciating trial. At 29,028 feet up in the troposphere, so little oxygen was reaching my brain that my mental capacity was that of a slow child. Under the circumstances, I was incapable of feeling much of anything except cold and
15 tired.

I'd arrived on the summit a few minutes after Anatoli Boukreev, a Russian climbing guide working for an American commercial expedition, and just ahead of Andy Harris, a guide on the New Zealand-based team to which I belonged. Although I was only slightly acquainted with Boukreev, I'd come to
20 know and like Harris well during the preceding six weeks. I snapped four quick photos of Harris and Boukreev striking summit poses, then turned and headed down. My watch read 1:17 P.M. All told, I'd spent less than five minutes on the roof of the world.

A moment later, I paused to take another photo, this one looking down
25   the Southeast Ridge, the route we had ascended. Training my lens on a pair
of climbers approaching the summit, I noticed something that until that moment had escaped my attention. To the south, where the sky had been perfectly clear just an hour earlier, a blanket of clouds now hid Pumori, Ama
Dablam, and the other lesser peaks surrounding Everest.
30   Later—after six bodies had been located, after a search for two others
had been abandoned, after surgeons had amputated the gangrenous right
hand of my teammate Beck Weathers—people would ask why, if the weather had begun to deteriorate, had climbers on the upper mountain not heed-
ed the signs? Why did veteran Himalayan guides keep moving upward,
35   ushering a gaggle of relatively inexperienced amateurs—each of whom had
paid as much as $65,000 to be taken safely up Everest—into an apparent
death trap?
Nobody can speak for the leaders of the two guided groups involved, because both men are dead. But I can attest that nothing I saw early on the af-
40   ternoon of May 10 suggested that a murderous storm was bearing down. To
my oxygen-depleted mind, the clouds drifting up the grand valley of ice known
as the Western Cwm looked innocuous, wispy, insubstantial. Gleaming in the
brilliant midday sun, they appeared no different from the harmless puffs of
convection condensation that rose from the valley almost every afternoon....

As Krakauer began his descent from the summit of Mt. Everest, he became ex-
tremely concerned because his oxygen tanks were running low. He knew he had to climb
down to the South Summit camp to get oxygen. On his way down, however, he ran into
a "traffic jam" of more than a dozen climbers trying to reach the summit. He stepped
aside to let them pass.

45   The traffic jam was comprised of climbers from three expeditions: the team I belonged to, a group of paying clients under the leadership of the celebrated New Zealand guide Rob Hall; another guided party headed by the American Scott Fischer; and a noncommercial Taiwanese team. Moving at the snail's pace that is the norm above 26,000 feet, the throng labored up the
50   Hillary Step one by one, while I nervously bided my time.

Harris, who'd left the summit shortly after I did, soon pulled up behind me. Wanting to conserve whatever oxygen remained in my tank, I asked him to reach inside my backpack and turn off the valve on my regulator, which he did. For the next ten minutes I felt surprisingly good. My head cleared. I ac-
55   tually seemed less tired than I had with the gas turned on. Then, abruptly, I sensed that I was suffocating. My vision dimmed and my head began to spin. I was on the brink of losing consciousness.

Instead of turning my oxygen off, Harris, in his hypoxically impaired state, had mistakenly cranked the valve open to full flow, draining the tank. I'd just
60   squandered the last of my gas going nowhere. There was another tank waiting for me at the South Summit, 250 feet below, but to get there I would have to descend the most exposed terrain on the entire route without the benefit of supplemental oxygen.

And first I had to wait for the mob to disperse. I removed my now useless
65   mask, planted my ice ax into the mountain's frozen hide, and hunkered on the ridge. As I exchanged banal congratulations with the climbers filing past, inwardly I was frantic: "Hurry it up, hurry it up!" I silently pleaded....

The climbers, many of them exhausted, passed Krakauer on their way to the summit. They were behind schedule. After they passed, Krakauer continued his descent to the South Summit.

It was after three o'clock when I made it down to the South Summit. By now tendrils of mist were streaming over the 27,923-foot top of Lhotse and
70   lapping at Everest's summit pyramid. No longer did the weather look so benign. I grabbed a fresh oxygen cylinder, jammed it onto my regulator, and hurried down into the gathering cloud. Moments after I dropped below the South Summit, it began to snow lightly and visibility went to hell.

Four hundred vertical feet above, where the summit was still washed in
75   bright sunlight under an immaculate cobalt sky, my compadres dallied to memorialize their arrival at the apex of the planet, unfurling flags and snapping photos, using up precious ticks of the clock. None of them imagined that a horrible ordeal was drawing nigh. Nobody suspected that by the end of that long day, every minute would count.

John Krakauer

Nine climbers from four expeditions, many of those whom Krakauer passed on his way down from the summit, perished in the freak storm on Mt. Everest on May 10, 1996. Impaired judgment seems to have been a big factor in their deaths.

After You Read

3   **Making Inferences.** Inferences are ideas or opinions that are not stated but that can be inferred or concluded from the information given. For example, if your friend says, "Nuts! I have to wear my heavy coat today," you can infer that he thinks it is cold outside. Work with a partner or in a group. In front of each inference, write the letter of the statement from the article that gives the basis for it.

_____d_____ 1. Weather can change very quickly in the mountains.

_____ 2. Climbing at high altitude causes problems with the respiratory (breathing) system.

_____ 3. Climbing at high altitude makes normal eating and sleeping difficult.

_____ 4. Mountain climbers are proud people who do not like to show their fear.

_____ 5. Lack of oxygen can make a person act in stupid ways.

a. I hadn't slept in fifty-seven hours. The only food I'd been able to force down over the preceding three days was a bowl of ramen soup and a handful of peanut M&Ms.

b. Weeks of violent coughing had left me with two separated ribs that made ordinary breathing an excruciating trial.

c. …so little oxygen was reaching my brain that my mental capacity was that of a slow child.

d. To the south, where the sky had been perfectly clear just an hour earlier, a blanket of clouds now hid Pumori, Ama Dablam, and the other lesser peaks surrounding Everest.

e. As I exchanged banal congratulations with the climbers filing past, inwardly I was frantic: "Hurry it up, hurry it up!"

4   **Getting the Meaning of Everyday Phrases.** Sometimes you know the meaning of each word but don't understand the whole phrase. You have to guess or infer the meaning from the context (general sense of the words before and after). With a partner or in a small group, write a brief explanation of the phrases in italics. Line numbers are given so you can look up more of the context if you need to.

1. I'd fantasized about this moment and *the release of emotion* that would accompany it… (line 5)
    The author is on the summit and expects to feel strong emotions that he had to hold back before.

2. I snapped four quick photos of Harris and Boukreev *striking summit poses*… (line 20)

    _____

3. All told, I'd spent less than five minutes *on the roof of the world.* (line 22)

    _____

4. A *blanket of clouds* now hid Pumori, Ama Dablam, and the other lesser peaks… (line 28)

    _____

5. Why did veteran Himalayan guides keep moving upward ...*into an apparent death trap*? (line 34)

_____

6. *The traffic jam* was comprised of climbers from three expeditions... (line 45)

_____

7. *Moving at the snail's pace* that is the norm above 26,000 feet... (line 48)

_____

8. ...my compadres dallied to memorialize their arrival at the apex of the planet...*using up precious ticks of the clock.* (line 75)

_____

Talk It Over

Discuss these questions in small groups.

1. What kinds of people climb Mt. Everest? What character traits or qualities do they have?
2. Do you think that many people want to climb this mountain simply because it is the highest? What does it symbolize for you? Would it be just as good to climb another mountain that is equally difficult or even more difficult to climb?
3. In your opinion, is it important for people to climb Mt. Everest for the sake of nationalism, so they can place the flag of their country at the top?
4. In general, do you like to take risks? What kinds of risks? Physical, intellectual, social, financial? Is the idea of danger exciting to you? Explain.

_____

5 **Words Expressing Emotion.** With a partner or in a small group, talk about the emotions that the narrator felt during the events he describes. He does not talk directly about his feelings, so we have to infer them from his words and actions. Which of the following emotions do you think he experienced: anger, delight, excitement, exhaustion, fear, frustration, happiness, panic, sadness, terror? When? Are there other emotions that should be added?

Making Connections

Use the Internet or the library to find information on one of the following topics.

- The first people to stand on the summit of Everest. Who were they? When and how did they achieve this goal? What happened to them afterward? What other famous climbers died trying before this successful attempt?

- Sherpas, money, and equipment. What does it take for a successful expedition? How many Sherpas must be employed? How much does it cost? What equipment is necessary? Do the Sherpas manage to make a good living this way? How do they live? What do they think about these expeditions?

- Statsitics of life and death. What percentage of those who try succeed in their quest for the summit? How many people have died trying? What kinds of injuries and impairment have climbers suffered as a result of their attempts to reach the top of the world's highest mountain?

- The controversy about *Into Thin Air* by John Krakauer. Why are many of the relatives of people mentioned in the book angry with the author? Why do some people feel that he should not have written the book at all? Who are the people who defend the book and why?

PART 2   The World We Lost

Before You Read

1 **Getting the Meaning from Context.** Read the following excerpts from the next selection and choose the best definition for each italicized word. Use the hints in parentheses to aid you.

1. In order to round out my study of wolf family life, I needed to know what the *den* was like inside—how deep it was, the diameter of the passage, the presence (if any) of a nest at the end of the *burrow*, and such related information.

   The *den* is the place where the wolves go to ___b___ .
   a. hunt
   b. sleep
   c. die

   A *burrow* is ___c___ .
   a. a pile of sticks and mud
   b. a young wolf or dog
   c. a hole dug by an animal

2. The *Norseman* came over at about fifty feet. As it roared past, the plane waggled its wings gaily in salute, then lifted to skim the crest of the wolf *esker*, sending a blast of sand down the slope with its propeller wash. (The word *esker* is not well known even to English speakers, but the reader can use clues from the context: the word *crest*, your knowledge of where the man is going, what happens when the propeller gets near the esker.)

   The *Norseman* is a type of ___c___ .
   a. animal
   b. wind
   c. plane

   An *esker* is ___a___ .
   a. a ridge of sand
   b. a small river
   c. a kind of fruit tree

3. My mouth and eyes were soon full of sand and I was beginning to suffer from *claustrophobia*, for the tunnel was just big enough to admit me. (*Phobia* is a term used in psychology to refer to a deep, irrational fear. If you remember that the word *for* means "because" when it starts a secondary clause, you will understand what fear is referred to by this word.)

   Claustrophobia is the unreasonable fear of ___b___ .
   a. high, open places
   b. small, enclosed places
   c. wild animals

4. Despite my close familiarity with the wolf family, this was the kind of situation where irrational but deeply ingrained *prejudices* completely overmaster reason and experience. (If you break up the word *prejudice*, you get the prefix *pre-* meaning "before," and the root *jud*, which also appears in words such as *judge* and *judgment*.)

   In this context, *familiarity* means ___c___ .
   a. similarity
   b. hatred
   c. acquaintance

   Prejudices are ___b___ .
   a. strong and warm emotions
   b. opinions formed with no basis in fact
   c. conclusions drawn from observation and action

5. It seemed *inevitable* that the wolves *would* attack me, for even a *gopher* will make a fierce defense when he is cornered in his den. (The word *even* is your best clue to the meaning of the first and third italicized words.)

   Inevitable means ___a___ .
   a. certain
   b. highly unlikely
   c. possible

A *gopher* is an animal that is __b__ .
a. large and dangerous
b. small and defenseless
c. similar to a wolf

6. I was *appalled* at the realization of how easily I had forgotten, and how readily I had denied, all that the summer *sojourn* with the wolves had taught me about them…and about myself.

Appalled means __b__ .
a. pleased
b. shocked
c. relieved

Sojourn means __c__ .
a. reading
b. weather
c. stay

Read

Do you ever have nightmares? What is your secret fear? Poisonous snakes? Earthquakes? Water? Fire? Everyone is afraid of something, and wild animals appear high on the list of terror for many people. Farley Mowat, the world-famous Canadian writer and adventurer, shared this fear, but he still accepted a job that meant living alone in the far north for many months in direct contact with packs of wolves. The Wildlife Service of the Canadian government hired him to investigate claims that hordes of blood-thirsty wolves were killing the arctic caribou (large animals of the deer family). Much to his surprise, Mowat discovered that the wolves were not savage killers, but cautious and predictable animals that usually tried to stay out of people's way. He gave names to the wolves he studied (Angeline, George, and so forth), and even became fond of them.

Later he wrote a book called *Never Cry Wolf* about his experiences. It became a best-seller and was made into a popular movie that has changed many people's ideas about wolves, although extermination campaigns against wolves still continue. The following selection is the last chapter of his book. It tells of an incident that led the author to an important discovery, not about the wolves but about himself. What do you think the title might mean? See if your idea of it changes as you read the story.

The World We Lost

In order to round out my study of wolf family life, I needed to know what the den was like inside—how deep it was, the diameter of the passage, the presence (if any) of a nest at the end of the burrow, and such related information. For obvious reasons I had not been able to make the investigation while the
5   den was occupied, and since that time I had been too busy with other work to get around to it. Now, with time running out, I was in a hurry.

I trotted across country toward the den and I was within half a mile of it when there was a thunderous roar behind me. It was so loud and unexpected that I involuntarily flung myself down on the moss. The *Norseman* came over
10 at about fifty feet. As it roared past, the plane waggled its wings gaily in salute, then lifted to skim the crest of the wolf esker, sending a blast of sand down the slope with its propeller wash. I picked myself up and quieted my thumping heart, thinking black thoughts about the humorist in the now rapidly vanishing aircraft.

15 The den ridge was, as I had expected (and as the *Norseman* would have made quite certain in any case), wolfless. Reaching the entrance to the burrow I shed my heavy trousers, tunic, and sweater, and taking a flashlight (whose batteries were very nearly dead) and measuring tape from my pack, I began the difficult task of wiggling down the entrance tunnel.

20 The flashlight was so dim it cast only an orange glow—barely sufficient to enable me to read the marks on the measuring tape. I squirmed onward, descending at a forty-five-degree angle, for about eight feet. My mouth and eyes were soon full of sand and I was beginning to suffer from claustrophobia, for the tunnel was just big enough to admit me.

25 At the eight-foot mark the tunnel took a sharp upward bend and swung to the left. I pointed the torch in the new direction and pressed the switch.

Four green lights in the murk ahead reflected back the dim torch beam.

In this case green was not my signal to advance. I froze where I was, while my startled brain tried to digest the information that at least two wolves were with me in the den.

Despite my close familiarity with the wolf family, this was the kind of situation where irrational but deeply ingrained prejudices completely overmaster reason and experience. To be honest, I was so frightened that paralysis gripped me. I had no weapon of any sort, and in my awkward posture I could barely have gotten one hand free with which to ward off an attack. It seemed inevitable that the wolves *would* attack me, for even a gopher will make a fierce defense when he is cornered in his den.

The wolves did not even growl.

Save for the two faintly glowing pairs of eyes, they might not have been there at all.

The paralysis began to ease and though it was a cold day, sweat broke out all over my body. In a fit of blind bravado, I shoved the torch forward as far as my arm would reach.

It gave just sufficient light for me to recognize Angeline and one of the pups. They were scrunched hard against the back wall of the den; and they were as motionless as death.

The shock was wearing off by this time, and the instinct for self-preservation was regaining command. As quickly as I could I began wiggling back up the slanting tunnel, tense with the expectation that at any instant the wolves would charge. But by the time I reached the entrance and had scrambled well clear of it, I had still not heard nor seen the slightest sign of movement from the wolves.

I sat down on a stone and shakily lit a cigarette, becoming aware as I did so that I was no longer frightened. Instead an irrational rage possessed me. If I had had my rifle I believe I might have reacted in brute fury and tried to kill both wolves.

The cigarette burned down, and a wind began to blow out of the somber northern skies. I began to shiver again; this time from cold instead of rage. My anger was passing and I was limp in the aftermath. Mine had been the fury of resentment born of fear: resentment against the beasts who had engendered naked terror in me and who, by so doing, had intolerably affronted my human ego.

I was appalled at the realization of how easily I had forgotten, and how readily I had denied, all that the summer sojourn with the wolves had taught me about them…and about myself. I thought of Angeline and her pup cowering at the bottom of the den where they had taken refuge from the thundering apparition of the aircraft, and I was shamed.

Somewhere to the eastward a wolf howled; lightly, questioningly. I knew the voice, for I had heard it many times before. It was George, sounding the wasteland for an echo from the missing members of his family. But for me it was a voice which spoke of the lost world which once was ours before we chose the alien role; a world which I had glimpsed and almost entered,…only to be excluded, at the end, by my own self.

Farley Mowat

After You Read

Talk It Over

In small groups, discuss the following questions.

1. Would you be afraid to study wild animals? Would you be able to spend a summer completely alone, away from all human company? What character traits (qualities) must a person have to do these things?

2. Farley Mowat writes in a personal, down-to-earth style. He is not afraid to tell about his faults and his feelings. In your opinion, what does this indicate about his character?

3. At a dramatic point in his story, Mowat interjects a bit of humor. He says, "In this case green was not my signal to advance." What does he mean by this? The use of humor at a very serious moment is called comic relief. What do you think of this technique?

4. How can you tell that Mowat has gotten to know the wolves as individuals and that he feels affection for them?

5. Have you ever seen wolves? Do you know of places other than Canada where they live?

6. In your opinion, should wolves be exterminated or not? Why?

Focus on Testing

Summarizing a Narrative

On essay tests, you may need to write the summary of a narrative. Most stories cannot be summarized in a single sentence, so the summary will have to be longer than a summary statement. Good summaries are brief and include all essential elements. So the best one tells the most in the fewest words.

Generally, narratives (fiction or nonfiction) follow these four steps for plot development:

1. conflict: the problem or difficult situation at the beginning. (After all, if everything were going fine, there would be no movement, no real story to tell.)
2. complication: the group of events or other factors that increase the conflict and make it more difficult.
3. climax: the high point or turning point of the action that occurs toward the end.
4. resolution: the ceasing or solution of the problem for better or for worse. Sometimes there is a happy ending and sometimes a sad one, depending on the author's view of reality and the point he or she wants to make.

Use these steps are guidelines to write narrative summaries. It is not easy to write a summary, so many writers do a rough copy first on a separate sheet of paper. Then they read it over and cross out the parts that are not essential. Finally, they write the final version on the test paper. Try this technique in the following exercise. Afterward, compare your summary with those of your classmates. Who has said the most in the fewest words? That person has the best summary.

Write a summary of Mowat's story in eight sentences (or fewer) by completing the following outline.

1. (conflict) In the far north, the Canadian writer Farley Mowat…
2. (complication) When he was within half a mile of his goal…
3. (climax) Suddenly in the darkness he saw…
4. (resolution) Afterward, Mowat realized…

2 **Expressing the Theme.** Mowat's story was based on true experience, but he chose, from among many true events, certain ones to tell for a particular reason, to show a certain general idea, or theme. Describe in one or two sentences what you consider the theme of the selection.

Making Connections

- On the Internet or at the library find information on the attempts to re-introduce wolves into certain parts of the United States, such as Yellowstone Park, by bringing them in from Canada. What groups are in favor of these programs? What groups are against them? Why?
- Read the book *Never Cry Wolf* by Farley Mowat, or see the movie based on it and write a brief report about it to share with the class.
- Find some stories about wolves from songs, folk tales or in the bookstore, and describe one of them to your classmates. What is the figure of the wolf that is usually presented? Do you think it is a true picture of the animal or not? Explain.

3 **Thinking Your Way Out of Danger.** Many times the only way to get out of a dangerous spot is with your brain. Read over the following imaginary situations; then work together in small groups and try to figure out how you would escape from each of them. The solutions are on page 35.

Situation A: The Windowless Prison

While participating in a revolution against an unjust tyrant, you are caught and thrown into a prison cell that has a dirt floor, thick stone walls, and no windows. There is only a skylight, very high above, to provide light and air. To prevent escape, there are no tables or chairs, only a very small mattress on the floor. Just before you are locked in, a comrade whispers to you that it is possible to escape through the skylight by digging a hole in the floor. How can you do this?

Situation B: The Cave of the Two Robots

Having entered a time machine, you have been whisked one thousand years into the future to find yourself at the mercy of a superior civilization. These creatures of the future choose to amuse themselves by playing games with you. They set you in a cave that has two doors at the end of it: one leads back to the time machine that would transport you safely home, and the other leads to a pit filled with horrible monsters. There are also two robots in the cave. They know the secret of the doors. One always tells the truth and one always lies, and you do not know which is which. According to the rules of their game, you are allowed to ask one question to one of the robots. What question should you ask? How can you know which door to choose?

What Do You Think?

Courting Danger

Many activities can be dangerous: mountain climbing, sky diving, bungee jumping, scuba diving. Even sports like downhill skiing, football, in-line skating, and horseback riding are dangerous at times. Do you participate in any of these activities, or do you have friends or relatives who do? Which do you consider the most dangerous? Why? In your opinion, when is it irresponsible to participate in dangerous activities? Explain.

Answers

"Thinking Your Way Out of Danger," page 34: Situation A: You simply dig a hole in the floor and use the dirt to build a ramp and them climb out through the skylight. Situation B: You should ask the question, "Which door would the other robot tell me to take to get to the time machine?" If you are asking the robot who always tells the truth, he will tell you the wrong door, because he knows the other robot lies. If you are asking the robot who always lies, he will tell you the wrong door too because he knows that the other robot always tells the truth. So you simply open the opposite door, get in your time machine, and go home.

Video Activities: Extreme Sports

Before You Watch.   Discuss these questions in small groups.

1.   What is the most dangerous sport you have tried? Why did you try a dangerous sport?
2.   What do you know about hang gliding and paragliding? Describe these sports.
3.   Have you ever meditated? What was it like?

Watch.   Complete the sentences.

1.   People enjoy hang gliding and paragliding because those sports are _____ .
     a.   peaceful
     b.   good exercise
     c.   safe
2.   Hang gliding and paragliding are similar to _____ .
     a.   riding in a plane
     b.   going up in a rocket ship
     c.   flying like a bird
3.   Tandem rides are for _____ .
     a.   one person
     b.   two people
     c.   three people

Watch Again.   Answer these questions in small groups.

1.   What is the name of the place that many people go to hang-glide?

     _____

2.   The narrator says, "To you and me it might be intimidating; to the veteran, it's blissful."
     a.   What is *it*?
     b.   Who are the veterans?
     c.   What are other words for *intimidating*?
     d.   What are other words for *blissful*?
3.   Circle the words that are used to describe hang gliding.
     a.   spiritual   d.   natural
     b.   holy   e.   ethereal
     c.   dreamlike

After You Watch.   Find an article about an extreme sport. Write a summary of the article. Your summary should answer these questions:
1.   What is the sport?
2.   Why is it dangerous?
3.   Where is it popular?
4.   Why do people do it?

Chapter 3

Sex and Gender

IN THIS CHAPTER

Down through the ages, the eternal "battle of the sexes" has been a popular topic. This chapter begins with a discussion of how technology and tradition blend to aid romance in today's Japan. Then a poem gives one man's view of the transforming power of love. An article about love and intimacy follows, in which contemporary psychologists reveal a possible explanation of why we fall in love with one person rather than with another.

PART 1 # For Better or Worse

Before You Read

1   **Distinguishing the General from the Specific.** The following article is from the *Wall Street Journal*, a newspaper best known for its business and financial news. This, however, is a feature article, one that deals with a topic of general human interest. Like many feature articles, it alternates between general statements (large, broad ideas) and specific information (small points, details, statistics, particular cases, and examples that illustrate or support the general statements). Take three minutes to skim the selection. Then answer the following questions about its overall organization.

1. Does the article begin with the general or the specific? Why do you think it begins this way?
2. At what point does it change?
3. How does it end?
4. How could you briefly describe its organization?

Read

What is the best way to find a husband or a wife? Should you let your family select a mate for you or should you date many people and try to "fall in love"? Many cultures have the tradition of arranged marriages. These are brought about by "matchmakers" who find and introduce possible candidates to a young person at the family's request and for a fee.

1.   What do you think of this practice?
2.   From the first phrase of the title, what can you infer about the author's point of view on arranged marriages?

In the article you will find out what the Japanese mean by being "wet" or "dry" when making a decision and how modern technology is aiding romance. Read for main ideas and see if you change some of your opinions about the best way to select a mate.

For Better or Worse, Arranged Marriages
Still Thrive in Japan

"He was a banker," Toshiko says of the first young man her parents set her up with. "He was so-o-o-o-o boring."

The second was an architect. He tried to impress her with his knowledge of the historic hotel where they had coffee. "He was wrong on almost every point," she sniffs.

The third, for some reason, "asked me a lot of questions about the French Revolution."

Seven more followed. She turned them all down. Just twenty-six, and seeing on the sly a boyfriend from the wrong side of the tracks, Toshiko was in no hurry to get married. With her Yale diploma, her colloquial English, and her very modern outlook on life, this rich family's daughter from Tokyo could almost pass for a rich family's daughter from Greenwich, Connecticut.

But Tokyo isn't Greenwich. Like most unmarried women here, Toshiko (it's not her real name; her parents read this newspaper) still lives with her mother and father. And like most parents here, they think that by the time a young woman reaches her mid-twenties she ought to be married. About a year ago, they began to pressure her to go through *omiai*, the ceremonial first meeting in the traditional Japanese arranged marriage.

Meet and Look

"It was such a drag to get up in the morning, because I knew at breakfast we would have another fight about this," Toshiko says. "I did my first *omiai* so I could have some peace at home."

These days lots of young Japanese do *omiai*, literally, "meet and look." Many of them, unlike Toshiko, do so willingly. In today's prosperous and increasingly conservative Japan, the traditional *omiai kekkon*, or arranged marriage, is thriving.

But there is a difference. In the original *omiai*, the young Japanese couldn't reject the partner chosen by his parents and their *nakodo*, or middleman. After World War II, many Japanese abandoned the arranged marriage as part of their rush to adopt the more democratic ways of their American conquerors. The Western *ren'ai kekkon*, or love marriage, came into vogue; Japanese began picking their own mates by dating and falling in love.

But the Western way was often found wanting in an important respect: It didn't necessarily produce a partner of the right economic, social, and educational qualifications. "Today's young people are quite calculating," says Chieko Akiyama, a social commentator.

No Strings

What seems to be happening now is a repetition of a familiar process in the country's history, the "Japanization" of an adopted foreign practice. The Western ideal of marrying for love is accommodated in a new *omiai* in which both parties are free to reject the match. "*Omiai* is evolving into a sort of stylized introduction," Mrs. Akiyama says.

Many young Japanese now date in their early twenties, but with no thought of marriage. When they reach the age when society decrees they should wed—in the middle twenties for women, the late twenties for men— they increasingly turn to *omiai*. Some studies suggest that as many as 40 percent of marriages each year are *omiai kekkon*. It's hard to be sure, say those who study the matter, because many Japanese couples, when polled, describe their marriage as a love match even if it was arranged.

These days, doing *omiai* often means going to a computer matching service rather than to a *nakodo*. The *nakodo* of tradition was an old woman who knew all the kids in the neighborhood and went around trying to pair them off by speaking to parents; a successful match would bring her a wedding invitation and a gift of money. But Japanese today find it's less awkward to reject a proposed partner if the *nakodo* is a computer.

Japan has about five hundred computer matching services. Some big companies, including Mitsubishi, run one for their employees. At a typical commercial service, an applicant pays $80 to $125 to have his or her personal data stored in the computer for two years and $200 or so more if a marriage results. The stored information includes some obvious items, like

education and hobbies, and some not-so-obvious ones, like whether a person is the oldest child. (First sons, and to some extent first daughters, face an obligation of caring for elderly parents.)

65 The customer also tells the computer service what he or she has in mind. "The men are all looking for good-looking women, and the women are all looking for men who can support them well," says a counselor at one service.

Whether generated by computer or *nakodo*, the introduction follows a ritual course. The couple, who have already seen each other's data and picture,
70 arrive at a coffee shop or computer-service meeting room accompanied by their parents and the *nakodo* or a representative of the service. After a few minutes of pleasantries, the two are left to themselves. A recent comedy movie had such a couple heading directly to one of Japan's "love hotels," which offer rooms by the hour; but ordinarily it takes love a good bit longer to flower, if it does at all.

75 And there still are those Japanese who consider love and marriage to be quite separate things. Here, in brief, are how three arranged marriages of the past twenty-five years unfolded.

The Asamis

Munehiro Asami was a twenty-eight-year-old office worker at a machine-parts
80 company. "I had a friend from childhood whose mother was very pushy," he says. "One day she stomped into my room and took a picture of me out of my picture album. She also left an *omiai* picture of a lady. I was to meet this girl and I didn't want to go."

Neither did the woman. She was Reiko Ohtsuka, a twenty-three-year-old
85 part-time office worker. She recalls how she "half jokingly" agreed to the meeting, then asked if it was too late to change her mind. It was.

But all was for the best, apparently. Mr. Asami warmly remembers the ritual as "like being introduced to a cute girl by your friend." Miss Ohtsuka discovered that her worries about what to talk about were unfounded. "We dated

90 for four months," she says, "fell in love, and got married."

The Watanabes

In 1972 he was five years out of Tokyo University, Japan's Harvard. He was working for a big Tokyo
95 bank. And, reflecting his heavy work schedule and a certain Japanese shyness, he had never had a date.

100 Mr. Watanabe—he doesn't want to be identified further—always intended to marry through *omiai*. "It's a good system," he says, because the partners don't waste time on someone who
105 doesn't meet their specifications. It's also realistic, he adds: "In love marriages, the two look only at each other's good points: We calculate the bad as well."

110 Mr. Watanabe was looking for a wife who, first and foremost, "would get along well with my father." To that end, he asked for someone from his home prefecture of Yamanashi. He also wanted a wife who wouldn't have to support her parents. Being himself a second son, he could qualify for a woman who
115 was also looking for a mate free of parental obligations.

Thus, after an introduction through his uncle, did Mr. Watanabe marry a second daughter from his hometown in early 1973. They now have two children. "Everyone wants to get married through love, but not everyone can," Mr. Watanabe says.

120 The Japanese like to think they are "wet" (emotional) compared with "dry" (rational) Westerners. But Mr. Watanabe thinks that "when it comes to marriage, we Japanese are dry."

The Azumas

Kikuko Azuma, who found her husband through *omiai* twenty-five years ago, says the custom is still "the shortest, most convenient way." She is recom-
125 mending it to her twenty-two-year-old daughter.

Mrs. Azuma was only twenty and just out of junior college when she wed. But she was eager to study in the United States and by coincidence was introduced to a twenty-seven-year-old trading company executive about to be
130 transferred to New York. He was from a well-to-do family, and Mrs. Azuma recalls being chauffeured to the *omiai* at an expensive Western restaurant. "I admired his social status," she says.

Then too, her own parents were having marital difficulties, and she feared that if they divorced she would seem a less desirable catch in a future *omiai*.
135 So she had to move quickly, even though "at twenty I hadn't given much thought to getting married."

Did she love him? "Love and marriage are different," Mrs. Azuma replies firmly. "I think after you get married, love eventually emerges." Does her husband of twenty-five years agree? "I don't know," she says. "I don't really know
140 him very well."

There is one other *omiai* success story to report. It is about Toshiko, the young sophisticate who opened this article. After coolly dismissing ten young men sent her way, she was intrigued by Number 11, a physician who had worked in Africa. A friend says he was the first guy Toshiko had met whom
145   she found "intellectually compatible" and who, more importantly, wasn't intimidated by her.

Toshiko herself isn't available for comment. She is in Fiji making wedding preparations.

Urban C. Lehner

After You Read

Focus on Testing

Improving Your Chances on Multiple-Choice Exams

Multiple choice is a common format on objective exams. You can use the following exercise to practice your strategy for this type of test. Do the exercise without looking back at the reading, as if this were an exam. Here are some tips to help you.

1. There is usually a time limit during a test, so first quickly look through the whole exercise and do the items you are sure of.
2. Next, if there is no penalty for guessing, take a guess at the remaining ones. Generally, if you are uncertain, choose an option in the middle, either b or c, rather than a or d. These tend to be used more for correct answers. If you are just guessing, keep the same letter consistently. Long statements in multiple choice tend to be true.
3. Afterward, go back to the reading, scan for the answers, and correct your work.

Choose the best way of finishing each statement, based on what you have just read.

1. The literal translation of the Japanese word *omiai* is _____ .
   a. ceremonial introduction
   b. meet and look
   c. computer wedding
   d. arranged marriage
2. After World War II, a new practice that came into fashion in Japan was _____ .
   a. divorce
   b. arranged marriage
   c. love marriage
   d. church wedding
3. In order to use the new commercial services for *omiai*, a person must _____ .
   a. pay money
   b. belong to a noble family
   c. go to a "love hotel"
   d. all of the above

4. Many Japanese do not want to marry _____ .
   a.   an oldest child
   b.   a youngest child
   c.   a middle child
   d.   a twin
5. The reason that this position in the family makes the person a less desirable marriage partner is that he or she _____ .
   a.   is usually very spoiled and arrogant
   b.   does not inherit any money or property
   c.   has to take care of his or her parents when they are older
   d.   must make all the food
6. In comparison with the time right after World War II, the practice of arranged marriages in Japan now seems to be _____ .
   a.   decreasing
   b.   increasing
   c.   about the same
   d.   completely finished

2   **Explaining the Meaning of Expressions and Phrases.** Find each phrase or expression in italics in the reading and guess what it means by looking at its context. Then write a short explanation of it.

1. He was wrong *on almost every point*,…(line 4)

   <u>   about almost everything he said   </u>

2. She *turned them* all *down.* (line 8)

   _____

3. Just twenty-six, and seeing *on the sly*…(line 8)

   _____

4. …a boyfriend *from the wrong side of the tracks*,…(line 9)

   _____

5. *"It was such a drag* to get up in the morning…(line 20)

   _____

6. …love marriage, *came into vogue*;…(line 31)

   _____

3   **Finding Support for General Ideas.** Find specific facts, statistics, and examples from the article to support the following general ideas.

1. In today's prosperous and increasingly conservative Japan, the traditional *omiai kekkon*, or arranged marriage, is thriving.
2. What seems to be happening now is a repetition of a familiar process in the country's history, the "Japanization" of an adopted foreign practice.
3. The Japanese like to think they are "wet" (emotional) compared with "dry" (rational) Westerners. But Mr. Watanabe thinks that "when it comes to marriage, we Japanese are dry."

4 **Drawing Conclusions from a Chart.** You can find specifics to support generalizations or you can do the reverse: make generalizations on the basis of specifics. The chart Months for Weddings in the U.S. gives specific statistics. Read the chart and write C in front of the one generalization that correctly describes the data. Write I in front of the others, which are incorrect.

Top 10 Months for Weddings in the U.S.			
Month	**Weddings**	**Month**	**Weddings**
1. June	256,000	6. October	221,000
2. August	242,000	7. December	184,000
3. May	231,000	8. April	175,000
4. July	228,000	9. November	174,000
5. September	227,000	10. February	166,000

Source: *National Center for Health Statistics*
Figures are for 1992 from a U.S. total of some 2,362,000 weddings, a decrease of 9000 from 1991.
March is at No. 11 with 145,000, and January is last with 112,000.

_____ 1.   Most Americans get married at Christmastime.

_____ 2   Americans do not care which month they get married in.

_____ 3.   Americans prefer to marry in months that begin with the letter J.

_____ 4.   Americans prefer warm weather for weddings.

_____ 5.   Americans prefer cold weather for weddings.

In a wedding in Guanajuato, Mexico, two relatives called the "godparents of the knot" put a rope around the bride and groom to show that they will be faithful to each other for life.

Talk It Over

In small groups, discuss the following questions.

1. According to the article, at what age is a woman expected to marry in Japan? A man? What do you think is the ideal age to marry? Why?

2. What are some of the advantages of arranged marriages? What are some of the disadvantages?

3. Do you think that arranged marriages are more or less likely to end in divorce? Why?

4. Does everyone have to get married? Can some people remain single and still lead a happy and complete life? Explain your opinion.

5. Did reading the article give you any new information? Did it change your views on how to select a marriage partner? Explain.

---

5   **Looking at Love.** Take a fresh look at love by reading the following poem by the English poet Alfred Edward Housman (1859–1936). Like many English poems, this one uses rhyme, the use of the same sounds at the end of the last words in certain lines (for example: *you/grew, brave/behave*). Read it aloud to enjoy the rhyme and rhythm, and take care to pronounce the word *again* in the second stanza in the British way (əge' ɪn) so that it will rhyme correctly.

Oh, When I Was in Love with You

Oh, when I was in love with you,
    Then I was clean and brave,
And miles around the wonder grew
    How well I did behave.

And now the fancy passes by,
    And nothing will remain,
And miles around they'll say that I
    Am quite myself again.

Talk It Over

In small groups, discuss the following questions.

1. Do you think that love can transform a person? How? In the poem, is the transformation permanent or temporary? Do you agree?

2. Is there a regular pattern of rhyme in the poem? Why do you think the poet used rhyme? What effect does it have on a reader?

3. How would you describe the tone of the poem? Do you think a woman would use this tone when talking about love? Why or why not?

| PART 2 | # Finding Real Love |

Before You Read

1 **Previewing a Reading for Its Organization.** The following reading is taken from the popular magazine *Psychology Today*. The word *psychology* comes from two Greek roots: *psycho*, meaning "breath, spirt, mind," and *logos*, meaning "reason" or "study of." Therefore, psychology is the science or study of the mind. An article on psychology often uses specific stories of real people to show general principles about the way the human mind works. These stories are called *case studies* (or *case histories*). Look at the following questions. Then skim the article to answer them.

- Where does the case study begin in this article: at the beginning, in the middle, or at the end?
- What are the names of the two people in the case study?
- Judging from the title and first few sentences, the article is about people's need for intimacy and an intimate relationship. What do you understand by an intimate relationship?

In your opinion, why do people buy this magazine and read articles like this?

2 **Scanning for More Exact, Concise, or Colorful Synonyms.** Synonyms are words that have similar meanings, but of course no two words ever mean exactly the same thing. Scan the reading selection for the synonyms that say almost the same thing as the words in parentheses but in a more exact, shorter, or more colorful way.

1. Human beings (desire intensely) ___*crave*___ intimacy.
2. …four mental health professionals discuss their ideas about how we (destroy by many small acts) _____ our intimate relationships….
3. The various decisions we make, and our behavior toward one another, are what (helps) _____ closeness or drive us apart.
4. We often choose partners who remind us of (important and meaningful) _____ people from our childhood….
5. …and we set out to (build again) _____ the patterns of our childhood.
6. She was instantly attracted to the tall, lean man with (an absent) _____ look in his eyes….
7. Abe, who had been standing alone, was delighted when Tara (came near to) _____ him….
8. It was not the kind of suffocating closeness he had always (feared greatly) _____…
9. …his mother, who used to enter his room uninvited and arrange his personal belongings with no regard to his (right to independence and secrecy) _____.
10. But occasionally, Abe would come home from work tired and (irritated)… _____.

11.   …and he responded the way he did with his mother: by (moving away) _____.

12.   She responded in the same way she did when her father withdrew: by (hanging on tightly) _____.

Read

One purpose of psychology is to help us understand why we act the way we do. Psychologists examine case studies and identify patterns of behavior that occur again and again. We are often not conscious of why we are behaving in certain ways. By analyzing the patterns, we can discover the hidden causes for our actions.

• Why do we feel immediately attracted to one person but not to another?

• Why do two people in an intimate relationship often interact beautifully at first, and later develop serious problems?

Read the article to find out some answers to these questions.

Finding Real Love
By Cary Barbor

Human beings crave intimacy, to love and be loved. Why then do people feel isolated in their intimate relationships?

We need to be close to other people as surely as we need food and water. But while it's relatively easy to get ourselves a good meal, it is difficult for
5   many of us to create and maintain intimacy with others, particularly a romantic partner. There are many variables that affect the quality of our relationships with others; it's difficult to pin it on one thing or another. But in this article, based on a symposium recently held at the annual American Psychological Association convention in Washington, D.C., four mental health professionals
10   discuss their ideas about how we sabotage our intimate relationships—and what we can do to fix them.

Choose to Lose?
Many factors influence the level of intimacy we enjoy in our relationships. The various decisions we make, and our behavior toward one another, are what
15   foster closeness or drive us apart. These decisions are all under our control, although we are influenced by old patterns that we must work to change.

The first decision we make about a relationship is the partner we choose. Whom we fall in love with determines the level of intimacy in our relationships, according to Ayala Malach Pines, Ph.D. who heads the behavioral sciences in
20   management program at Ben-Gurion University in Israel. We often choose partners who remind us of significant people from our childhood—often our parents—and we set out to recreate the patterns of our childhood. Let's look at an example:

Tara met Abe at a party. She was instantly attracted to the tall, lean man
25   with a faraway look in his eyes. Abe, who had been standing alone, was delighted when Tara approached him with her open smile and outstretched hand. She was not only beautiful, but she struck him as warm and nurturing as well. The conversation between them flowed instantly. It felt comfortable and easy. Eventually, they fell in love, and after a year, they were married.

30   The intimacy between them also felt terrific to Abe. It was not the kind of suffocating closeness he always dreaded—the kind of intrusive closeness he experienced as a child with his mother, who used to enter his room uninvited and arrange his personal belongings with no regard to his privacy. But Tara was different. She did not intrude.

35   But occasionally, Abe would come home from work tired and annoyed. All he wanted was a drink and to sit with the paper until he could calm down and relax. Seeing him that way, Tara would become concerned. "What is going on?" she would ask anxiously. "Nothing," he would answer. Sure that there was something very wrong, and assuming that it must be something
40   about her or their marriage, Tara would insist that he tell her. She reminded him of his mother, and he responded the way he did with his mother: by withdrawing. To Tara, this felt similar to the way her father behaved. She responded in the same way she did when her father withdrew: by clinging. The struggle between them continued and became more and more intense over
45   time, with Tara demanding more intimacy and Abe demanding more space.

Recreating the Family

Like Abe and Tara, people choose partners who help them recreate their childhood struggles. Tara fell in love with a man with "a faraway look in his eyes," and subsequently had to struggle for greater intimacy. Abe fell in love
50   with a woman who was "warm and nurturing," then spent a lot of energy struggling for more space.

Tara's unresolved intimacy issues complement Abe's. For example, one partner (often the woman) will fight to break down the defenses and create more intimacy while the other (often the man) will withdraw and create dis-
55   tance. So the "dance of intimacy" follows: If the woman gets too close, the man pulls back. If he moves too far away, she pursues, and so on.

To achieve greater intimacy, the partners must overcome the anxiety that compels them to take their respective parts in that dance. In the example, Tara needs to control her abandonment anxiety and not pursue Abe when he
60   withdraws, and Abe needs to control his engulfment anxiety when Tara pursues him and not withdraw. Working to overcome these anxieties is an opportunity to resolve childhood issues and can be a major healing experience for both partners.

After You Read

3   **Arranging Events in a Sequence.** The order in which events are described is not always the order in which they actually occurred. The following events are from the case study described in the article. Put them in the order in which they occurred in real life, by writing a letter in front of each one, with A for the first and H for the last.

_____ 1. Tara and Abe fell in love.

_____ 2. Tara began to cling to Abe.

_____ 3. Tara would become concerned and insist on talking about what was wrong.

_____ 4. Tara and Abe met at a party.

_____ 5. Abe would come home tired and annoyed.

___A___ 6. Tara wanted more closeness with her father, and Abe more respect for his privacy from his mother.

_____ 7. Abe began to withdraw from Tara.

_____ 8. Tara and Abe got married.

4   **Identifying Causes.** The article points out common patterns in the behavior of people involved in intimate relationships. Complete each statement to show the cause for the behavior described.

1. According to Dr. Ayala Malach, we often fall in love with someone because he or she...reminds us of a significant person from our childhood _____.

2. Tara was first attracted to Abe because he had _____.

3. Abe was first attracted to Tara because she seemed _____.

4. Tara began to cling more and more to Abe because she felt that he _____.

5. Abe began to withdraw more and more from Tara because he felt that she _____.

Talk It Over

In small groups, discuss the following questions.

1. In simple words, what went wrong between Abe and Tara? Do you think this is a common pattern of behavior?

2. What do you think is meant in the article by the "dance of intimacy"?

3. Do most people really look for someone to love who reminds them of one of their parents? Can it be the opposite? Explain.

4. Is it hard to find love? What is meant in the title by "real love"? What other kinds of love are there, and how do you know when love is real?

5   **Writing the Ending.** What happened to Abe and Tara? Did they get a divorce? Did they make up and "live happily ever after"? Did their parents come to visit? Did they go to a marriage counselor? Alone or in a small group, write an ending of 10 to 15 sentences for the case study of Abe and Tara.

What Do You Think?

How Men and Women Communicate

A well-known "pop (popular) psychology" book in North America is called *Men Are From Mars, Women Are From Venus*. The book talks about the differences in the styles of communication between the sexes and why they have such difficulty understanding one another. Venus (women), says author John Gray, have different values from Mars (men). "A woman's sense of self is defined through her feelings and the quality of her relationships." But "Martians (men) value power, competency, efficiency, and advancement. Their sense of self is defined through their ability to achieve results." What do you think of these definitions? Would they be correct for men and women in other cultures? Why do you think men and women have difficulty understanding and communicating with one another?

Video Activities: Seeking Love

Before You Watch.   Discuss these questions in small groups.

1. What are some ways to meet people?
2. Which ways are the most effective?
3. What is the most important quality to seek in a boyfriend or a girlfriend?

Watch.   Answer these questions in small groups.

1. What does the narrator say is probably what most of us want and need the most? _____
2. Check the ways of finding a mate that are mentioned in this video segment.
    a. ___ using a dating service
    b. ___ placing personal advertisements
    c. ___ getting involved in activities that you enjoy
    d. ___ asking friends to help you meet someone
3. Put a check (✓) next to things that you should do and an (x) next to things that you shouldn't do on a first date.
    a. ___ Ask creative questions.
    b. ___ Dress well.
    c. ___ Be someone that you're not.
    d. ___ Ask questions to find out about your date's financial status.

Watch Again.   Circle the correct answers.

1. What does Dr. Jim Soulis say you should do before you start looking for a mate?
    a. look into yourself
    b. lose weight and buy new clothes
    c. read books about relationships
2. Dr. Jim Soulis says that the most important quality you must have to find love is ____.
    a. good looks
    b. money
    c. intelligence
    d. confidence
3. Which three things does Victoria Parker tell her clients to do?
    a. meditate
    b. think positively
    c. study themselves
    d. listen to a tape recorder
    e. become active in things they enjoy
4. Judy Knoll says that _____ personal ads are not effective.
    a. imaginative
    b. negative
    c. boastful

5. Men should never _____ .
   a.   pay for a woman's friends
   b.   compliment a woman on a part of her body
   c.   call a woman when they said that they would

6. Men don't like women who _____ .
   a.   become attached too quickly
   b.   ask them a lot of questions
   c.   make a lot of money

After You Watch.   Find an article about dating or marriage in a newspaper or a magazine. Use the article to improve your reading speed.

1. First estimate the number of words in the reading by counting the number of words in two or three lines, taking the average, and then multiplying the average by the number of lines in the text.

2. Write down the time and begin reading. Remember to use clustering to increase your speed. When you are finished, figure out the number of words per minute. This is your reading speed.

3. Finally, read the article again more slowly. How many important ideas did you miss? If you missed a lot, then you should try to read more slowly.

Chapter 4

Mysteries Past and Present

IN THIS CHAPTER

When does the part of human nature that is selfish and barbaric take over in some-one? One of the classic puzzle stories of the English language focuses on the com-plex motivations of human nature and the human heart. The next selection examines how the legendary dragon helped modern Chinese scholars unravel an important mystery of their past and restore their cultural confidence.

The Lady or the Tiger?

Before You Read

1   **Skimming and Scanning.** Since this story has a surprise ending, you will probably enjoy it more if you don't skim the whole selection in advance. Just look at the title and skim the first half to get a general idea of what the story is about. Next, scan the appropriate paragraphs to answer the following questions about the narrative elements of *setting, character,* and *plot* ~~plot~~

1.   What do you find out about the *setting* (the where and when) from the first paragraph? _In the very olden time_

2.   Which of the *characters* is presented first? _semibarbaric king_

3.   Since the tone is playful and ironic, you might have to read over the first three paragraphs several times to understand the description of this character. Do you think he is kind or cruel? Humble or arrogant? What other qualities does he have?

   _____

4.   It is obvious that in this story the setting and characterization are given first and the *plot* (action) comes later. By skimming over the first part and looking at the title, what can you guess about the plot?_____

   _____

   _____

2   **Getting Meaning from Structure and Context.** One skill that can help you guess the meanings of words better is breaking the words down into smaller parts and looking for clues within the surrounding context. Practice this skill by writing definitions for the italicized words in the following sentences taken from the reading.

1.   In the very olden time, there lived a *semibarbaric* king, who was a man of exuberant fancy and of an authority so irresistible that, at his will, he turned his varied fancies into facts. (lines 1–3) (To understand the meaning of the prefix *semi-*, first notice that *barbaric* can be associated with the following negative-sounding words from the surrounding context: *authority, irresistible,* and *at his will.* Then notice that *exuberant fancy* is not negative-sounding so the king can't be all that barbaric.)

   semibarbaric:

   _____

2.   He was greatly given to *self-communing*, and when he and himself agreed upon anything, the thing was done. (lines 3–4) (The clue to the meaning here is in the following words from the context: *he and himself agreed….*)

   self-communing:

   _____

3. This vast amphitheater, with its encircling galleries,…was an agent of poetic justice in which crime was punished, or virtue rewarded, by the decrees of an *impartial* and *incorruptible* chance. (lines 11–14) (Both words begin with prefixes that mean the same thing; both have smaller words—*partial* and *corrupt*—in them.)
    impartial: _____

    incorruptible: _____

4. He was subject to no guidance or influence but that of the *aforementioned* impartial and incorruptible chance. (lines 25–26)
    aforementioned: _____

5. The moment that the case of the criminal was thus decided,…great wails went up from the hired mourners posted on the outer rim of the arena, and the vast audience, with bowed heads and *downcast* hearts, wended slowly their *homeward* way, mourning greatly….(lines 29–33)
    downcast: _____

    homeward: _____

6. As is usual in such cases, she was the *apple of his eye* and was loved by him above all humanity. (lines 65–66) (Here it is a phrase, not a word, you must break into smaller parts. When you do that, the phrase doesn't make any literal sense, but can you guess the meaning from the latter part of the sentence?)
    apple of his eye: _____

7. In *afteryears* such things became *commonplace* enough, but then they were, in no slight degree, novel and startling. (lines 79–80)
    afteryears: _____

    commonplace: _____

Read

The following story, written by the American writer Frank Stockton (1834–1902), has been considered a classic "brainteaser" ever since it first appeared. Perhaps this is because it builds up to an intensely dramatic moment, a moment during which a single act will decide between life and death, between the greatest sense of relief and the most horrifying pain. The story is presented as it was originally written, with no adaptation. The vocabulary is difficult, so you should not try to understand every word. Read to understand the main ideas only.

The Lady or the Tiger?

In the very olden time, there lived a semibarbaric king, who was a man of exuberant fancy and of an authority so irresistible that, at his will, he turned his
varied fancies into facts. He was greatly given to self-communing, and when
he and himself agreed upon anything, the thing was done. When everything
moved smoothly, his nature was bland and genial; but whenever there was a
little hitch, he was blander and more genial still, for nothing pleased him so
much as to make the crooked straight, and crush down uneven places.

Among his borrowed notions was that of the public arena, in which, by
exhibitions of manly and beastly valor, the minds of his subjects were refined
and cultured.

But even here the exuberant and barbaric fancy asserted itself. This vast
amphitheater, with its encircling galleries, its mysterious vault, and its unseen
passages, was an agent of poetic justice in which crime was punished, or
virtue rewarded, by the decrees of an impartial and incorruptible chance.

When a subject was accused of a crime of sufficient importance to interest the king, public notice was given that on an appointed day the fate of the
accused person would be decided in the king's arena.

When all the people had assembled in the galleries, and the king, surrounded by his court, sat high up on his throne of royal state on one side of
the arena, he gave a signal, a door beneath him opened, and the accused
subject stepped out into the amphitheater. Directly opposite him, on the other
side of the enclosed space, were two doors, exactly alike and side by side.
It was the duty and the privilege of the person on trial to walk directly to these
doors and open one of them. He could open either door he pleased. He was
subject to no guidance or influence but that of the aforementioned impartial
and incorruptible chance. If he opened the one, there came out of it a hungry

tiger, the fiercest and most cruel that could be procured, which immediately sprang upon him and tore him to pieces as a punishment for his guilt. The moment that the case of the criminal was thus decided, doleful iron bells were clanged, great wails went up from the hired mourners posted on the outer rim of the arena, and the vast audience, with bowed heads and downcast hearts, wended slowly their homeward way, mourning greatly that one so young and fair, or so old and respected, should have merited so dire a fate.

But if the accused person opened the other door, there came forth from it a lady, the most suitable to his years and station that His Majesty could select among his fair subjects; and to this lady he was immediately married, as a reward of his innocence. It mattered not that he might already possess a wife and family, or that his affections might be engaged upon an object of his own selection. The king allowed no such arrangements to interfere with his great scheme of punishment and reward. The exercises, as in the other instance, took place immediately, and in the arena. Another door opened beneath the king, and a priest, followed by a band of choristers, and dancing maidens blowing joyous airs on golden horns, advanced to where the pair stood side by side, and the wedding was promptly and cheerily solemnized. Then the gay brass bells rang forth their merry peals, and the people shouted glad hurrahs, and the innocent man, preceded by children strewing flowers on his path, led his bride to his home.

This was the king's semibarbaric method of administering justice. Its perfect fairness is obvious. The criminal could not know out of which door would come the lady. He opened either he pleased, without having the slightest ideas whether, in the next instant, he was to be devoured or married. On some occasions the tiger came out of one door, and on some, out of the other. The decisions were not only fair—they were positively decisive. The accused person was instantly punished if he found himself guilty, and if innocent, he was rewarded on the spot, whether he liked it or not. There was no escape from the judgments of the king's arena.

The institution was a very popular one. When the people gathered together on one of the great trial days, they never knew whether they were to witness a bloody slaughter or a hilarious wedding. This element of uncertainty lent an interest to the occasion which it could not otherwise have attained. Thus the masses were entertained and pleased, and the thinking part of the community could bring no charge of unfairness against his plan; for did not the accused person have the whole matter in his own hands?

The semibarbaric king had a daughter as blooming as his most rosy fancies, and with a soul as fervent and imperious as his own. As is usual in such cases, she was the apple of his eye and was loved by him above all humanity. Among his courtiers was a young man of that fineness of blood and lowness of station common to the heroes of romance who love royal maidens. This royal maiden was well satisfied with her lover, for he was handsome and brave to a degree unsurpassed in all this kingdom, and she loved him with an ardor that had enough of barbarism in it to make it exceedingly warm and strong. This love affair moved on happily for many months, until one day, the king happened to discover its existence. He did not hesitate or waver in regard to his duty. The youth was immediately cast into prison, and a day was appointed for his trial in the king's arena. This, of course, was an especially important occasion, and His Majesty, as well as all the people, was greatly interested in the workings and development of this trial. Never before had such a case occurred—never before had a subject dared to love the daughter of a king. In afteryears such things became commonplace enough, but then they were, in no slight degree, novel and startling.

80   The tiger cages of the kingdom were searched for the most savage and relentless beasts, from which the fiercest monster might be selected for the arena, and the ranks of maiden youth and beauty throughout the land were carefully surveyed by competent judges, in order that the young man might have a fitting bride in case fate did not determine for him a different destiny. Of 85 course, everybody knew that the deed with which the accused was charged had been done. He had loved the princess, and neither he, she, nor anyone else thought of denying the fact. But the king would not think of allowing any fact of this kind to interfere with the workings of the court of judgment, in which he took such great delight and satisfaction. No matter how the affair turned 90 out, the youth would be disposed of, and the king would take pleasure in watching the course of events which would determine whether or not the young man had done wrong in allowing himself to love the princess.

The appointed day arrived. From far and near the people gathered and thronged the great galleries of the arena, while crowds, unable to gain ad- 95 mittance, massed themselves against its outside walls. The king and his court were in their places, opposite the twin doors—those fateful portals, so terrible in their similarity!

All was ready. The signal was given. A door beneath the royal party opened, and the lover of the princess walked into the arena. Tall, beautiful, 100 fair, his appearance was greeted with a low hum of admiration and anxiety. Half the audience had not known so grand a youth had lived among them. No wonder the princess loved him! What a terrible thing for him to be there!

As the youth advanced into the arena, he turned, as the custom was, to bow to the king. But he did not think at all of that royal personage; his eyes 105 were fixed upon the princess, who sat to the right of her father. Had it not been for the barbarism in her nature, it is probable that lady would not have been there. But her intense and fervid soul would not allow her to be absent on an occasion in which she was so terribly interested. From the moment that the decree had gone 110 forth that her lover would decide his fate in the king's arena, she had thought of nothing, night or day, but 115 this great event and the various subjects connect- ed with it. Pos- 120 sessed of more power, influence, and force of char- acter than anyone who had ever be- fore been interest- 125 ed in such a case,

she had done what no other person had done—she had possessed herself of the secret of the doors. She knew in which of the two rooms behind those doors stood the cage of the tiger, with its open front, and in which waited the lady. Through these thick doors, heavily curtained with skins on the inside, it was impossible that any noise or suggestion should come from within to the person who should approach to raise the latch of one of them. But gold and the power of a woman's will had brought the secret to the princess.

Not only did she know in which room stood the lady, ready to emerge, all blushing and radiant, should her door be opened, but she knew who the lady was. It was one of the fairest and loveliest of the damsels of the court who had been selected as the reward if the accused youth should be proved innocent of the crime of aspiring to one so far above him; and the princess hated her. Often had she seen, or imagined that she had seen, this fair creature throwing glances of admiration upon the person of her lover, and sometimes she thought these glances were perceived and even returned. Now and then she had seen them talking together. It was but for a moment or two, but much can be said in a brief space. It may have been on most unimportant topics, but how could she know that? The girl was lovely, but she had dared to raise her eyes to the loved one of the princess, and, with all the intensity of the savage blood transmitted to her through long lines of wholly barbaric ancestors, she hated the woman who blushed and trembled behind the silent door.

When her lover turned and looked at her, his eye met hers as she sat there paler and whiter than anyone in the vast ocean of anxious faces about her, he saw, by that power of quick perception which is given to those whose souls are one, that she knew behind which door crouched the tiger, and behind which stood the lady. He had expected her to know it. He understood her nature, and his soul was assured that she would never rest until she had made plain to herself this thing, hidden to all other lookers-on, even to the king. The only hope for the youth in which there was any element of certainty was based upon the success of the princess in discovering the mystery, and the moment he looked upon her he saw she had succeeded.

Then it was that his quick and anxious glance asked the question, "Which?" It was as plain to her as if he shouted it from where he stood. There was not an instant to be lost. The question was asked in a flash; it must be answered in another.

Her right arm lay on the cushioned parapet before her. She raised her hand, and made a slight, quick movement toward the right. No one but her lover saw her. Every eye but his was fixed on the man in the arena.

He turned, and with a firm and rapid step he walked across the empty space. Every heart stopped beating, every breath was held, every eye was fixed immovably upon that man. Without the slightest hesitation, he went to the door on the right and opened it.

Now, the point of the story is this: Did the tiger come out of that door, or did the lady?

The more we reflect upon this question, the harder it is to answer. It involves a study of the human heart which leads us through roundabout pathways of passion, out of which it is difficult to find our way. Think of it, fair reader, not as if the decision of the question depended upon yourself, but upon that hot-blooded, semibarbaric princess, her soul at a white heat beneath the combined fires of despair and jealousy. She had lost him, but who should have him?

How often, in her waking hours and in her dreams, had she started in wild horror and covered her face with her hands as she thought of her lover opening the door on the other side of which waited the cruel fangs of the tiger!

180   But how much oftener had she seen him at the other door! How in her grievous reveries had she gnashed her teeth and torn her hair when she saw his start of rapturous delight as he opened the door of the lady! How her soul had burned in agony when she had seen him rush to meet that woman, with her flushing cheek and sparkling eye of triumph; when she had seen him lead her forth, his

185   whole frame kindled with the joy of recovered life; when she had heard the glad shouts from the multitude, and the wild ringing of the happy bells; when she had seen the priest, with his joyous followers, advance to the couple, and make them man and wife before her very eyes; and when she had seen them walk away together upon their path of flowers, followed by the tremendous shouts of the hi-

190   larious multitude, in which her one despairing shriek was lost and drowned!

Would it not be better for him to die at once, and go to wait for her in the blessed regions of semibarbaric futurity?

And yet, that awful tiger, those shrieks, that blood!

Her decision had been indicated in an instant, but it had been made after

195   days and nights of anguished deliberation. She had known she would be asked, she had decided what she would answer, and without the slightest hesitation, she had moved her hand to the right.

The question of her decision is one not to be lightly considered, and it is not for me to presume to set up myself as the one person able to answer it.

200   So I leave it with all of you: Which came out of the opened door—the lady or the tiger?

Frank Stockton

After You Read

3   **Phrases That Describe Characters.** Read the following phrases from the story that describe the different characters—the *k*ing, the *p*rincess, and the *c*ourtier (the princess's lover). Then decide which character each phrase describes and write *k, p,* or *c* in the appropriate blanks. Next compare your work with a partner. Finally, scan the story to check your answers.

_____ C___   1.   fineness of blood and lowness of station

_____ K___   2.   pleased…to make the crooked straight

_____ K___   3.   bland and genial

_____ P___   4.   hated the woman…behind the silent door

_____ C___   5.   power of quick perception

_____ K___   6.   allowed no…arrangements to interfere with his great scheme of punishment and reward

_____ P___   7.   hot-blooded, semibarbaric

Talk It Over

In small groups, discuss the following questions.

1. What do you think of the king's method of administering justice? The author states that by it the minds of the people were "refined and cultured" and that "its perfect fairness is obvious." Does he really mean this or is he being ironic? Explain.

2. In your opinion, are there some advantages to living in a kingdom like the one described? Do you think that most of the king's subjects probably lead fairly happy lives or not? Why?

3. Do any leaders in the world today have characters and governments similar to this king's? Explain.

4. How would you describe the character of the princess? Is she like her father or not?

---

4 **Identifying Support for Hypotheses.** What do you think was behind the door—the lady or the tiger? Why? Some parts of the story (certain words, phrases) support one hypothesis and some support the other. Check either "lady" or "tiger" for each of the following statements to show which hypothesis it supports. Be prepared to explain your choice. If you think a statement supports neither, put a 0 in front of each. If you think a statement supports both, check both.

1. The semibarbaric king had a daughter as blooming as his most rosy fancies, *and with a soul as fervent and imperious as his own.*

    _____ lady   _____ tiger

2. This royal maiden *was well satisfied with her lover,* for he was handsome and brave to a degree unsurpassed in all this kingdom, and *she loved him with an ardor that had enough of barbarism in it to make it exceedingly warm and strong.*

    _____ lady   _____ tiger

3. It was one of the *fairest and loveliest* of damsels of the court who had been selected as the reward of the accused youth,…*and the princess hated her.*

    _____ lady   _____ tiger

4. *Often had she seen,* or imagined that she had seen, *this fair creature throwing glances of admiration upon the person of her lover, and sometimes* she thought *these glances were perceived and even returned.*

    _____ lady   _____ tiger

5. When her lover turned and looked at her, his eye met hers as she sat there *paler and whiter* than anyone in the vast ocean of anxious faces…

    _____ lady   _____ tiger

6. He understood her nature, and his soul was assured that she would never rest until she had made plain to herself this thing, hidden to all other lookers-on.…

    _____ lady   _____ tiger

7. *Without the slightest hesitation,* he went to the door on the right and opened it.

    _____ lady   _____ tiger

8. But *how much oftener* had she seen him at the other door! How in her grievous reveries had she *gnashed her teeth and torn her hair when she saw his start of rapturous delight* as he opened the door of the lady!

    _____ lady   _____ tiger

5   **Formulating an Argument.** Join a small group and follow these steps.

1.   Discuss whether the lady or the tiger was behind the door in the story. Try to reach a unanimous decision (one agreed on by everybody). Use quotations from the preceding exercise or find others to support your position. If there is not a unanimous decision, keep a record of how many group members chose the lady and how many chose the tiger.

2.   After five to ten minutes, choose one member of your group to report the decision to the class and present the main argument(s) or reason(s) for the choice. If the decision was not unanimous, present the statistics to the class—for example, tiger: 3 to 2, or lady: 4 to 1.

3.   To see how the class as a whole decided, choose a class member to write on the board the tally (record) of how many group members chose the lady and how many chose the tiger.

If you do not have time for a class discussion, your teacher may ask you to write a paragraph about your answer to the central question of the story. Here is an outline to follow and complete. Write your completed paragraph on separate paper.

1.   Begin by writing a topic sentence similar to this one.
I believe that the princess in Frank Stockton's story chose the (lady/tiger).

2.   Write three to five sentences to support your topic sentence argument. For example, state reasons for your decision, using the author's descriptions of the princess's character.
One reason is that the princess (had an intense and fervid soul/was by nature barbaric like her father).

3.   Write the last sentence—your conclusion. Try to summarize your previous arguments:
Because the princess (had a kind and loving soul/was a jealous, spiteful person), it is more likely that she pointed to the door that concealed the (lady/tiger).

6   **Identifying the Theme.** In a truly good story, the author wants to make a point. This point is the most important narrative element in a story—the *theme*. The other narrative elements—*setting, characters,* and *plot*—all contribute to the *theme*. What do you think is the theme of "The Lady or the Tiger?"? Check (✓) the theme that best fits the story.

_____   Kings with too much power are always unjust.

_____   Women have deeper emotions than men and therefore are more passionate.

_____ It is difficult to truly know the human heart and its pathways of passion.

_____ People under a king (subjects) always suffer.

Now write down a reason for your choice. Refer to the story. Next compare your work, first with a partner, and then with the class.

PART 2 # It All Started with Dragon Bones

Before You Read

1   **Scanning for Synonyms.** Practice your scanning skill and learn key vocabulary by finding synonyms in the reading for the italicized words.

1. The beginning of this century was a *discouraging* time for Chinese intellectuals.

    _____

2. They doubted the abilities of their own people and feared they were *basically* incapable of operating foreign machines.

    _____

3. There was a general mood of *discontent* with the wisdom of the past.

    _____

4. Many Chinese historians were looking for proof of their traditions to meet *Western* scientific standards.

    _____

5. Old records described the *reigning periods* of the Yin and Chou families.

    _____

6. According to Chinese religion, dragons were powerful cosmic forces that would *light up* people's minds and inspire them with *wonder*.

    _____

7. Could anyone *decode* the mysterious marks *engraved* on the so-called dragon bones?

    _____

8. One man was about to make a *clear soup* from some old bones when he saw *picture writing symbols* on them.

    _____

9. Ancient rulers had employed *fortune tellers* who used these bones to *predict* the weather or the sex of unborn children.

    _____

Does anybody believe in dragons? We think of them as mythical, fire-breathing beasts that exist only in the pages of storybooks. But even though they don't really exist, can they affect us? Can they influence our knowledge and our history? The title of the selection suggests that something important began with the bones of these legendary reptiles. Read to find out how myths can influence history.

Read

It All Started with Dragon Bones

The beginning of the twentieth century was a low point in Chinese history. Drought, famine, and disease troubled the common people. Opium addiction spread, and the government was powerless to stop it, for British guns protected the drug importers. Because of economic dominance, China was

5   forced to bow before the superior weaponry and technology of countries it had once considered inferior.

Even worse, a cultural tradition three thousand years old was falling apart beneath the impact of Western scientific thought, further demoralizing Chinese intellectuals. Chinese writers published articles claiming that their own

10 people were inherently incapable of operating foreign machines, let alone inventing new ones. A mood of self-doubt, of dissatisfaction with old wisdom, extended into every branch of study.

Pushed by Occidental standards for scientific proof, Chinese historians studied their ancient records with increased skepticism. Were the stirring his-

15 tories of the earliest dynasties Yin and Chou only legends? Were there enough hard facts to prove that Confucius really lived? Some Western scholars even cast doubt on the foundation stone of Chinese culture, its written language, by suggesting that Chinese characters had been imported from the Middle East in ages long past.

20   Then something happened to restore confidence in ancient tradition. A small coincidence struck a spark that would later become a light brilliant enough to illuminate the dim reaches of Chinese history. Here, then, is the story of this coincidence.

     The farmers around the village of Hsiao T'un in northern Hunan Province
25 sometimes earned extra money from a most unusual crop: pieces of bone turned up by the plow or by heavy rain. It was well known then that a dragon sheds its bones as a snake sheds its skin. Dragons have always played a starring role in Chinese folklore, religion, and philosophy.

     To the common mind, dragons are generally good creatures (unlike the
30 Western dragon, which is pictured as an evil monster in league with the devil) associated with rain, rivers, and mists, and with the emperor. Taoism, a native Chinese religion, later developed a complex mythology featuring the dragon as a mythical force of cosmic power who appears for a moment to fill man with awe, then disappears into the mist. The Buddhist sect called Ch'an in
35 China and better known in the West by its Japanese name, Zen, elevates the dragon to a philosophical symbol for the flash of Truth that comes to enlighten the thinker. Traditional healers believed that ground-up dragon bones could cure women's diseases, dysentery, and malaria, as well as a number of other maladies.

40   The farmers of Hsiao T'un could not be sure the bones they found came from dragons. Some had strange symbols scratched on them. Crosses and straight and curved lines could be deciphered, and even sketchy pictures. Might dragon bones carry these marks? Probably not. But the pharmacies in Peking wanted dragon bones, and the farmers needed money, so they
45 scraped off the peculiar markings and sent the bones to Peking.

     Fortunately, one farmer did not scrape well, and a piece of marked bone was sold by a Peking pharmacist to a scholar who was ill. Imagine the sick man's astonishment when he recognized, on an object he was about to grind up for medicinal broth, a written message from China's mythical past!

50 The year was 1899. Tantalized by the mysterious "dragon bone" hieroglyphics, a small group of Chinese scholars collected quantities of inscribed
bones from the fields around Hsiao T'un. Five years passed before enough
symbols could be deciphered to reveal the true nature of the "dragon bones."

They were a record of a people who called themselves Shang, and ruled
55 lands in the area some four thousand years ago. Here was objective proof for
the existence of a dynasty called "Yin" (about 1766–1122 B.C.) by its Chou
conquerors, part of a heroic epoch of Chinese history, described until then
only in semilegendary histories.

The objects embedded in the fields of Hsiao T'un came not from drag-
60 ons but from turtles and cattle. Shang kings sought to learn the future through
their diviners, who inscribed royal questions on a carefully scraped and pol-
ished bone. The inscribed oracle shells and bones were partially drilled in
prescribed patterns. Heat was applied, and the course of the resulting cracks,
determined by ancestral spirits, indicated answers to their questions.

65 Shang oracle bones provide intriguing glimpses of life in China four thousand years ago. Kings then yearned to know the results of military campaigns
and hunting expeditions. They asked spirits to forecast the weather, the sex
of unborn children, the outcome of diseases bothering the royal family. Yet
Shang oracle bones raise more questions than they answer. Like a tiny flash-
70 light played over a dark room filled with unknown objects, they give us a frag-
mented understanding of the Shang people.

Raymond Chang and Margaret Scrogin Chang

Focus on Testing

Improving Your Chances on True/False Exams

True or false is a common kind of objective exam. Here are some tips to help improve your chances on this kind of exam.

1. There is usually a time limit during a test, so first quickly look through the whole exercise and do the items you are sure of.

2. Next, *if there is no penalty for guessing*, take a guess at the remaining items. Usually more answers are true than false. Exceptionally long statements tend to be false. If you cannot decide how to answer, mark either *true* or *false*, and answer all remaining items with the same choice.

You can use the following exercise to practice using the tips. Do the exercise as if it were an exam; don't look back at the reading.

Write T (true) or F (false) in front of each statement.

_____ 1. At the beginning of the twentieth century, China found itself humiliated and controlled militarily and economically by cultures it had once considered unimportant.

_____ 2. Chinese writers and intellectuals of this time paid no attention to Western scientific thought and maintained that the ancient wisdom of their culture was superior.

_____ 3. Some Western scholars even suggested that the Chinese written language had been invented by the British.

_____ 4. Just as in Western tradition, the Chinese dragon has always been portrayed as an evil monster in league with the devil.

_____ 5. In the Chinese Buddhist sect called Ch'an (known as Zen in Japan), the dragon was a symbol for the flash of Truth that enlightens a person.

_____ 6. The farmers from the village of Hsiao T'un used to scrape off the strange symbols from the bones before selling them.

_____ 7. Fortunately, a scholar in Peking bought a bone for medicine and recognized a symbol that had not been scraped off.

_____ 8. The symbols on the bones were substantially decoded in 1899.

_____ 9. In reality, the "dragon bones" were from cattle and turtles.

_____ 10. These bones had been used in ages past for the purpose of answering questions about the future.

Now go back to the reading, scan for the answers, and correct your work. Correct false statements to make them true.

After You Read

2   The main point of the previous selection is that the discovery of the "dragon bones" led to restored Chinese confidence in its history. Although the authors do not directly say it, this was the result of Chinese scholars being able to refute (prove false) Western doubt over the origins of the Chinese written language. Why were these scholars able to do this? Write your answer in a short paragraph. Refer to the reading to do so. Then compare your paragraph with a partner's.

Talk It Over

In small groups, discuss the following questions.

1.   The authors mention "a small coincidence" that was eventually to provide an important key to Chinese history. What is this coincidence?
2.   Do you think that the origins of the Chinese language would have been discovered some day even without this coincidence? Why or why not?
3.   Have you heard of any other legends or mysteries from the past that people used to laugh at but that were later discovered to be true?
4.   Do people from the U.S. have the same attitude toward tradition and history as the people in China? Explain.

---

3   **Summarizing an Article.** Write a summary of the selection "It All Started with Dragon Bones," using these guidelines.

1.   Write a one-sentence thesis statement describing the main point of the article. To do this, mention the problem described at the beginning and the resolution to it.
2.   Go back to the middle of the article and write three to five sentences that tell the story that supports the author's thesis.
3.   Finish with a brief concluding sentence. One way of doing this is to start out *In conclusion* (or *Thus, Therefore*, or *In this way*) and then repeat the main point in different words and shorter form.

Around the Globe

Stories Behind Words: Words with Origins in Mythology

The article describes some Chinese scholars as being "*tantalized* by the mysterious dragon bone hieroglyphics." *Tantalized* is one of many English words that have their origins in myths and legends of the past (in this case, Greek and Roman ones). The meaning of the verb *tantalize* is a very particular one: "to promise or show something desirable to a person and then take it away; to tease by arousing hope." Many (but not all) English dictionaries give you a brief indication of a word's origins in brackets before or after the explanation of the meaning. For *tantalize* the following explanation is given: [>Tantalus]. This means that you should look up the name *Tantalus* to find out the word's origins, and if you do, you will find out that in Greek mythology, Tantalus was a king who was punished in the lower world with eternal hunger and thirst; he was put up to his chin in water that always moved away when he tried to drink it and with fruit on branches above him placed just a little bit out of his reach. Can you see why his name was changed into a verb meaning "to tease or torment by arousing desire"?

Another example is the word *siren*, familiar to us as the mechanical device that makes such an alarming sound when police cars, ambulances, or fire engines approach. This word also has its origins in Greek mythology. The traveler Odysseus (Ulysses to the Romans) made his men plug their ears so that they wouldn't hear the dangerous voices of the *sirens*, creatures who were half bird and half woman and who lured sailors to their deaths on sharp rocks. So the word came to be associated both with a loud sound and with danger!

When someone speaks of a "*jovial* mood" or a "*herculean* effort," he or she is using words with origins in mythology. Look these words up to find their meaning and relationship to myths.

Many common words, such as the names for the days of the week and the months of the year, also come from mythology. *Wednesday* derives from the ancient Norse king of the gods, Woden, and *Thursday* was originally *Thor's day*, in honor of Thor, the god of thunder. Do you know which of the days of the week was named in honor of a Roman god? There is also a planet named for him. Another one of the planets is named for the Roman god of war because it is red, and one of the months is named for him too. Can you guess which one? In fact, all the planets, except the one we live on, bear names that come from Roman mythology, including the planet that is farthest away from the sun and for that reason was called after the Roman god of the dead. This god has also given his name to one of the chemical elements. Do you know what his name is? Several other elements have names that come from mythology, too.

It seems that myths and legends live on in the English language.

Talk It Over

In small groups, discuss the following questions.

1. What are the days of the week called in the language of your culture? Do their names relate to any myths or legends?
2. What about the names of the months, the planets, and the chemical elements?
3. Can you think of any ways that your language and culture preserve the ancient beliefs of your ancestors? Explain.

4 **Using Research Sources.** In small groups, prepare a brief report about one of the following unsolved mysteries. Each person should use a different source (book, magazine article, etc.). You should discuss in class beforehand how to find the information in the library from printed sources and on the Internet. The first person will explain what the phenomenon is, then the others will read in turn a small section about it from their sources.

1. the Yeti (also known as the Abominable Snowman)
2. UFOs
3. the Loch Ness monster
4. werewolves
5. the Lost Continent of Atlantis
6. ESP
7. the Bermuda Triangle
8. vampires
9. the *Llorona* of Mexico
10. psychic surgery

Making Connections

Use the Internet to find information about a present-day unsolved mystery—Bigfoot (also known as Sasquatch). Go to the following Website and read about Bigfoot.

http://www.n2.net/prey/bigfoot/

On the Website find the "Contact Us" listing and send an e-mail asking for more information.

See if you can find other "Contact Us" listings at Websites for the ten unsolved mysteries in the previous activity. Send e-mail questions you'd like to ask.

Around the Globe

Over the past several decades, the U.S., Canada, and Europe have received a great deal of media and even research attention over unusual phenomena and unsolved mysteries. These include UFOs as well as sightings and encounters with "nonhuman creatures" such as Bigfoot, Yeti (also known as the Abominable Snowman), and the Loch Ness monster. Only recently has Latin America begun to receive some attention as well. Although the mysteries of the Aztec, Mayan, and Inca civilizations have been known for centuries, now the public is also becoming aware of unusual, paranormal phenomena in countries such as Peru and Mexico. Puerto Rico has also been at the center of a great deal of media attention about unusual happenings.

The Nazca "lines" of Peru were discovered in the 1930s. These lines are deeply carved into a flat, stony plain, and form about 300 intricate pictures of animals such as birds, a monkey, and a lizard. Seen at ground level, the designs are a jumbled senseless mess. The images are so large that they can only be viewed at a height of 1,000 feet—meaning from an aircraft. Yet there were no aircraft in 300 B.C., when it is judged the designs were made. Nor were there then, or are there now, any nearby mountains ranges from which to view them. So how and why did the native people of Nazca create these marvelous designs? One answer appeared in 1969, when the German researcher and writer Erich von Daniken proposed that the lines were drawn by extraterrestrials as runways for their aircraft. The scientific community did not take long to scoff at and abandon von Daniken's theory. Over the years several other theories have been put forth, but none has been accepted by the scientific community.

Today there is a new and heightened interest in the Nazca lines. It is a direct result of the creation of the Internet. Currently there are over 60 sites dedicated to this mystery from Latin America's past, and even respected scientists have joined the discussion through e-mail and chat rooms.

As for Mexico and Puerto Rico, their unusual phenomena do not go back in time quite as far as the Nazca lines. These present-day unsolved mysteries include the appearance in various parts of Mexico of a creature that is said to be "half human and half bear." This "Bearman," or "Hombre Oso" in Spanish, has been sighted in wilderness areas ranging from the arid plains of Chihuahua to Veracruz on the Gulf Coast. In Puerto Rico, it is the "chupacabras," or "goatsucker" in English—a panther-like creature with red "alien-shaped" eyes and a long, snake-like tongue that appears at night and sucks the blood of farmers' goats until they are dead. One much scoffed-at theory is that the *chupacabras* is a creature from outer space.

Will the Internet help explain these unsolved mysteries? Perhaps it is a step in the right direction.

Gerry Strei

Are there any present-day unsolved mysteries in your home country? If so, write down the information you know. You can also collect additional information from friends or relatives in your home country or from the Internet. Then share the information with the class.

5   **Solving Riddles.** A riddle is a mini-mystery or little puzzle in the form of a question asked in such a way that it requires some cleverness to answer it. Often you must look at the whole question in a manner that is not at first obvious. Riddles are popular in most cultures and are often humorous. Some are silly and some are sophisticated, but they can all be fun. These refer to letters of the alphabet and to the dictionary. Match the answers to the riddles.

1. Why is the letter *e* lazy?
2. What is the end of everything?
3. What begins with a *t*, ends with a *t*, and has *t* in it?
4. Why is an island like the letter *t*?
5. What four letters frighten a thief?
6. Which is easier to spell, seventeen or eighteen?
7. Why is *smiles* the longest word in the dictionary?
8. Where does Thursday come before Wednesday?
9. What's the definition of *minimum*?

a. Because it is in the middle of *water*
b. In the dictionary
c. Because it is always in *bed*
d. A teapot
e. Because there is a *mile* in between its first and last letter
f. "A small mother"
g. The letter *g*
h. 17 (Seventeen) because it is spelled with more "ease" (e's)
i. O-I-C-U!

What Do You Think?

The Secret of Fire Walking

The firewalkers of Fiji, Hawaii, and the Cook Islands walk over blazing hot coals without flinching. When they come out of the fire, there is no sign of burns or blisters on their feet. Yet this is not always the case. One firewalker in the 1940s who had not prepared properly "spiritually and mentally" was so badly injured that both legs had to be amputated. What do you think is the secret of fire walking? What do you think is the "proper" preparation? What do people gain by accomplishing something like this? Have you heard of similar things in other cultures?

Video Activities: Abduction by Aliens

Before You Watch.   Discuss these questions in small groups.

1. Do you think that people from other planets have visited Earth? Have you ever seen a UFO (Unidentified Flying Object)?

2. *Abduct* means the same as _____.
    a. borrow   b. kidnap   c. visit

Watch.   Answer these questions in small groups.

1. Ruth Foley says that she _____ .
    a. has been abducted by people from outer space
    b. was born in outer space
    c. has visited other planets

2. What do the abductors look like? Write a description.

    _____

    _____

    _____

3. According to Ruth, what is the abductors' purpose?
    a. to perform medical tests
    b. to ask people about life on Earth
    c. to tell people about their planet

4. People in Indiana say that _____ burned the ground near a house in Indiana.
    a. an abductor   b. a light   c. a spaceship

5. The author of *Secret Life* _____ abductions really happen.
    a. isn't sure if   b. is positive that   c. doesn't believe that

Watch Again.   Write answers to these questions.

1. How old was Ruth Foley when she was first abducted?
    _____

2. Who once saw Ruth being abducted?
    _____

3. What was the year of the abduction in Indiana?
    _____

4. How long did it take for the grass to grow on the burned spot?
    _____

5. Who is John Mack and what did he write?
    _____

6. What does John Mack believe?
    _____

After You Watch.   Work in groups of three or four. Read and take notes on articles about UFOs from different sources. Compare the information you've found. Do the articles agree, or are they contradictory?

Chapter 5

Transitions

IN THIS CHAPTER

Human life is a series of transitions, both ordinary and extraordinary. The first selection shows how confronting the modern urban environment for the first time causes changes in some people in developing countries. Next is the story of Inna, a Russian immigrant to Canada who left her family, native land, and culture years ago and now eagerly awaits a visit from her only brother.

PART 1   # Conversations in Malaysia

Before You Read

1   **Making Comparisons.** Although the title of the first selection uses the word *conversations*, the following reading is more like an interview. In what way is an interview different from a conversation? Compare the following descriptions and write *i* in the blank for *interview* or *c* for *conversation*.

_____ 1. Different persons share information by expressing their views about something.

_____ 2. Person A asks Person B questions about Person B.

_____ 3. Two individuals exchange ideas about a particular topic.

_____ 4. Someone tries to find out information about another person by asking that person questions.

_____ 5. Because Person B has information that Person A thinks is important, Person A asks B questions and records the answers.

2   **Understanding Change of Speakers 1.** While reading, it is important to take note of which person is speaking in each paragraph. How can you tell when the speaker changes? Skim the selection to get a general idea of how you can tell when a different person is speaking. Note that there are 25 paragraphs. A new paragraph usually signals a change in speaker.

Check the ways to tell when there is a change of speakers.

_____ 1. the content of each paragraph—by what the speaker (or writer) is saying

_____ 2. the length of each paragraph

_____ 3. usually by the back-and-forth movement (exchange) from one speaker (one paragraph) to the other (next paragraph)—first the author speaks, then Shafi, then the author, then Shafi, and so on.

_____ 4. the verb tenses in each paragraph

_____ 5. the punctuation—a paragraph that is a question from one speaker (ends in a ?) is usually followed by an answer from the other speaker.

_____ 6. the different styles of speech of the speakers—for example, the author speaks standard English, while Shafi uses nonstandard English—that is, he makes a lot of grammatical errors.

3 **Understanding Change of Speakers 2.** Here are some other observations about the change of speakers in the selection. Answer the questions that follow. (You might want to number the paragraphs 1 through 25 before you answer.)

1. Sometimes the author tells you directly who the speaker for a paragraph will be. In which paragraph(s) does this happen?

   _____

2. There's one paragraph in which both the author and Shafi relate information. Which paragraph is it?

   _____

3. In that paragraph, how is the way Shafi relates the information different from the author's way?

   _____

4. What is the total number of paragraphs spoken by Shafi?

   _____ .

Read

The following selection is taken from the book *Among the Believers: An Islamic Journey* by V. S. Naipaul, one of the most renowned writers of English of our times. It is his interview of Shafi, a young Muslim man in Kuala Lumpur, the capital city of Malaysia. Shafi used to live in a village and finds that life in the big city is very different. Think for a moment about what it would be like to move from a very small village to a modern city. What aspects of the urban lifestyle do you imagine would appeal to him? Which aspects would disturb him or cause him trouble? As you read, try to understand Shafi's point of view. At the same time, notice what elements in his background would give him this point of view.

Conversations in Malaysia

Shafi worked for the Muslim cause. He didn't wear Arab clothes. But he understood the young men who did. Shafi had come to Kuala Lumpur from a village in the north. The disturbance of the move was still with him.

5 Shafi said: "When I was in the village the atmosphere is entirely different. You come out of the village. You see all the bright lights, you begin to sense the materialistic civilization around you. And I forgot about my religion and my commitments—in the sense that you had to pray. But not to the extent of going out and doing nasty things like taking girls and drinking and gambling and drugs. I didn't lose my faith. I simply forgot to pray, forgot responsibilities. Just

10 losing myself. I got nothing firm in my framework. I just floating around and didn't know my direction."

I said, "Where did you live when you came to Kuala Lumpur?"

He didn't give a straight answer. At this early stage in our conversation concreteness didn't come easily to him. He said, "I was living in a suburb

15 where I am exposed to materialistic civilization to which I had never been exposed before. Boys and girls can go out together. You are free from family control. You are free from society who normally criticize you in a village when

you do something bad. You take a goat, a cow, a buffalo—somewhere where the goat is being tied up all the time—and you release that goat in a bunch

20 of other animals: The goat would just roam anywhere he want to go without any strings."

"Is that bad for the goat?"

"I think the goat would be very happy to roam free. But for me I don't think that would be good. If goat had brains, I would want to say, 'Why do you want

25 to roam about when you are tied and being fed by your master and looked after? Why do you want to roam about?'"

I said, "But I want to roam about."

"What do you mean by being free? Freedom for me is not something that you can roam anywhere you want. Freedom must be within the definition of a

30 certain framework. Because I don't think we are able to run around and get everything. That freedom means nothing. You must really frame yourself where you want to go and what you want to do."

"But didn't you know what you wanted to do when you came to Kuala Lumpur?"

35 "The primary aim was education. That was a framework. But the conflict of this freedom and the primary aim is there, and I consider this is the problem I faced and many of my friends face."

"Other people in other countries face the same problem."

Shafi said, "Do they face the same restrictions of family life as I do?"

40 "What restrictions?"

"Religious restrictions. You have that frame with you. Religious tradition, family life, the society, the village community. Then you come into the city, where people are running, people are free. The values contradict.

"You see, in the village where I was brought up we have the bare mini-

45 mum. We have rice to eat, house to live. We didn't go begging. In the city you can buy a lunch at ten dollars (Malaysian dollars, $2. 20 to the American). Or in a stall you can have a lunch for fifty cents. That excess of nine-fifty which the city dwellers spend will be spent by us on other purposes. To us, with our framework and tradition and religion, that is excessiveness.

50   "Sometimes my wife feels that we should go back to the village, and I also feel the same. Not running away from the modern world, but trying to live a simpler, more meaningful life than coming to the city, where you have lots of waste and lots of things that is not real probably. You are not honest to yourself if you can spend fifty cents and keep yourself from hunger, but instead
55   spend ten dollars.

     "I will tell you about waste. Recently the government built a skating rink. After three months they demolished it because a highway going to be built over it. They are building big roads and highways across the villages. And whose lorries are passing by to collect the produce of the poor and to dump
60   the products that is manufactured by the rich at an exorbitant price—colour TVs, refrigerators, air conditioners, transistor radios?"

     "Don't people want those things?"

     "In the end they are going to use the colour TVs—which the people enjoy—to advertise products to draw people into wasteful living."
65   "Village life—wouldn't you say it is dull for most people?"

     "The village? It's simple. It's devoid of—what shall I say?—wastefulness. You shouldn't waste. You don't have to rush for things. My point about going back to the kampong is to stay with the community and not to run away from development. The society is well knit. If someone passed away there is an
70   alarm in the kampong, where most of us would know who passed away and when he is going to be buried, what is the cause of death, and what happened to the next of kin—are they around? It's not polluted in the village. Physical pollution, mental, social."

     "Social pollution?"

75   "Something that contradicts our customs and traditions. A man cannot
          walk with a woman who doesn't belong to his family in the kampong. It is for-
          bidden."
                "Why is it wrong?"
                "The very essence of human respect and dignity comes from an hon-
80   ourable relationship of man and woman. You must have a law to protect the
          unit of your society. You need your family to be protected. When the girls come
          from the villages to Kuala Lumpur, they don't want to be protected by the law."

After You Read

4   **Finding Support for Main Ideas.** Check the statement in each group that expresses
one of Shafi's ideas. Remember that you are looking for Shafi's ideas, not those of the
author. Then find at least two examples in the reading that support or illustrate that idea.

1.   _____   City life is better than village life because it gives more freedom.

     _____   City life is not as good as village life because it lacks structure.

2.   _____   People in the city are wasteful.

     _____   People in the village are dull.

3.   _____   The city offers many wonderful products—color TVs, refrigerators, and so
             on—that improve people's lives.

     _____   The village (kampong) offers a sense of community that improves people's
             lives.

5   **Paraphrasing.** The verb *paraphrase* means "to rephrase or restate a text by clarifying
it or by making it more concise." One way to paraphrase a text is to rewrite it. The following opinions are taken from the reading selection. In your own words, paraphrase
them—rewrite them in a clear and concise manner.

1.   "He didn't give a straight answer. At this early stage in our conversation concrete-
     ness didn't come easily to him."

     _____

     _____

     _____

     _____

2.   "You take a goat, a cow, a buffalo—somewhere where the goat is being tied up all
     the time—and you release that goat in a bunch of other animals: The goat would
     just roam anywhere he want to go without any strings."

     _____

     _____

     _____

     _____

3. "In the end they are going to use the colour TVs—which the people enjoy—to advertise products to draw people into wasteful living."

_____

_____

_____

_____

4. "It's not polluted in the village. Physical pollution, mental, social."

_____

_____

_____

_____

Talk It Over

In small groups, discuss the following questions.

1. In your opinion, why does Shafi have problems adjusting to city life?
2. Do you agree or disagree with Shafi's ideas about the city and the village? In which place would you live more happily? Explain.
3. When Shafi gives an example of the excesses of city life, he talks about the difference between a lunch of ten dollars and one of fifty cents. He speaks as if the nine dollars and fifty cents were simply thrown away and would not benefit anyone in any way. What might an urban person argue in defense of the ten-dollar lunch?

6 **Interviewing a Classmate.** Work with a partner and follow these steps:

1. Ask your partner to identify some important transition that he or she has made—for example, a move from one country to another, a change of lifestyle, a change of job, a marriage, and so on.
2. Write down four or five questions to ask your partner about his or her transition. Try to focus on how the other person's point of view has changed or is changing because of the transition. For example, you might write "How do you view the freedom a single person has now that you're married?"
3. Ask your partner the questions. On a piece of paper, take notes on the answers. Then hand your notes in to the teacher or share them with the class.

7 **Recognizing Vocabulary Differences.** Most people learn either the British or American form of English. Canadians speak in their own style, which contains some elements in common with each of the others. Could you tell which type was being used by the author and the young man he interviewed in Malaysia? Two words that immediately stand out as the British form of English are *lorries* and *honourable*. Americans do not use the word *lorry*, and many of them would not even know what it means; instead they say truck. *Honourable* would be spelled *honorable*—without the *u*—by an American. Can you find any other British words or spellings in the interview?

How good are you at spotting differences in vocabulary and spelling between the two types of English? Do you know which of the two types has retained the longer, more old-fashioned way of spelling certain words and which one now spells them in a shorter way?

Test your skill at making this distinction by guessing which of the words in the following pairs is American and which is British.

Vocabulary

1. subway/underground
2. (electric) flex/cord
3. stove/cooker
4. (car) hood/bonnet
5. flashlight/torch

Spelling

1. programme/program
2. cheque/check
3. color/colour
4. catalogue/catalog
5. behavior/behaviour

What Do You Think

The Refugee Problem

In 1975, there were 2.5 million refugees in the world. Today there are over 20 million. The war in the former Yugoslavia alone has left more than 3. 7 million displaced persons. Whether it be for reasons of war, economics, political persecution, or changes in borders, the world is filled with mass migrations of refugees. In your opinion, what is the obligation of stable and prosperous countries toward these refugees? How many should be allowed to enter prosperous nations? Which refugees should be accepted and which ones turned away?

PART 2

Grisha Has Arrived

Before You Read

1   **Selecting Adjectives to Fit the Context.** Well-chosen adjectives bring the characters and setting of a story to life. Adjectives from the story are given in the list, along with their definitions. Fill in the blanks with the appropriate adjectives. If you cannot guess a word from its definition and context, scan the story for it.

Adjective	Definition
exhausted	very, very tired, completely fatigued
exquisite	unusually beautiful and fine
Herculean	very difficult (like the tasks of Hercules)
inebriated	drunk, intoxicated by alcohol or emotion
indefatigable	untiring, incapable of fatigue
mundane	ordinary, without special meaning
marshy	swampy, soft and wet like a swamp or marsh
prosaic	dull, unimaginative, like prose (instead of poetry)
rejuvenated	brought back to youth, made young again
shabby	worn out, poor, dilapidated

1.   Grandma would put on her blue-checkered apron and seem instantly _rejuvenated_.
2.   Their _____ , sooty kitchen suddenly became bright and cheerful.
3.   The stove would become the airport in the "_____ forest."
4.   There was an amber brooch, perfumes, books, wooden spoons, and a small _____ box from Boris.
5.   Grisha was _____ by these bright photographs and looked at his sister with admiration.
6.   Grisha took childish pleasure in everything and was very enthusiastic. He was _____ in his activity.
7.   The mountain of goods on the living room floor grew…but the shopping list hardly got shorter…. It was a _____ task.
8.   She had expected a very significant moment in her life—the family reunion—and it had turned out to be very _____, even _____.
9.   Suddenly Inna felt _____.

2 **Scanning for Information.** The story begins with a *flashback*—the description of a scene that happened earlier, before the time of the main story. Scan lines 1–24 to find out when the flashback occurred to Inna, the main character. Then check the appropriate blank. Remember that *scan* means to "search for specific information," so you might want to begin by scanning for the main character's name.

_____ in her childhood

_____ late in her teens

_____ when she was an adult

Read

> What is it like to leave your home and move to another country? Many people go through this transition. They often speak of being "uprooted," like a tree that has been transplanted into new ground. The following story was written by a Russian who left her native country and immigrated to western Canada. It describes the visit to a Russian-Canadian woman from her brother Grisha at a time when goods and commodities were very difficult to obtain in Russia. The situation has changed and many Russians now say, "Back then we had money, but there was nothing to buy; today there is plenty to buy, but we have no money!" In either case, there is a great difference in the material standard of living between Russia and Canada. In your opinion, what problems can this cause between relatives living in the two countries? Read the story to see if this creates problems for Inna and her brother Grisha.

3 **Predicting Story Events.** As you read this story, try to think ahead of the plot by asking yourself, "What will happen next?" Predicting action helps comprehension. The text will be interrupted in a few places and you will be asked questions about what you've just read and about what you think will happen next. Check the story to correct your answers.

Grisha Has Arrived*

Whenever Grisha was expected in the apartment on Novosibirskaya Street, Babushka made some pirozhki filled with meat and cabbage.† She would put on her blue-checkered apron and seem instantly rejuvenated. Little Inna would seal these pirozhki on a wooden board while Babushka presided over the
5 boiling oil. Their shabby, sooty kitchen suddenly became bright and cheerful. In this way Grisha's arrival became forever linked to an expectation of joyful festivity.

He would rush in, thin and pale. At once the long hallway, dimly lit by a single electric bulb, was filled with lively bustle. They played in the kitchen. It

---

*The story has been shortened but not changed in any other way.

†Two Russian words are used in this sentence, *Babushka* (Grandmother) and *pirozhki* (meat pies), which many English speakers know and others would guess from the context. Later in the story, the Russian word *dacha* (country house) is used.

10   was warmer there. Babushka covered the large stove with an oilcloth. The stove would become the airport in the "marshy forest. " Grisha made paper airplanes and launched them skillfully from the stove towards the electric light. The small, white airplanes briefly shone against the soot-covered ceiling and fell into the dark space near the door.

15   Grisha would bring his tin soldiers. He was a guerrilla leader and little Inna was a doctor. They always played the same war game. Inna's military hospital was located in Babushka's room. Could Inna ever forget this narrow room with the fireplace and the photograph of a young woman on the dressing table? There, among various treasures with which Inna was not allowed 20   to play, was a carved box with letters.

         Later she would read these yellowed sheets which Babushka had preserved so carefully. They were letters from her mother who had died in a labour camp. Inna could not remember her parents. She had been raised by Babushka, while Grisha had been adopted by relatives of their father.

25   Memory is a strange thing! In its vast foggy valleys one's past is kept untouched. Now, when forty-two-year-old Inna was on the way to the airport to meet her brother coming from Moscow, the smell of the swamp grass suddenly released distant memories of frying pirozhki, of childhood, of bliss….

A conflict does not always mean a problem. Sometimes it is just a change. In this case the conflict that begins the story is the arrival of Grisha. In the flashback, what do we learn of Inna and Grisha's family? Why is he especially important to Inna? What do you think she expects from his visit?

Finish this statement to predict what happens next.

When Inna sees Grisha she will be _____ .

a.   happy to see he has not changed at all
b.   surprised to see he is dressed in shabby clothes
c.   sad to find he is very depressed.

---

30   On the stairs of the airport Inna came face to face with Grisha, but did not recognize him at first. His hair had gone completely grey and he seemed shorter. She was struck at once by how badly he was dressed. He was wearing a brown raincoat fit only for picking mushrooms. His worn out shoes were of an indefinable colour. Grisha was carrying a small suitcase.

35   They embraced, kissed, and walked slowly to her car. Grisha was telling her excitedly about the flight across the ocean, about the last days before departure, how frightened he had been that he might fall ill and be unable to come.

         Inna was listening to Grisha happily and distractedly. She realized that he must be tired from lack of sleep, but why this pathetic shabbiness? Why 40   would Yelena have allowed him to leave home in this Godforsaken state? They had a marvelous apartment and dacha. Both were working, and Grisha earned substantial amounts from translations.

45 As though he had read her mind, Grisha said: "Do you know, all our acquaintances advised me to travel in my oldest clothes so that I could discard them without regret here. They said that you, my sister, anyway would clothe me and Yelena and our children."

50 Maybe it was because she had no family of her own that Inna was very attached to Grisha's children. She gave them expensive presents and spoiled them, especially his oldest daughter, Lyuba. Inna tolerated Yelena, no more than that. Her relationship with her brother's wife had gone wrong from the very beginning. Probably deep down Inna envied Yelena....

They soon reached home. Inna put a bowl with fruit on the table and a bottle of French wine which she had bought yesterday to welcome Grisha.

55 Grisha opened his suitcase and brought out presents from himself and Yelena, from Lyuba and Yura who had already had families of their own, and from Inna's numerous friends and relatives. There was an amber brooch, perfumes, books, wooden spoons, and a small exquisite box from Boris. He had put a sheet of paper with comical verses for Inna's birthday into the box. How many years had passed since she had seen his familiar bold handwriting?

60 Inna had been a young girl in Moscow when she had become involved with Boris, who was much older. On various occasions he had left his wife to move in with Inna. At other times he had left her to return to his family. Inna had been his friend, his mistress, his graduate student, and eventually his coworker in the laboratory. This pattern of life had continued up to the time of

65 her leaving Moscow.

Brother and sister sat on the balcony, smoking and talking almost till dawn. From the twelfth floor there was a view over Edmonton and the dark river valley spanned by a bridge. Below them the street lights shone moistly.

Why did Grisha arrive in shabby clothing? What do we find out about Inna's relationship with Grisha's wife and children? What do we find out about Boris?

Finish this statement to predict what happens next.

Grisha will show a great interest in his sister's _____ .
a. thoughts and feelings
b. work and ambitions
c. possessions and appliances

Grisha walked about the apartment inspecting Inna's habitation. For a while, he remained in the bedroom where, beside the bed, there was a large desk with a computer. On the chest of drawers, he found their mother's faded photograph in its walnut frame, that had stood in Babushka's room. In the kitchen, he wanted to know how the dishwasher worked and opened the door to the microwave oven.

Inna made a bed for Grisha on the living room sofa. The following morning she got up as early as usual. She was tired from lack of sleep and took two Tylenol tablets before going into the kitchen to prepare breakfast. Grisha was up already and was doing yoga exercises on the balcony.

After breakfast they went for a walk and then to the university. Inna showed Grisha her laboratory. As it was a holiday, the university campus was deserted. They ate in a small Chinese restaurant. The evening was spent sitting on the balcony. Inna brought out albums with photographs taken on various trips: one to France and Spain, another to the Scandinavian countries, still another to South America, and finally one to Indonesia and Hong Kong.

Grisha was inebriated by these bright photographs and looked at his sister with admiration.

They were drinking tea with cake when Grisha suddenly asked:

"How much does a Lada cost here?"

"I don't know, perhaps around five thousand or maybe seven. Why do you want to know?" Inna was very surprised.

"You see, it can be paid for here, and Yura would be able to get it in Moscow. Many people buy them in this way for their relatives. "

"Really? They buy a whole car?"

"Of course, they can't buy it in pieces, can they?" Grisha started laughing.

The magnitude of his expectations and naive faith in her financial prowess struck Inna like a splash of cold water. All her achievements, of which she had been so proud only yesterday, were reduced to rubble and lost their significance.

100   The woman in the rocking chair was suddenly middle-aged and lonely.
      "For myself, I bought a secondhand car and that was almost seven years
ago."
      Inna cut herself short. In the depth of Grisha's eyes as in two dark mirrors
she saw herself as she must have appeared to him—a rich world traveller.

What do we learn about Inna's work and lifestyle? What impresses Grisha? Why does Inna suddenly feel old and lonely?

Finish this statement to predict what happens next.

Inna and her brother will spend a lot of their time _____ .
a.   talking
b.   traveling
c.   shopping

---

105   Every morning Grisha got up early and did yoga exercises frantically.
      Then he went to the swimming pool. The highrise building in which Inna lived
      had a sauna and whirlpool in the basement. Grisha took childish pleasure in
      everything and was very enthusiastic. He was indefatigable. Inna took a va-
      cation in order to devote herself completely to her brother.
      She showed him the sports complex which belonged to the university.
110   They pushed a shopping cart around the superstore which was the size of an
      airplane hangar. They bought groceries and Grisha had his picture taken
      against a backdrop of mountains of fruits and vegetables and colourful cans
      of cat food.
      They spent a whole day at West Edmonton Mall, the world-famous shop-
115   ping centre. They wandered through the shops, inspected Fantasyland, and,
      while there, took a trip in a submarine. They had lunch in a French café.
      The mountain of goods on the living room floor grew and threatened to
      become Mt. Everest, but the shopping list hardly got shorter. A sheepskin coat
      for Lyuba, high winter boots for Yura's wife, a waterproof coat for Yelena, a
120   videotape recorder, some kind of rings for the camera of the sister of Lyuba's
      husband, a Japanese walkman radio for Yura and a mouthpiece for a trum-
      pet belonging to some person unknown to her. It was a herculean task.
      Grisha had excellent taste and an unfailing sense for what was beautiful
      and very expensive. He said to Inna: "We must buy this blouse for Lyuba."
125   The blouse was certainly unusually pretty. Inna would have bought it for her-
      self if it had been on sale.
      Goodness, how she had waited for him, her only brother! She would have
      liked to complain to him of her loneliness, the fact that her job was only a tem-
      porary five-year contract, and that her future looked extremely uncertain. After
130   all was said and done, the trips that she had taken to conferences and sem-
      inars were all that she possessed.
      His visit lasted over two weeks and, not counting the first evening, when
      they had sat on the balcony and smoked, there had not been a free moment
      when they could have had a heart-to-heart talk. She wondered if such a talk
135   was even possible. She had expected a very significant moment in her life—
      the family reunion—and it had turned out to be very prosaic, even mundane.

140 The gap between brother and sister was widening at an alarming rate. His trip gradually became transformed into a giant shopping expedition to North America. Each day spent wandering through stores moved them further apart into mutual incomprehension.

Once Inna took Grisha to dinner with Lyova who (amazing coincidence!) had been Grisha's fellow pupil in the eighth grade of Moscow school #214. Inna's and Grisha's arrival was eagerly awaited in the elegant two-storey house overlooking the ravine. Other guests were drinking cocktails on the wooden
145 veranda surrounded by creepers. Later on, there was a barbecue on the lawn. Grisha was enthusiastic about the barbecued meat, which he had never tasted before. For dessert, Lyova's wife brought out a basket carved out of a pineapple filled with large, fresh strawberries.

Grisha soaked up all this like a sponge. He committed it to memory, imag-
150 ining how he would relate every minute detail in Moscow. To Grisha, Inna's new life must seem just such a fragrant pineapple-strawberry basket, which only lacked immortality to be perfect.

Suddenly Inna felt exhausted. She felt that she was participating in some sort of farce, that she was on stage and Grisha was viewing her from the back
155 of a hall without being able to hear her. The loneliness became unbearable.

How do Inna and Grisha spend their time together? Do you think they are enjoying themselves at Lyova's party? Why or why not?

Finish this statement to predict what happens next.

Before Grisha leaves, Inna will _____ .

a. have a heart-to-heart talk with him about her situation
b. get angry with him about his selfishness
c. remain silent about her true feelings

People were laughing on the veranda. In the house Lyova demonstrated his new stereo system with the compact disk player to Grisha. Through the open window Inna could see Grisha's forced smile and the sweat droplets on his forehead. She felt sorry for him and wanted more than anything for him to
160 leave as soon as possible.

She went down from the veranda and walked along the path to the ravine. The air smelt fresh and moist. From that angle her friend's brightly lit house seemed even grander.

"I wonder how Boris would have behaved?" she thought. "Was it possi-
165 ble that he, too...?"

"Experience determines consciousness." Inna remembered the long-forgotten Marxist formula.

During the last days before leaving, Grisha could talk only of the customs inspection in Moscow. He flew off on July 15th.
170 "Next time I will bring Yelena," Grisha promised when leaving.

From the airport, Inna drove straight to work. She was sad and felt like crying. The small white airplane of her childhood vanished in the empty blue sky.

Tanya Filanovsky, translated from Russian by Ruth Schachter

After You Read

Focus on Testing

Avoiding "Traps" in Standardized Vocabulary Tests

Many vocabulary tests are similar to the following exercise. Each item is a sentence with a word in bold type, and this is followed by four choices. You must choose the best synonym or definition for the word in bold. Here are some tips to help you avoid the "traps" that often accompany this test design.

1. The choices may include a word that sounds and looks like the word in bold and begins with the same letter. It is usually (but not always) wrong. Do not choose a word because of its similar sound or appearance. Choose it because its meaning is similar. Five items in the following exercise have choices like this. Which numbers are they? _____

2. The choices may include an antonym of the word in bold. Because we learn by association, it is easy to fall into this trap and choose a word that means exactly the opposite of the correct one. Four of the items in the following exercise have antonyms among the choices. Which numbers are they?_____

3. The answer key may be in another section or on a different page. Be careful to fill in the correct circle. Sometimes it helps to "say the letter in your mind" until you have filled it in.

Choose the word or phrase that best explains the meaning of the word(s) in bold type and darken the appropriate letter in the answer column. If necessary, scan for the word(s) in the story to see them in another context. Words are given in the order they appear in the story.

1. …Babushka **presided over** the boiling oil.
    A. pressed down on   **Answer**
    B. carried away, removed   (A)   (B)   (C)   (D)
    C. lit the fire under
    D. was in charge of, watched out for

2. At once the long hallway…was filled with lively **bustle**.
    A. inactivity   **Answer**
    B. games   (A)   (B)   (C)   (D)
    C. children
    D. movement

3. Later she would read these **yellowed** sheets….
    A. colorful   **Answer**
    B. mellowed   (A)   (B)   (C)   (D)
    C. aged
    D. sunny

4. Inna was listening to Grisha happily and **distractedly**.
   A. absentmindedly, not carefully
   B. noticeably, intentionally
   C. carefully, with great attention
   D. clearly, without hearing surrounding noises

   Answer Ⓐ Ⓑ Ⓒ Ⓓ

5. Why would Yelena have allowed him to leave home in this **Godforsaken state**?
   A. God-loving country
   B. Godless part of a country
   C. sloppy, neglected condition
   D. unforgiven, unpardoned way

   Answer Ⓐ Ⓑ Ⓒ Ⓓ

6. Probably deep down Inna **envied** Yelena….
   A. was jealous of
   B. became tired of
   C. watched out for
   D. felt sorry for

   Answer Ⓐ Ⓑ Ⓒ Ⓓ

7. …his expectations and **naive** faith in her financial prowess struck Inna like a splash of cold water.
   A. wise, insightful
   B. innocent, simple
   C. happy, smiling
   D. negative, terrible

   Answer Ⓐ Ⓑ Ⓒ Ⓓ

8. All her achievements…were **reduced to rubble**….
   A. found in a field
   B. examined by the police
   C. made to seem unimportant
   D. proudly destroyed

   Answer Ⓐ Ⓑ Ⓒ Ⓓ

9. …Inna and Grisha's arrival was eagerly awaited in the elegant two-storey house overlooking the **ravine**.
   A. narrow river
   B. small road
   C. narrow valley
   D. rushing water

   Answer Ⓐ Ⓑ Ⓒ Ⓓ

10. She felt that she was participating in some sort of **farce**.
    A. face lift
    B. serious drama
    C. ridiculous comedy
    D. funny dance

    Answer Ⓐ Ⓑ Ⓒ Ⓓ

Talk It Over

In small groups, discuss these questions.

1. What went wrong with Grisha's visit to his sister Inna?
2. Do you think that Inna should buy a car for Grisha's son Yura? Why or why not?
3. What quotation of Karl Marx does Inna remember at the end of the story? Why does it seem important to her? What do you think of it?
4. The story begins and ends with the image of an airplane. What does the airplane represent in Inna's memory of childhood? What does the airplane represent at the end?
5. Which is more important to you: family feeling or material success? In your opinion, why are these two aspects of life often in conflict?

Making Connections

Immigrants to the United States can find information and communicate with each other on the Internet. For information from the Immigration and Naturalization Service (INS), go to its Web site at www.ins.usdoj.gov. There you can find out the latest laws regarding immigration rulings about visas, forms to obtain and fill out, and other important information. To find other information about immigration, simply type in the following phrase on a common search engine: *Immigrant information*. To share information with other immigrants, type in: *Immigrant chat rooms*.

4 **Identifying Spelling Differences.** Look at the differences between American and British spelling described on page 82. Americans would write *labor camp, color, center, colorful*. How are these words spelled in Tanya Filanovsky's story that was translated by a Canadian? Can you explain why Canadian spelling is more like British spelling than American spelling? (The answer has to do more with history than with geography.)

1. labor camp   _____
2. gray   _____
3. color   _____
4. center   _____
5. colorful   _____

5 **Summarizing a Story.** Write a summary (from six to nine sentences) of the story "Grisha Has Arrived," following these guidelines. To review the story elements, see Part 1 of Chapter 4.

1. Identify the two main characters and setting, and state the conflict. (1–2 sentences)
2. Describe the complication, in this case involving Grisha's actions and Inna's needs and feelings. (2–3 sentences)
3. Describe the climax (crisis, or high point of the plot) that occurs at Lyova's party and brings a new insight (way of thinking) to Inna. (1–2 sentences)
4. State the resolution at the end. (1–2 sentences)

6   **Role Playing.** Work with a partner. One of you plays the role of Grisha, who is visiting your city. The other one plays the role of a radio commentator interviewing Grisha with the following questions. After you finish, the radio commentator may be asked to tell the class about Grisha's impressions.

1.   How are things with your wife and children in Russia now?
2.   Why have you come here to visit?
3.   What has impressed you most about our city?
4.   What is your greatest wish?

Around the Globe

There are numerous refugees around the globe. What exactly is a refugee? The commonly accepted definition is "a person who has fled his or her country because of persecution." Many countries receive refugees and try to help them resettle. The majority of refugees are in the developing world. At the end of 1999, the Middle East hosted the largest number of refugees—5.8 million. Each year, thousands of refugees apply for admission to various countries. In 1999, over 85,000 refugees applied and were admitted to the United States.

What do you know about refugees? Have you or a relative or friend ever been a refugee? What about someone you know? Share your answers to these questions with the class.

Find out information about refugees on the Internet. Simply use a search engine and type in the words "refugee information." A good Website you can go to is *www.refugees.org*.

Video Activities: College Graduation

Before You Watch.   Discuss these questions in small groups.

1.   Have you ever attended a graduation ceremony? What happened at the ceremony?
2.   How many years do people usually have to study to become doctors?

Watch.   Circle the correct answers to the following questions.

1.   Why is Mrs. Christianson so happy?
    a.   She's graduating from college.
    b.   Her son is becoming a doctor.
    c.   She has just immigrated to the United States.
2.   Louis Christianson says that his mother gave him a love of _____ .
    a.   education   b.   medicine   c.   Mexico
3.   Louis decided to become a doctor _____ .
    a.   when he was young   b.   in high school   c.   after high school

Watch Again.   Match the speakers to the quotations.

_____ 1.   I'd love to share with you some stories about the medical students soon to be physicians before you.

_____ 2.   I did a major in philosophy, so I had no plans to go to medical school.

_____ 3.   Nine years ago Christianson was graduating from Madison High School.

_____ 4.   I still see him as my baby.

_____ 5.   We are delighted.

a.   narrator

b.   graduation speaker

c.   Mr. Christianson

d.   Louis Christianson

e.   Mrs. Christianson

After You Watch.   Find an account of a graduation from a newspaper. Scan the article for these facts. Keep track of the time it takes you to find the information. Work as fast as you can.

1.   Where was the graduation?
2.   How many students were graduating?
3.   Who were the main speakers?

Chapter 6

The Mind

IN THIS CHAPTER

Many scientists speak of the mind as the "new frontier," the most dynamic area of research. The first selection discusses some amazing results of psychologists who have been studying people with an extraordinary ability to remember or memorize. Then Edgar Allan Poe provides an inside look at the disordered and diseased mind of a madman. Finally, there is a timed reading about a very unusual American man.

| PART 1 | # A Memory for All Seasonings |

Before You Read

1 **Anticipating the Reading.** Before beginning to read an article, it's helpful to try to anticipate what it will be about and determine what associations you have with the topic. Answer the following questions. Then share your answers with a partner.

1. Look at the title. It's rather unusual. What do you think it means?

_____

_____

2. The article you are about to read is about different kinds and aspects of human memory. When you think of a person with an extraordinary memory, what is the first question that comes to your mind?

_____

_____

3. Is there something practical you might learn from this reading?

_____

_____

4. What is the earliest event in your life that you can remember and approximately how old were you when it occurred?

_____

_____

_____

_____

5. Why do you suppose you can remember the event?

_____

_____

Read

Memory is one of the most important functions of the mind. Without our memories, we would have no identity. The following article is about a mnemonist, a person with an extraordinary power to remember. The title includes a pun, a form of humor based on a play on words. The usual phrase to describe something constant and dependable is *for all seasons*. Here the phrase is changed to *for all seasonings*. *Seasonings* is another word for spices, such as salt, pepper, and curry. What hint does this give you about the mnemonist? Early in the article you will find out.

A Memory for All Seasonings

One evening two years ago, Peter Polson, a member of the psychology department at the University of Colorado, took his son and daughter to dinner at Bananas, a fashionable restaurant in Boulder. When the waiter took their orders, Polson noticed that the young man didn't write anything down. He just
5 listened, made small talk, told them that his name was John Conrad, and left. Polson didn't think this was exceptional: There were, after all, only three of them at the table. Yet he found himself watching Conrad closely when he returned to take the orders at a nearby table of eight. Again the waiter listened, chatted, and wrote nothing down. When he brought Polson and his children
10 their dinners, the professor couldn't resist introducing himself and telling Conrad that he'd been observing him.

The young man was pleased. He wanted customers to notice that, unlike other waiters, he didn't use a pen and paper. Sometimes, when they did notice, they left him quite a large tip. He had once handled a table of nineteen
15 complete dinner orders without a single error. At Bananas, a party of nineteen (a bill of roughly $200) would normally leave the waiter a $35 tip. They had left Conrad $85.

Polson was impressed enough to ask the waiter whether he would like to come to the university's psychology lab and let them run some tests on him.
20 Anders Ericsson, a young Swedish psychologist recently involved in memory research, would be joining the university faculty soon, and Polson thought that he would be interested in exploring memory methods with the waiter. Conrad said he would be glad to cooperate. He was always on the lookout for ways to increase his income, and Polson told him he would receive $5 an hour to be a
25 guinea pig.

Conrad, of course, was not the first person with an extraordinary memory to attract attention from researchers. Alexander R. Luria, the distinguished Soviet psychologist, studied a Russian newspaper reporter named Shereshevskii for many years and wrote about him in *The Mind of a Mnemonist*
30 (Basic Books, 1968). Luria says that Shereshevskii was able to hear a series

of fifty words spoken once and recite them back in perfect order fifteen years later. Another famous example of extraordinary memory, the conductor Arturo Toscanini, was known to have memorized every note for every instrument in 250 symphonies and 100 operas.

35   For decades the common belief among psychologists was that memory was a fixed quantity; an exceptional memory, or a poor one, was something with which a person was born.

This point of view has come under attack in recent years; expert memory is no longer universally considered the exclusive gift of the genius, or the

40   abnormal. "People with astonishing memory for pictures, musical scores, chess positions, business transactions, dramatic scripts, or faces are by no means unique," wrote Cornell psychologist Ulric Neisser in *Memory Observed* (1981). "They may not even be very rare." Some university researchers, including Polson and Ericsson, go a step further than Neisser. They believe that

45   there are no physiological differences at all between the memory of a Shereshevskii or a Toscanini and that of the average person. The only real difference, they believe, is that Toscanini trained his memory, exercised it regularly, and wanted to improve it.

Like many people with his capacity to remember, Toscanini may also have

50   used memory tricks called mnemonics. Shereshevskii, for example, employed a technique known as *loci*. As soon as he heard a series of words, he mentally "distributed" them along Gorky Street in Moscow. If one of the words was "orange," he might visualize a man stepping on an orange at a precise location on the familiar street. Later, in order to retrieve "orange," he would take

55   an imaginary walk down Gorky Street and see the image from which it could easily be recalled. Did the waiter at Bananas have such a system? What was his secret?

John Conrad would be the subject of Anders Ericsson's second in-depth study of the machinations of memory. As a research associate at Carnegie-

60   Mellon University in Pittsburgh, Ericsson had spent the previous three years working with William Chase on an extensive study of Steve Faloon, an undergraduate whose memory and intellectual skills were considered average. When Ericsson and Chase began testing Faloon, he could remember no more than seven random digits after hearing them spoken once. According to gen-

65   erally accepted research, almost everyone is capable of storing five to nine random digits in short-term memory. After twenty months of working with Chase and Ericsson, Faloon could memorize and retrieve eighty digits.

"The important thing about our testing Faloon is that researchers usually study experts," Chase says. "We studied a novice and watched him grow into

70   an expert. Initially, we were just running tests to see whether his digit span could be expanded. For four days he could not go beyond seven digits. On the fifth day he discovered his mnemonic system and then began to improve rapidly."

Faloon's intellectual abilities didn't change, the researchers say. Nor did

75   the storage capacity of his short-term memory. Chase and Ericsson believe that short-term memory is a more or less fixed quantity. It reaches saturation quickly, and to overcome its limitations one must learn to link new data with material that is permanently stored in long-term memory. Once the associations have been made, the short-term memory is free to absorb new informa-

80   tion. Shereshevskii transferred material from short-term to long-term memory

by placing words along Gorky Street in Moscow. Faloon's hobby was long-distance running, and he discovered that he could break down a spoken list of eighty digits into units of three or four and associate most of these with running times.

To Faloon, a series like 4, 0, 1, 2 would translate as four minutes, one and two-tenths seconds, or "near a four-minute mile"; 2, 1, 4, 7 would be encoded as two hours fourteen minutes seven seconds, or "an excellent marathon time." When running didn't provide the link to his long-term memory, ages and dates did; 1, 9, 4, 4 is not relevant to running, but it is "near the end of World War II."

Chase and Ericsson see individual differences in memory performance as resulting from previous experience and mental training. "In sum," they write, "adult memory performance can be adequately described by a single model of memory."

Not every student of psychology agrees with Chase and Ericsson, of course. "I'm very suspicious of saying that everyone has the same kind of memory," says Matthew Erdelyi, a psychologist at Brooklyn College. "In my research," he says, "I find that people have very different memory levels. They can all improve, but some levels remain high and some remain low. There are dramatic individual differences."

It is unlikely that there will be any agreement among psychologists on the conclusions that they have thus far drawn from their research. The debate about exceptional memory will continue. But in the meantime it is interesting to look deeper into the mind of a contemporary mnemonist.

Ericsson and Polson, both of whom have tested Conrad over the past two years, believe that there is nothing intellectually outstanding about him. When they began testing Conrad's memory, his digit scan was normal: about seven numbers. His grades in college were average.

Conrad himself says that he is unexceptional mentally, but he has compared his earliest memories with others' and has found that he can recall things that many people can't. His first distinct memory is of lying on his back and raising his legs so that his mother could change his diapers. As a high school student he didn't take notes in class—he says he preferred watching the girls take notes—and he has never made a list in his life. "By never writing down a list of things to do, and letting it think for me," he says, "I've forced my memory to improve."

Conrad does believe that his powers of observation, including his ability to listen, are keener than most people's. Memory, he says, is just one part of the whole process of observation. "I'm not extraordinary, but sometimes people make me feel that way. I watch them and realize how many of them have disorganized minds and memories and that makes me feel unusual. A good memory is nothing more than an organized one."

One of the first things Conrad observed at Bananas was that the head-waiter, his boss, was "a very unpleasant woman." He disliked being her subordinate, and he wanted her job. The only way he could get it was by being a superior waiter. He stayed up nights trying to figure out how to do this; the idea of memorizing orders eventually came to him. Within a year he was the headwaiter.

"One of the most interesting things we've found," says Ericsson, "is that just trying to memorize things does not insure that your memory will improve.

It's the active decision to get better and the number of hours you push your-self to improve that make the difference. Motivation is much more important than innate ability."

135   Conrad began his memory training by trying to memorize the orders for a table of two, then progressed to memorizing larger orders.

He starts by associating the entree with the customer's face. He might see a large, heavy-set man and hear "I'd like a big Boulder Steak." Some-times, Peter Polson says, "John thinks a person looks like a turkey and that customer orders a turkey sandwich. Then it's easy."

140   In memorizing how long meat should be cooked, the different salad dressings, and starches, Conrad relies on patterns of repetition and variation. "John breaks things up into chunks of four," Ericsson says. "If he hears 'rare, rare, medium, well-done,' he instantly sees a pattern in their relationship. Sometimes he makes a mental graph. An easy progression—rare, medium-
145   rare, medium, well-done—would take the shape of a steadily ascending line on his graph. A more difficult order—medium, well-done, rare, medium—would resemble a mountain range."

The simplest part of Conrad's system is his encoding of salad dressings. He uses letters: B for blue cheese; H for the house dressing; O for oil and vine-
150   gar; F for French; T for Thousand Island. A series of orders, always arranged according to entree, might spell a word, like B-O-O-T, or a near-word, like B-O-O-F, or make a phonetic pattern: F-O-F-O. As Ericsson says, Conrad re-members orders, regardless of their size, in chunks of four. This is similar to the way Faloon stores digits, and it seems to support Chase and Ericsson's
155   contention that short-term memory is limited and that people are most com-fortable working with small units of information.

One of the most intriguing things about Conrad is the number of ways he can associate material. Another is the speed with which he is able to call it up from memory. Ericsson and Polson have also tested him with animals, units
160   of time, flowers, and metals. At first, his recall was slow and uncertain. But with relatively little practice, he could retrieve these "orders" almost as quick-ly as he could food.

"The difference between someone like John, who has a trained memory, and the average person," says Ericsson, "is that he can encode material in
165   his memory fast and effortlessly. It's similar to the way you can understand English when you hear it spoken. In our tests in the lab, he just gets better and faster." "What John Conrad has," says Polson, "is not unlike an athletic skill. With two or three hundred hours of practice, you can develop these skills in the same way you can learn to play tennis."

Stephen Singular

After You Read

Study Skills

John Conrad spoke of the importance of having an organized mind for developing one's memory. In this section, two skills will be presented to help you organize materials for study: underlining and marginal glossing.

Underlining

Before underlining, read the material once. Then scan the reading, underlining key words and phrases that relate to main ideas and important statistics or examples that support them. Underline only about 20 to 30 percent of the material. Many students underline with felt pens, often using one color for main concepts and a different color for statistics and examples.

Another effective method is to underline main ideas and circle or draw rectangles around names, terms, or statistics you want to remember. Supporting ideas can be underlined with broken lines. Practice underlining a few different ways until you find a method you like.

Marginal Glossing

Marginal glossing is another way to organize material for study. A marginal gloss is a note in the margin of your book summarizing the material next to it. When you study, these notes stand out and remind you of other points as well. This saves time because you do not reread everything, only the brief notes. You can also try to think of questions that might be asked on a test and write these questions in the margins.

2 **Underlining and Glossing.** Here are the first eight paragraphs from a "Memory for All Seasonings" with underlining and marginal glosses done for the first four paragraphs. Look over the four paragraphs that have been marked. Then finish the remaining paragraphs by underlining and glossing them yourself. Afterward, compare your work with your classmates. You should find that the first part of the comprehension quiz is quite easy after this preparation.

Peter Polson, from University Colo. Psy. Dept., saw a waiter at Bananas Restaurant with an amazing memory. The waiter was John Conrad.

Conrad did not write his orders. He memorized all of them.

One evening two years ago, (Peter Polson,) a member of the psychology department at the University of Colorado, took his son and daughter to dinner at Bananas, a fashionable restaurant in Boulder. When the waiter took their orders, Polson noticed that the young man didn't write anything down. He just listened, made small talk, told them that his name was (John Conrad) and left. Polson didn't think this was exceptional: There were, after all, only three of them at the table. Yet he found himself watching Conrad closely when he returned to take the orders at a nearby table of eight. Again the waiter listened, chatted, and wrote nothing down. When he brought Polson and his children their dinners, the professor couldn't resist introducing himself and telling Conrad that he'd been observing him.

The young man was pleased. He wanted customers to notice that, unlike other waiters, he didn't use a pen and paper. Sometimes, when they did no-

15

tice, they left him quite a large tip. He had once handled a table of nineteen complete dinner orders without a single error. At Bananas, a party of nineteen (a bill of roughly $200) would normally leave the waiter a $35 tip. They had left Conrad $85.

Polson invited Conrad to the lab for further memory study for $5 an hour.

20

Polson was impressed enough to ask the waiter whether he would like to come to the university's psychology lab and let them run some tests on him. Anders Ericsson a young Swedish psychologist recently involved in memory research, would be joining the university faculty soon, and Polson thought that he would be interested in exploring memory methods with the waiter. Conrad said he would be glad to cooperate. He was always on the lookout for ways to increase his income, and Polson told him he would receive $5 an hour to be a guinea pig.

25

Other people with amazing memories include a Russian reporter named Shereshevskii and the conductor Arturo Toscanini.

30

Conrad, of course, was not the first person with an extraordinary memory to attract attention from researchers. Alexander R. Luria, the distinguished Soviet psychologist, studied a Russian newspaper reporter named Shereshevskii for many years and wrote about him in *The Mind of a Mnemonist* (Basic Books, 1968). Luria says that Shereshevskii was able to hear a series of fifty words spoken once and recite them back in perfect order fifteen years later. Another famous example of extraordinary memory, the conductor Arturo Toscanini, was known to have memorized every note for every instrument in 250 symphonies and 100 operas.

35

For decades the common belief among psychologists was that memory was a fixed quantity; an exceptional memory, or a poor one, was something with which a person was born.

40

This point of view has come under attack in recent years; expert memory is no longer universally considered the exclusive gift of the genius, or the abnormal. "People with astonishing memory for pictures, musical scores, chess positions, business transactions, dramatic scripts, or faces are by no means unique," wrote Cornell psychologist Ulric Neisser in *Memory Observed* (1981). "They may not even be very rare." Some university researchers, including Polson and Ericsson, go a step further than Neisser. They believe that there are no physiological differences at all between the memory of a Shereshevskii or a Toscanini and that of the average person. The only real difference, they believe, is that Toscanini trained his memory, exercised it regularly, and wanted to improve it.

45

50

Like many people with his capacity to remember, Toscanini may also have used memory tricks called mnemonics. Shereshevskii, for example, employed a technique known as loci. As soon as he heard a series of words, he mentally "distributed" them along Gorky Street in Moscow. If one of the words was "orange," he might visualize a man stepping on an orange at a precise location on the familiar street. Later, in order to retrieve "orange," he would take an imaginary walk down Gorky Street and see the image from which it could easily be recalled. Did the waiter at Bananas have such a system? What was his secret?

55

John Conrad would be the subject of Anders Ericsson's second in-depth study of the machinations of memory. As a research associate at Carnegie-Mellon University in Pittsburgh, Ericsson had spent the previous three years working with William Chase on an extensive study of Steve Faloon, an undergraduate whose memory and intellectual skills were considered average. When Ericsson and Chase began testing Faloon, he could remember no more

60

65 | than seven random digits after hearing them spoken once. According to generally accepted research, almost everyone is capable of storing five to nine random digits in short-term memory. After twenty months of working with Chase and Ericsson, Faloon could memorize and retrieve eighty digits.

3   **Recalling Information.** Based on what you have just read, choose the best way of finishing each statement.

1. The psychology professor discovered John Conrad's incredible ability to memorize _____.
   a. in school
   b. on a test
   c. in a restaurant

2. Conrad agreed to let the professor study his memory because _____.
   a. Conrad was interested in psychology
   b. Conrad wanted to increase his income
   c. Conrad needed to improve his memory

3. The famous Russian mnemonist Shereshevskii used a memory trick called *loci* to remember objects by _____.
   a. associating them with events in Russian history
   b. imagining them placed along a street in Moscow
   c. picturing each one in his mind in a different color

4. The memory trick used by Steve Faloon was the association of certain numbers with _____.
   a. running times
   b. important dates
   c. both of the above
   d. none of the above

5. Conrad had been _____.
   a. a gifted student
   b. a below-average student
   c. an average student

6. Part of Conrad's motivation for developing memory tricks to aid him as a waiter was _____.
   a. his desire to get his boss's job
   b. his great admiration for the headwaiter
   c. his fear of not finding any work

7. Imagine that four customers have requested that their steaks be cooked in the following way: well-done, medium, medium-rare, rare. According to John Conrad's "mental graph" technique, this order would be remembered as _____.
   a. a steadily ascending line
   b. a steadily descending line
   c. a mountain range

8. From this article a careful reader should infer that _____.

   a. everyone has about the same memory capacity and can develop a superior memory through practice and motivation

   b. a good or bad memory is an ability that a person is born with and cannot change to any great degree

   c. there is still no conclusive evidence as to whether outstanding memories are inborn or developed

Study Skills

Earlier you were instructed to underline and gloss the important points in part of an article to help you review it. Another way to organize information for study is to make a study map.

   Study mapping is a method of taking notes. It is unique in that an entire article or even a chapter of a textbook is mapped on just one page. To make a map, you must select the major and minor points of the article or chapter. Then arrange them in graph form. Students who enjoy drafting, charts, or symbols tend to like mapping. No exact method of map making is standard. Figures or shapes, lines, and arrows can be used. Some students prefer treelike designs for their maps; others use circles, octagons, or squares.

   Like underlining, mapping should be done after the first reading. A study map of the preceding paragraph follows.

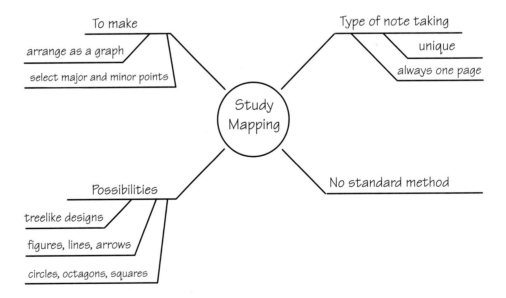

4 **Finishing a Study Map.** Look at the incomplete study map for "A Man for All Seasonings" that follows. Work with a partner or a small group and finish the map. Compare your work afterward with your other pairs or small groups. Did you add too much information? Too little?

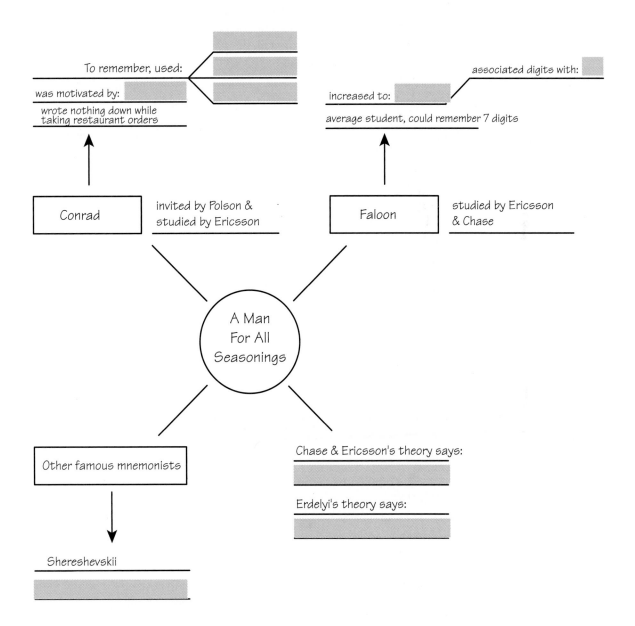

5   **Applying Concepts from the Reading.** Several different mnemonic systems (memory tricks) are described in the reading. Working in small groups, show that you have understood these tricks by applying them to the following situations. A list of the systems with line references is given in case you want to review them.

a. *loci* (imagining objects in a familiar place), used by Shereshevskii, lines 50–56
b. number association, used by Steve Faloon, lines 85–90
c. physical appearance association, used by John Conrad, lines 136–139
d. mental graph or picture, used by Conrad, lines 140–147
e. word or sound pattern association, used by Conrad, lines 148–153

1.   You want to remember the names of all the psychologists mentioned in this article: Polson, Ericsson, Luria, Neisser, Chase. How would you do this using word or sound pattern association?

2.   You want to remember to buy the following items at the grocery store: apples, milk, rice, pepper, salad dressing, and olives. How would you do this, using *loci*? How would you do it using word or sound pattern association? Which system would be better for you?

3.   You have just a minute or two to look at the alphabetical list of exam grades and want to remember the grades of seven of your friends. What kind of mental graph would you picture in your mind to remember them in the following order: A, D, A, D, B, C, B?

4.   You want to remember the combinations for the locks you use for your bicycle, your school locker, and your gym locker: 0915, 1220, 1492. How could you do this, using number association? Can you think of any other way of doing it?

5.   You are at a dinner party and want to remember the names of the four other guests: a very tall lady named Mrs. Stemski; a large, heavy-set man named Mr. Barnes; a cheerful young woman with a big smile named Miss Rich; and a sad-looking young man named Mr. Winter. How could you use physical appearance association to remember their names?

Talk It Over

In small groups, discuss the following questions.

1.   In what other professions, besides that of a waiter, is it useful to have a good memory? Why?

2.   Do you know or have you heard of any people (besides those mentioned in the article) who have extraordinary memories?

3.   What techniques, other than those mentioned in the preceding exercise, are sometimes used to aid memory?

4.   Are there some situations in life when it is important to develop the ability to forget rather than to remember? If so, how can this be done? Explain.

6 **Finding Support for or Against a Hypothesis.** As the article points out, some psychologists today believe that extraordinary memories are simply the result of development through hard work and the application of a system. According to them, an average person could achieve a superior memory if he or she tried hard enough. Find evidence from the article to support this hypothesis and write it in the blanks:

_____

_____

_____

Now find evidence from the article that goes against this hypothesis:

_____

_____

_____

What is your opinion of this controversial question?

_____

_____

_____

When you finish, compare and share your work with a partner and then in a small group.

PART 2   The Tell-Tale Heart

Before You Read

1 **Getting the Meaning of Words from Context.** Some words and expressions in the next selection are now archaic (no longer used in modern English). Many English-speaking readers would not be familiar with them. However, they would have little trouble following the story because the context provides many clues. Read the following sentences from the Edgar Allan Poe story that follows and select a modern word or expression to replace the old-fashioned one in italics. Remember to use the context to help you.

1. "How, then, am I mad? *Hearken!* and observe how healthily—how calmly I can tell you the whole story." (lines 4–5)
   a. Speak!
   b. Listen!
   c. Go away!

2. "It is impossible to say how first the idea entered my brain, but once conceived, it haunted me day and night. *Object* there was none. Passion there was none…. For his gold I had no desire." (lines 7–13)
   a. fear
   b. purpose
   c. argument

3. "Now this is the point. You *fancy* me mad. Madmen know nothing. But you should have seen <u>me</u>." (lines 21–23)

   a. like

   b. imagine

   c. offend

4. "Presently I heard a slight groan, and I knew it was the groan of mortal terror. It was not a groan of pain or of grief—oh, no!—it was the low stifled sound that arises from the bottom of the soul…. I knew the sound well. Many a night…it has welled up from my own *bosom*…." (lines 61–64)

   a. house

   b. chest

   c. able

5. "I knew what the old man felt, and pitied him…. His fears had been ever since growing upon him. …He had been saying to himself—'It is nothing but the wind in the chimney….' Yes, he had been trying to comfort himself with these suppositions: but he had found all *in vain*. All *in vain*; because Death…had stalked with his black shadow before him, and enveloped the victim." (lines 66–74)

   a. useless

   b. successful

   c. harmful

6. "But, for many minutes, the heart beat on with a muffled sound. This, however, did not *vex* me; it would not be heard through the wall. *At length* it ceased. The old man was dead." (lines 105–107)

   vex

   a. delight

   b. confuse

   c. irritate

   at length

   a. soon

   b. after a while

   c. in a moment

7. "I took my visitors all over the house. I *bade* them search—search well." (lines 129–130)

   a. bathed

   b. invited

   c. refused

8. "They sat, and while I answered cheerily, they chatted of familiar things. But, *ere long*, I felt myself getting pale and wished them gone." (lines 136–137)

   a. too long, after many hours

   b. before long, in a short while

   c. too long, with too much time

Read

It is not only science that brings us a better understanding of the human mind. Throughout the ages writers of fiction have also examined the mind. The famous American poet and short-story writer Edgar Allan Poe was born in Boston, Massachusetts, in 1809. He died forty years later after a stormy but productive life that included wild sprees of drinking and gambling and numerous love affairs as well as a great deal of serious journalistic and literary writing. His works are still popular today, and several have served as the basis for modern plays and movies. He is best known for his tales of horror, such as "The Tell-Tale Heart."

The following story is told from the point of view of a madman who commits a terrible crime. Many psychologists and criminologists have felt that Poe describes with great accuracy the inner workings of a severely disordered mind. What do you know, from reading or from personal contact, about madness (insanity)? What are some of the characteristics of the thinking, perception, or speech of a person that show he or she is insane? Watch for examples of these characteristics in the story.

2   **Getting Meaning from Context.** As you read the story, skip words or expressions you do not understand and then go back and reread after you see more of the context.

The Tell-Tale Heart

True—nervous—very, very dreadfully nervous I had been and am; but why will you say that I am mad? The disease had sharpened my senses—not destroyed—not dulled them. Above all was the sense of hearing acute. I heard all things in the heaven and in the earth. I heard many things in hell. How, then,
5   am I mad? Hearken! and observe how healthily—how calmly I can tell you the whole story.

It is impossible to say how first the idea entered my brain; but once conceived, it haunted me day and night.
10   Object there was none. Passion there was none. I loved the old man. He had never wronged me. He had never given me insult. For his gold I had no desire. I think it was his eye! Yes, it was this! He
15   had the eye of a vulture—a pale blue eye, with a film over it. Whenever it fell upon me, my blood ran cold; and so by degrees—very gradually—I made up my mind to take the life of the old man,
20   and thus rid myself of the eye forever.

Now this is the point. You fancy me mad. Madmen know nothing. But you should have seen me. You should have

25 seen how wisely I proceeded—with what caution—with what foresight—with what dissimulation I went to work! I was never kinder to the old man than during the whole week before I killed him. And every night, about midnight, I turned the latch of his door and opened it—oh, so gently! And then, when I had made an opening sufficient for my head, I put in a dark lantern, all closed, closed, so that no light shone out, and then I thrust in my head. Oh, you would

30 have laughed to see how cunningly I thrust it in! I moved it slowly—very slowly, so that I might not disturb the old man's sleep. It took me an hour to place my whole head within the opening so far that I could see him as he lay upon his bed. Ha!—would a madman have been so wise as this? And then, when my head was well in the room, I undid the lantern cautiously—oh so cau-

35 tiously—cautiously (for the hinges creaked)—I undid it just so much that a single thin ray fell upon the vulture eye. And this I did for seven long nights—every night just at midnight—but I found the eye always closed; and so it was impossible to do the work; for it was not the old man who vexed me, but his Evil Eye. And every morning, when the day broke, I went boldly into

40 the chamber, and spoke courageously to him, calling him by name in a hearty tone, and inquiring how he had passed the night. So you see he would have been a very profound old man, indeed, to suspect that every night, just at twelve, I looked in upon him while he slept.

Upon the eighth night I was more than usually cautious in opening the

45 door. A watch's minute hand moves more quickly than did mine. Never before that night, had I *felt* the extent of my own powers—of my sagacity. I could scarcely contain my feelings of triumph. To think that there I was, opening the door, little by little, and he not even to dream of my secret deeds or thoughts. I fairly chuckled at the idea; and perhaps he heard me; for he moved on the

50 bed suddenly, as if startled. Now you may think that I drew back—but no. His room was as black as pitch with the thick darkness (for the shutters were close fastened, through fear of robbers), and so I knew that he could not see the opening of the door, and I kept pushing it on steadily, steadily.

I had my head in, and was about to open the lantern, when my thumb

55 slipped upon the tin fastening, and the old man sprang up in bed, crying out—"Who's there?"

I kept quite still and said nothing. For a whole hour I did not move a muscle, and in the meantime I did not hear him lie down. He was still sitting up in the bed listening;—just as I have done, night after night, hearkening to the

60 death watches in the wall.

Presently I heard a slight groan, and I knew it was the groan of mortal terror. It was not a groan of pain or of grief—oh, no!—it was the low stifled sound that arises from the bottom of the soul. I knew the sound well. Many a night, just at midnight, when all the world slept, it has welled up from my own bosom,

65 deepening, with its dreadful echo, the terrors that distracted me. I say I knew it well. I knew what the old man felt, and pitied him, although I chuckled at heart. I knew that he had been lying awake ever since the first slight noise, when he had turned in the bed. His fears had been ever since growing upon him. He had been trying to fancy them causeless, but could not. He had been

70 saying to himself—"It is nothing but the wind in the chimney—it is only a mouse crossing the floor." Yes, he had been trying to comfort himself with these suppositions: but he had found all in vain. *All in vain*; because Death, in approaching him had stalked with his black shadow before him, and en-

75

veloped the victim. And it was the mournful influence of the unperceived shadow that caused him to feel—although he neither saw nor heard—to *feel* the presence of my head within the room.

When I had waited a long time, very patiently, without hearing him lie down, I resolved to open a little—a very, very little crevice in the lantern. So I

80

opened it—you cannot imagine how stealthily, stealthily—until, at length a single dim ray, like the thread of the spider, shot from out the crevice and fell full upon the vulture eye.

It was open—wide, wide open—and I grew furious as I gazed upon it. I saw it with perfect distinctness—all a dull blue with a hideous veil over it that chilled the very marrow in my bones; but I could see nothing else of the old

85

man's face or person: for I had directed the ray, as if by instinct, precisely upon the damned spot.

And have I not told you that what you mistake for madness is but overacuteness of the senses?—now, I say, there came to my ears a low, dull, quick sound, such as a watch makes when enveloped in cotton. I knew that sound

90

well, too. It was the beating of the old man's heart. It increased my fury, as the beating of a drum stimulates the soldier into courage.

But even yet I refrained and kept still. I scarcely breathed. I held the lantern motionless. I tried how steadily I could maintain the ray upon the eye. Meantime the hellish tattoo of the heart increased. It grew quicker and quick-

95

er, and louder and louder every instant. The old man's terror must have been extreme! It grew louder, I say, louder every moment—do you mark me well? I have told you that I am nervous: so I am. And now at the dead hour of the night, amid the dreadful silence of that old house, so strange a noise as this excited me to uncontrollable terror. Yet, for some minutes longer I refrained

100

and stood still. But the beating grew louder, louder! I thought the heart must burst. And now a new anxiety seized me—the sound would be heard by a neighbor! The old man's hour had come! With a loud yell, I threw open the lantern and leaped into the room. He shrieked once—once only. In an instant I dragged him to the floor, and pulled the heavy bed over him. I then smiled

105

gaily, to find the deed so far done. But, for many minutes, the heart beat on with a muffled sound. This, however, did not vex me; it would not be heard through the wall. At length it ceased. The old man was dead. I removed the bed and examined the corpse. Yes, he was stone, stone dead. I placed my hand upon the heart and held it there many minutes. There was no pulsation.

110

He was stone dead. His eye would trouble me no more.

If you still think me mad, you will think so no longer when I describe the wise precautions I took for the concealment of the body. The night waned, and I worked hastily, but in silence. First of all I dismembered the corpse. I cut off the head and the arms and the legs.

115

I then took up three planks from the flooring of the chamber, and deposited all between the scantlings. I then replaced the boards so cleverly, so cunningly, that no human eye—not *even* his—could have detected anything wrong. There was nothing to wash out—no stain of any kind—no blood-spot whatever. I had been too wary for that. A tub had caught all—ha! ha!

120

When I had made an end of these labors, it was four o'clock—still dark as midnight. As the bell sounded the hour, there came a knocking at the street door. I went down to open it with a light heart,—for what had I now to fear? There entered three men, who introduced themselves, with perfect suavity, as

125

officers of the police. A shriek had been heard by a neighbor during the night; suspicion of foul play had been aroused; information had been lodged at the police office, and they (the officers) had been deputed to search the premises.

I smiled,—for *what* had I to fear? I bade the gentlemen welcome. The shriek, I said, was my own in a dream. The old man, I mentioned, was absent in the country. I took my visitors all over the house. I bade them search—

130

search *well*. I led them, at length, to his chamber. I showed them his treasures, secure, undisturbed. In the enthusiasm of my confidence, I brought chairs into the room, and desired them *here* to rest from their fatigues, while I myself, in the wild audacity of my perfect triumph, placed my own seat upon the very spot beneath which reposed the corpse of the victim.

135

The officers were satisfied. My *manner* had convinced them. I was singularly at ease. They sat, and while I answered cheerily, they chatted of familiar things. But, ere long, I felt myself getting pale and wished them gone. My head ached, and I fancied a ringing in my ears: but still they sat and still chatted. The ringing became more distinct:—it continued and became more

140

distinct: I talked more freely to get rid of the feeling: but it continued and gained definiteness—until, at length, I found that the noise was *not* within my ears.

No doubt I now grew very pale;—but I talked more fluently, and with a heightened voice. Yet the sound increased—and what could I do? It was a

145

low, dull, quick sound—much such a sound as a watch makes when enveloped in cotton. I gasped for breath—and yet the officers heard it not. I talked more quickly—more vehemently; but the noise steadily increased.

150 I arose and argued about trifles, in a high key and with violent gesticulations; but the noise steadily increased. Why *would* they not be gone? I paced the floor to and fro with heavy strides, as if excited to fury by the observations of the men—but the noise steadily increased. Oh God! what *could* I do? I foamed—I raved—I swore! I swung the chair upon which I had been sitting, and grated it upon the boards, but the noise arose over all and continually increased. It grew louder—louder—*louder*! And still the men chatted pleasant-
155 ly, and smiled. Was it possible they heard not? Almighty God!—no, no! They heard!—they suspected!—they *knew*!—they were making a mockery of my horror!—this I thought, and this I think. But anything was better than this agony! Anything was more tolerable than this derision! I could bear those hypocritical smiles no longer! I felt that I must scream or die! and now—again!—
160 hark! louder! louder! louder! *louder*!

"Villains!" I shrieked, "dissemble no more! I admit the deed!—tear up the planks! here, here!—it is the beating of his hideous heart!"

Edgar Allan Poe

After You Read

3 **Recalling Information.** Choose the best way of finishing each statement, based on what you have just read.

1. The narrator believes that he suffers from acute nervousness that has _____.
    a. destroyed the power of his senses
    b. increased the power of his senses
    c. driven him mad
2. The motive for the murder was _____.
    a. a strong desire for the victim's money
    b. an intense hatred for the victim
    c. a dislike of the victim's eye
3. During the week before he killed the old man, the narrator's manner toward him was very _____.
    a. kind
    b. angry
    c. indifferent
4. Each night just at midnight, he thrust into the old man's room a _____.
    a. black cat
    b. chain
    c. lantern
5. On the eighth night, the old man awakened because of a noise and then _____.
    a. went right back to sleep
    b. began to call for help
    c. sat up waiting in terror

6. After a while, the murderer heard a sound that increased his fury and that he thought was _____.

   a. a watch enveloped in cotton

   b. the neighbors coming to enter the house

   c. the beating of his victim's heart

7. The murderer disposed of the old man's body by putting it _____.

   a. in the garden

   b. under the floor

   c. into the chimney

8. At four in the morning, three police officers arrived because neighbors had complained of _____.

   a. the lights

   b. some knocking

   c. a shriek

9. The officers found out the truth because _____.

   a. the murderer confessed

   b. a neighbor had told them

   c. there was a bloodstain on the floor

Talk It Over

In small groups, discuss the following questions.

1. Give three statements the narrator makes to prove he is sane. Then show how the author indicates to us that these claims are not true.

2. We are not told what relationship the murderer had to the old man or why they lived together. What did you imagine about this?

3. To whom do you think the murderer is telling this story and for what reason?

4. What do you think the author means by the term "evil eye"? Have you ever heard of people who believe in the "evil eye"? According to this belief, you can suffer bad luck or illness if you are looked at by someone who has this power. What do you think is the origin of this belief? Why do you think the narrator of the story was so disturbed by the old man's eye?

5. Various interpretations have been given to explain the loud beating that the narrator hears during the police visit. Do you agree with any of the following interpretations? Or do you have some other interpretation? Explain.

   a. It is simply a clock or other normal sound that seems louder to him because of his guilt.

   b. It is really the beating of his own heart, which becomes stronger as he gets more and more nervous.

   c. It is the old man's ghost taking revenge on him.

4 **Summarizing from Different Points of View.** What really happened when the three police officers came to search the narrator's house? What did he do or say to make them so suspicious that they stayed to chat with him? The events are presented from his point of view, but we must read "between the lines" in order to see what really happened. We must take into account the narrator's character and pinpoint the places in which he describes events incorrectly. Pretend you are one of the police officers. Summarize what you think really happened. Write your summary in the form of brief notes of explanation on the following lines. After you finish, compare your notes with those of two other "police officers" (classmates). Try to come up with a summary that the three of you agree about. Then share your work with the class.

_____

_____

_____

_____

5 **Identifying Elements in a Story.** Most horror stories focus on certain narrative elements in order to provoke terror. Very often an author will use a special description of a character or of the setting to "frighten" the reader. Of course, the plot or story line is primarily about horror. Listen to the story (either from a commercial recording or a class reading) or carefully look through it and fill in the information requested here. After you finish, compare your work with a partner and then with the class.

A character description that "frightened" me: _____

_____

_____

_____

Something from the setting that "frightened" me was _____

_____

_____

_____

What Do You Think?

Mental illness in many ways remains a mystery to us. Some scientists think that it is hereditary, passed down from parents to children in the genes. Others think it is caused by the environment, perhaps by some trauma in a person's experience or by brain damage at the time of birth. Today, most experts feel that mental illness is caused by a combination of these factors, but they do not agree on how to treat it. One method of treatment is to lock up mentally ill people in hospitals and even prisons to separate them from society. Another method is to place these people in halfway houses under the care of guardians who supervise them and allow them to mix with other people for some hours of the day. In some places mentally ill patients are given drugs, and in other places they receive many hours of counseling and talk therapy of the type pioneered by Sigmund Freud (1856–1939), the inventor of psychoanalysis. What do you think is the cause of mental illness? How should it be treated? How is mental illness treated in other cultures?

Focus on Testing

Reading for Speed

Most tests have a time limit, so good reading speed can be a great asset. As you already know, two ways to read for speedy comprehension are **skimming** the text or **scanning** it. For example, if all you want to find out is a general idea of what the reading is about, skim the text by letting your eyes quickly roam across the page or even down the middle of it, looking for clues. If you need specific information, like a description of a particular character, you can scan for the name of that character—that is, run your eyes quickly through the passage until you find the character's name. For both types of speed reading, remember not to read every word and sometimes, not even every phrase or sentence.

Try reading the following selection, "May's Boy," by scanning the article to find out the answer to these questions:

1. Who is May? _____
2. Who is Leslie Lemke? _____
3. Why is he famous? _____

Now time yourself and see if you can read the article and correctly do the exercise that follows it in five minutes.

May's Boy

Oshkosh, WI (AP)—It was only fitting that this concert be held in a church. After all, it had to do with miracles. Leslie Lemke, whose name has become synonymous with the savant syndrome,* meaning an "island of genius," has come to be even more associated with the term "miracle of love."

Blind, retarded, palsied, Leslie, who has to be led to the piano by his sister, Mary Parker, can play any piece of music he's ever heard.

Last Sunday, his genius came through more strongly than ever. This day he was playing for a special lady—his mother, May—who was celebrating her 93rd birthday and her last scheduled public appearance with him.

It was she who had taken him in and told her own children, "God has something special in mind for Leslie." But even she could not have known what "May's boy," as Leslie has come to be known, could accomplish.

Walter Cronkite used May and Leslie as his "Christmas miracle" years ago. Since then, Leslie has appeared on "That's Incredible," "Donahue," "60 Minutes," and finally, served as a prototype for the film *Rain Man*. He's played the piano for the King of Norway and appeared in Japan. Japanese television sent a crew to film Leslie for its Discovery program at the concert held both at the Seventh-Day Adventist Church in Neenah and St. John Lutheran Church in Oshkosh. "There Was a Lady May Who Prayed for a Miracle," a song written especially for May, was sung by Leslie as his mother, now suffering from Alzheimer's disease, was wheeled next to the piano.

"Day by day and year by year, she stuck by his side. Others thought it hopeless, but he never even cried," he sang in the presence of May's children, grandchildren, great-grandchildren, and even a few great-great-grandchildren.

---

*The "savant syndrome" is the name given to the condition of certain people who are very retarded but have a special genius for one subject or skill, often for mathematics or music. Their general intelligence is usually so low that they cannot lead an independent life, but in their one area of genius, they show extraordinary aptitude that is far above the average.

A spark of recognition lit May's eyes as the song continued, and her family came up to embrace her, though the years when she actually outtalked Donahue on the program are gone. All that is left is the loving glance she casts toward Leslie, as he plays the piece that has become his theme song, Tchaikovsky's Piano Concerto No. 1.

It was that piece May and Joe Lemke heard in the night a decade and a half ago when they were awakened by beautiful music and discovered their profoundly handicapped boy at the piano. It was the miracle May had told her family would come. From that night on, Leslie has been researched, lauded, filmed.

His ability to hear any piece of music just once, imprint it in his brain, and repeat it on the piano on command and in its entirety has brought him fame. No one knows how many pieces are forever locked in his memory. He can play and sing hundreds of songs at will—spirituals, ballads, arias, marches, ragtime, folksongs, and the classics. And yet, seconds before he appears before the crowd, he sits in a chair, head bowed, eyes shut, hand gnarled, unaware of his surroundings, waiting for his sister, Mary, to come and take him to the piano.

As soon as he sits down at the piano bench and lifts his head heavenward, his palsied fingers spread across the keys and praise the Lord with "How Great Thou Art." In the front pew, May's own hands lift in adoration.

Maya Penikis

6   **Recalling Information.** Choose the best answer to fit the blank.

1. May is Leslie Lemke's ____.
   a. teacher
   b. mother
   c. doctor

2. Leslie Lemke is ____.
   a. a retarded man with the ability to sing, dance, and play classical music on television and in the movies
   b. a piano player of very low intelligence who can play from memory any song he has ever heard
   c. a genius who has learned to play many different musical instruments with near perfection

Talk It Over

In small groups, discuss the following questions.

1. In your opinion, how important was May in Leslie's success?
2. What lesson can most people learn from the case of Leslie Lemke?
3. How many minutes did it take you to read this article?
4. When do you like to read fast? When and why do you like to read slowly?

Making Connections

Choose a favorite e-mail address that you haven't memorized yet. Try memorizing it by using one of the mnemonic tricks you practiced in this chapter. Next choose a favorite Internet Website URL (address) beginning with www. Use another mnemonic trick to memorize it. Share your experiences with a partner and with the class.

Now try looking up this URL on the Internet: *http://www.frii.com/~geomanda/mnemonics.html*. It's a Website devoted to mnemonics. Not only can you read all about mnemonics at this site, including hundreds of mnemonic tricks, you can also send in your own favorite mnemonic trick to the e-mail address attached to the Website: *geomanda@frii.com*.

Video Activities: Social Phobia

Before You Watch.   Answer these questions in small groups.

1. A phobia is _____.
    a. a need   b. a fear   c. an idea
2. What kinds of phobias do you know of?

Watch.   Answer these questions in small groups.

1. What kind of phobia does Katherine Whizmore suffer from? _____
2. Circle the things that people with this disorder believe.
    a. People are judging them all of the time.
    b. People want to physically hurt them.
    c. People are unfair to them.
3. Which kinds of treatments help these people?
    a. education about their illness
    b. antidepressant drugs and behavioral therapy
    c. surgery

Watch Again.   Choose the correct answers.

1. By the age of 20, Katherine Whizmore was afraid to _____ .
    a. go to work
    b. cross the street
    c. go shopping alone
2. How many Americans suffer from this disease?
    a. 100 million   b. 1 million   c. 10 million
3. This disease usually begins in _____ .
    a. college   b. high school   c. junior high school
4. *Panicked* means _____ .
    a. confident   b. very frightened   c. sick
5. *Impaired* means _____ .
    a. afraid   b. extraordinary   c. injured
6. *Scrutiny* means _____ .
    a. correction   b. inspection   c. destruction
7. *Harshly* means _____ .
    a. fairly   b. kindly   c. cruelly
8. *Struggle* means to _____ .
    a. fight   b. give up   c. win

After You Watch.   Find an article on different phobias in an encyclopedia or a psychology magazine. As you read, underline and/or highlight the important ideas. When you are finished, make a study map of the article.

Chapter 7

Working

IN THIS CHAPTER

Most people spend a third of their lives working. Many factors determine whether their work brings them pleasure, compensation, and fulfillment, or boredom and frustration. First, we meet a man who has an unusual line of work and loves it. Secondly, the president and CEO of a large company gives us his opinion on the secret of being a good manager. In the third part, we learn about women who work in jobs that used to be only open to men.

| PART 1 | # Stone Carver |

Before You Read

1 **Predicting from the Title and Illustrations.** Look at the title and illustrations of the article. Is there any part you don't understand? Which of the items in the following list do you *not* expect to find in the article? Explain.

- a description of movies that Nicolas Cage has acted in
- a description of various pieces of sculpture in San Francisco
- information about the life and work of a sculptor
- information about the habits of dragons, lizards and salamanders

2 **Scanning for Words.** Read each definition or description. Then scan the reading to find the word that matches it, using the line number to guide you.

1. A compound word for a place where things are stored (line 1) ____warehouse____
2. An adjective meaning "common, not very special" (line 2) _____
3. A word for the projecting shelf or ledge above a fireplace that serves as a place to put things (line 5) _____
4. An adjective describing the style popular during the times of Queen Victoria of England, 1837–1901 (line 5) _____
5. A synonym for *choices* (line 6) _____
6. Two words describing a style of the 1930s that used curves and ornaments (line 12) _____
7. A compound word for the outstanding features that mark a particular place (line 16) _____
8. A word starting with u that means "decorative vases or jars" (line 21) _____
9. A three-word phrase for a work you do because you enjoy it (line 26) _____
10. A synonym for *carved* or *sculpted* (line 43) _____
11. The name of the machine used for lifting very heavy objects (line 51) _____
12. A word that means "a journey to a holy place or a place of inspiration" (line 68) _____

(far left) The clay model for the dreadful dragon fireplace.
(left) The sculptor carving a stone in his studio.

Read

Manuel Palos spends most weekends working alone in his studio in San Francisco, but he doesn't mind. He feels very lucky: "I really enjoy my life. There are people who are born to be something and who find out early enough to enjoy the rest of their lives doing what they want. That's the trick." Palos is a sculptor. He carves statues and other objects out of stone or marble, makes castings in bronze, and restores historic buildings. He also runs a school for sculptors in Puerto Vallarta, Mexico, where the art and craft of sculpting stone is passed on to people from all over the world. What is it like to work as a sculptor? How did Palos get started in it? And why does this work inspire so much passion? The article that follows from the *San Francisco Chronicle* gives the answers.

The San Francisco Sculptor Who Created Nicolas Cage's "Dreadful Dragon"

Kristine M. Carber

In an old warehouse in an industrial section of town, San Francisco sculptor Manuel Palos takes the plebeian fireplace and turns it into a monumental work of art.

5   Plaster molds representing many periods and styles line the walls of his shop. Pinned on one wall is a sketch of a mantel for a restored Victorian house. " I will give the owner two options," says Palos, who wears jeans and a black T-shirt covered with white plaster dust. A green beret partially hides his curly, gray-flecked hair. "One will be traditional, the other softer and rounder in scale."

10   Over the course of his 30-year career, Palos has designed many fireplaces for businesses and private residences. Two are in San Francisco hotels: The Galleria Park has an 8-foot-by 8-foot Art Nouveau style with undulating curves, while the Villa Florence has a traditional European design.... Another fireplace is in the First Interstate Bank, and he counts among

15   his personal clients the Gallo family and Donald Trump.*

Worked on many S.F. landmarks

Palos also has worked on many of The City's famous landmarks. He resculpted six life-sized mythological figures at the California Palace of the Legion of Honor in Lincoln Park and made eight 13-foot-tall eagles for the Pacific

20   Bell's San Francisco headquarters. He worked on the old City of Paris building when Neiman Marcus* moved in and restored friezes and urns at the Academy of Sciences in Golden Gate Park. He is working on a bronze medallion to go outside San Francisco's Hall of Justice.

But it is the "Dreadful Dragon" fireplace for actor Nicolas Cage's Pacific

25   Heights home that is his most memorable piece. " Every time I talk about it I get excited," says Palos. "It was challenging, but it was also a labor of love.

Cage stopped by Palos' studio one morning last year wearing a baseball hat and ripped jeans. " I didn't know who he was," Palos says. "He told me he wanted a fireplace made out of stone."

30   "I asked him if he had a design and he said he wanted a dragon. I thought he was kidding, so I played along. I told him I could make a huge

dragon from the floor to the ceiling with the mouth as the opening. He looked at me and said, 'That's exactly what I want.'" Cage left a deposit and that's when Palos got "scared"—"I had to make the dragon I proposed."

35 *By the book*

Using a children's book about dragons, Palos sketched a design. When it was approved, he made a clay model before casting the real thing in stone.

For nearly five months, Palos labored over the sculpture. Cage wanted black limestone and the 13-foot-tall-by-ten-foot-wide piece required 4½ tons;
40 Palos moved to a studio in Mexico because that was the only place he could find enough.

"Every line had to match," says Palos of the bends and sinewy coils. He chiseled the dragon's nostrils to flare and created fiery-looking eyes. He used pneumatic tools to carve the hooked beak, scales and fang-like teeth for max-
45 imum control. "If any part of the face broke, I would have to start over." When finished, the sculpture was loaded on a truck and Palos drove it back to the United States himself.

Heavy-duty installation

Cage's San Francisco house is a Victorian and before the fireplace could be
50 installed, the walls and the foundation had to be reinforced to hold the weight. It took a crane to lift the fireplace from the street to the house.

Palos and four assistants rolled it up a ramp and in the front door. It had been shipped in 13 pieces and was reassembled using a special scaffold and pulley system. Stainless steel pins and epoxy secured it while Palos
55 carved and shaped it to fit the entire living room wall. At the end of three weeks, everything was in place.

The son of a shoemaker, Palos moved to San Francisco from Zacatecas, Mexico, while in his early 20s to learn how to sculpt. He took a job making molds and models, studying English at night. "My teachers encouraged me
60 to travel," he says, so he spent several months visiting museums and galleries throughout Europe. "I learned from the masters, but I developed my own style."

Palos opened his own studio in San Francisco 26 years ago. Eight people work for him, including his daughter, Alexandra, who helps in the office.
65 He prefers to sculpt on weekends when things are quiet and he can " really produce."

'They think I am Sicilian'

Every year Palos makes a six-week pilgrimage back to Europe to the small town of Carrara, Italy, known for its marble, which Michelangelo* used to
70 sculpt the Pieta.

"They think I am Sicilian," says Palos, who is fluent in Italian.

A showroom adjoins his studio where much of his artistic work—torsos, fountains, statues and urns—is on display.

Not everything is classical in style. A scale model of the "Dreadful Drag-
75 on" leans against one wall and a woman's head carved out of sleek black Belgian marble is in the contemporary mode.

When asked about his favorite, it is still the "Dreadful Dragon," he says. "Cage came to my studio and shook my hand when it was all over," Palos recalls. "He said, 'You are an artist.'"
80 "I told him it takes two."

After You Read

3 **Forming Adjectives from Nouns.** There are many ways to change nouns into adjectives. Can you recall the adjectives used in the article that are related to the nouns in italics? Write them in the blanks provided.

1. A section of town where there is a lot of *industry* is an _____ section.
2. A work of art that is large and important like a *monument* is a _____ work of art.
3. Hair that is full of *curls* is _____ hair.
4. A mantel made according to *tradition* is a _____ mantel.
5. A design that comes from *Europe* is a _____ design.
6. Statues of figures from Greek and Roman *mythology* are _____ statues.
7. A piece of art that stays in your *memory* is a _____ piece.
8. A job that presents a *challenge* is a _____ job.
9. A house built in the style of Queen *Victoria* is a _____ house.
10. A person who is from Sicily is a _____ person.
11. Marble that is from Belgium is _____ marble.

4 **Recalling Information.** Choose the best way of completing each statement, based on what you have just read.

1. Manuel Palos designs and builds works of art for _____ .
   a. hotels and other businesses
   b. private residences
   c. San Francisco landmarks
   d. all of these

2. He found inspiration for the dragon design of Nicolas Cage's fireplace in _____ .
   a. the Legion of Honor
   b. the Academy of Sciences
   c. a children's book
   d. the public zoo

3. In order to find enough black limestone for this work, Palos had to move temporarily to _____ .
   a. Italy
   b. Mexico
   c. Greece
   d. Arizona

4. If any part of the face of the dragon had broken, Palos would have had to _____ .
   a. pay a lot of money to have it fixed
   b. start over from the beginning
   c. give up the whole job
   d. find a new design

5. As a young man, Palos immigrated to the United States from his native country, _____ .
   a. Mexico
   b. Ireland
   c. Germany
   d. Italy

6. He opened up his own studio many years ago and now _____ .
   a. still works completely alone
   b. works with one other sculptor
   c. has eight people working for him, including his daughter
   d. has given up the sculpting and only works on the designs

7. Every year Palos returns for inspiration to _____ .
   a. Italy
   b. France
   c. Greece
   d. South America

 **5** **Finding the Basis for Inferences.** With a partner or in a small group, scan the reading to find and explain the basis for the following inferences about Manuel Palos.

1. Palos's sculpture is well known in San Francisco.
2. He has a sense of humor.
3. He is emotional about his work.
4. He is a perfectionist.
5. He is not afraid to take risks.
6. He works hard to please his clients.

Talk It Over

In small groups, discuss the following questions.

1. Manuel Palos immigrated to the United States from Mexico as a young man. What factors do you think helped him to achieve success?

2. Why do you think he loves his work so much? Is this common? Why do some people dislike what they do for a living or feel indifferent to it?

3. What is your idea of the perfect kind of work? Do you want to lead a balanced life with some of your time and energy devoted to other things? Or do you want to find a profession that takes all of your energy and time because you love it so much? Explain.

4. Which is more important for your future happiness: where you will live or what work you will do? Why?

5. Would you like to work for the rich and the famous? Why or why not?

Making Connections

From the library or on the Internet, find information about one of the following subjects. Then bring it to class and discuss it in a small group.

- The life and work of a classical sculptor, like the Italian master Michelangelo (whose famous statue, the *Pieta*, is referred to in the article) or the French sculptor Auguste Rodin

- The work being done now by Manuel Palos and his associates in San Francisco and Puerto Vallarta, or by other contemporary sculptors

- Information about another style for decorating homes and public buildings, different from the classical style generally used by Palos, such as postmodern, art nouveau, art deco, or the Asian philosophy of Feng Shui

- Current exhibits of sculpture at museums or galleries near you

PART 2   # A Lifetime of Learning to Manage Effectively

Before You Read

1   **Understanding Idiomatic Phrases.** Sometimes you recognize every word in a phrase but still do not understand the meaning of the whole phrase in the special (idiomatic) way it is being used. Usually, if you keep reading, you will find a clue to the meaning—an example, an explanation, or a contrasting phrase. All the following italicized phrases from the selection have these kinds of clues except the first one. Scan the article for each phrase and write a definition or explanation; then write the words that provided clues to the meaning. (Line references are given to make scanning faster.)

1.   raw brain power (line 2) (In this case there are no clues. You have to think of the more common usage of raw when applied to foods and extend the meaning.)
      intelect
      definition:

      _____

      _____

2.   broad human beings (line 18)
      definition:

      _____

      _____

      clue:

      _____

      _____

3.   sense of integrity (line 26)
      definition:
      make judgment

      _____

      clue:

      _____

      _____

4.   cut corners (line 37)
      definition:
      cut expenses

      _____

      clue:

      _____

      _____

5.   in the short run (line 38)
     definition:
     right now

     clue:

6.   hard knocks (line 65)
     definition:
     learning and making mistakes

     clue:

Read

Have you ever worked for someone you really liked and admired? Have you had the opposite experience—working for someone you disliked and did not respect? If so, you know that a manager or boss can make a great difference in the quality of an employee's work. The following article is written by Ralph Z. Sorenson, president and chief executive officer (CEO) of Barry Wright Corporation, a manufacturer of computer accessories and other products. He gives his opinion on the kind of person who makes a good manager and explains how his views on this subject have changed over the years.

A Lifetime of Learning to Manage Effectively

Years ago, when I was a young assistant professor at the Harvard Business School, I thought that the key to developing managerial leadership lay in raw brain power. I thought the role of business schools was to develop future managers who knew all about the various functions of business—to teach them

5   how to define problems succinctly, analyze these problems and identify alternatives in a clear, logical fashion, and, finally, to teach them to make an intelligent decision.

My thinking gradually became tempered by living and working outside the United States and by serving seven years as a college president. During

10 my presidency of Babson College, I added several additional traits or skills that I felt a good manager must possess.

①The first is the _ability to express oneself_ in a clear, articulate fashion. Good oral and written communication skills are absolutely essential if one is to be an effective manager.

"These executive decisions are never easy."

15   2 Second, one must possess that intangible set of qualities called *leader-ship skills*. To be a good leader one must understand and be sensitive to peo-ple and be able to inspire them toward the achievement of common goals.

3   Next I concluded that effective managers must be *broad human beings*
20   who not only understand the world of business but also have a sense of the cultural, social, political, historical, and (particularly today) the international aspects of life and society. This suggests that exposure to the liberal arts and humanities should be part of every manager's education.

Finally, as I pondered the business and government-related scandals that
have occupied the front pages of newspapers throughout the seventies and
25   early eighties, it became clear that a good manager in today's world must
4   have *courage and a strong sense of integrity.* He or she must know where to draw the line between right and wrong.

That can be agonizingly difficult. Drawing a line in a corporate setting sometimes involves having to make a choice between what appears to be
30   conflicting "rights." For example, if one is faced with a decision whether or not to close an ailing factory, whose interests should prevail? Those of stock-holders? Of employees? Of customers? Or those of the community in which the factory is located? It's a tough choice. And the typical manager faces many others.

35   Sometimes these choices involve simple questions of honesty or truth-fulness. More often, they are more subtle and involve such issues as having to decide whether to "cut corners" and economize to meet profit objectives that may be beneficial in the short run but that are not in the best long-term inter-ests of the various groups being served by one's company. Making the right
40   choice in situations such as these clearly demands integrity and the courage to follow where one's integrity leads.

But now I have left behind the cap and gown of a college president and put on the hat of chief executive officer. As a result of my experience as a corporate CEO, my list of desirable managerial traits has become still longer.

It now seems to me that what matters most in the majority of organizations is to have reasonably intelligent, hard-working managers who have a sense of pride and loyalty toward their organization; who can get to the root of a problem and are inclined toward action; who are decent human beings with a natural empathy and concern for people; who possess humor, humility, and common sense; and who are able to couple drive with "stick-to-it-iveness" and patience in the accomplishment of a goal.

It is the *ability to make positive things happen* that most distinguishes the successful manager from the mediocre or unsuccessful one. It is far better to have dependable managers who can make the right things happen in a timely fashion than to have brilliant, sophisticated, highly educated executives who are excellent at planning and analyzing, but who are not so good at implementing. The most cherished manager is the one who says "I can do it," and then does.

Many business schools continue to focus almost exclusively on the development of analytical skills. As a result, these schools are continuing to graduate large numbers of MBAs and business majors who know a great deal about analyzing strategies, dissecting balance sheets, and using computers—but who still don't know how to manage!

As a practical matter, of course, schools can go only so far in teaching their students to manage. Only hard knocks and actual work experience will fully develop the kinds of managerial traits, skills, and virtues that I have discussed here.

Put another way: The best way to learn to manage is to manage. Companies such as mine that hire aspiring young managers can help the process along by:

- providing good role models and mentors
- setting clear standards and high expectations that emphasize the kind of broad leadership traits that are important to the organization, and then rewarding young managers accordingly
- letting young managers actually manage

Having thereby encouraged those who are not only "the best and the brightest" but *also* broad, sensitive human beings possessing all of the other traits and virtues essential for their managerial leadership to rise to the top, we just might be able to breathe a bit more easily about the future health of industry and society.

Ralph Z. Sorenson

After You Read

2 **Highlighting and Marginal Glossing.** Use the preceding article to practice underlining and marginal glossing (discussed in Chapter 6). (You may want to make a photocopy of the article first.) Write your marginal gloss for lines 52–58. Compare your gloss with the glosses written by your classmates. Use your underlined and glossed copy to help you with the following exercises.

_____

_____

_____

_____

_____

_____

3 **Recalling Information.** Choose the best way of finishing each statement, based on what you have just read.

1. The author's work experience includes _____ .
   a. college teaching and administration
   b. working outside the United States
   c. business management
   d. all of the above

2. Since he believes managers should be broad human beings, he would like to see their education focused on business and also on _____ .
   a. the humanities and liberal arts
   b. computers and high technology
   c. accounting and finance

3. For him, a manager should have leadership skills; a good leader is one who _____.
   a. defines problems succinctly
   b. understands and inspires people
   c. expresses his or her ideas clearly
   d. none of the above

4. One of the experiences that convinced him of the need for a sense of integrity in managers was _____ .
   a. a conversation with a high government official
   b. the discovery of dishonesty among students
   c. reading about scandals in the newspapers

5. According to Sorenson, when facing a decision about the possible closing of a factory that is not profitable, a manager should consider the interests of _____ .
   a. the stockholders and customers
   b. the employees
   c. the community
   d. all the above

6. He thinks that managers should think not just of what is profitable in the short run but also of _____ .

    a.   how to "cut corners" to meet objectives
    b.   the long-term interests of those involved
    c.   the fastest way to make money for the company

7. In his view at present, the trait that distinguishes the successful manager from the mediocre is _____ .

    a.   high academic achievement
    b.   the ability to get things done
    c.   a critical and analytical mind

8. Companies that hire young managers ought to _____ .

    a.   let them manage right away
    b.   put them under the authority of an older manager
    c.   give them a training course

4   **Applying Inferences to a Specific Situation.** Now that you have read Sorenson's article, imagine that he is looking for a new manager for a department of his company and has received the following descriptions of three candidates for the position. Based on what he says in the article, what can you infer about his reaction to these candidates? Working in small groups, decide which one he would probably hire and why. Support your opinion for or against each candidate with specific statements from the reading.

Candidate A

- graduated with high honors from a top East Coast university
- majored in business, minored in computer science
- won two prizes for inventing new computer programs
- was chess champion of the university for two years
- received a medal for highest academic achievement in her senior year
- was described by her teachers as "brilliant, analytical, clear-thinking"

Candidate B

- graduated with above-average marks from a large Midwestern state university
- majored in history, minored in business
- spent two summers traveling through Europe and the Orient
- won a national essay contest
- was secretary of a debate club
- was active in community activities—for example, neighborhood cleanup drive, fund-raising for new senior citizens' center
- worked part-time for three years as assistant manager of the school bookstore in order to finance his education
- was described by his teachers as "well-liked, honest, industrious"

Candidate C

- graduated with honors from a well-known California university
- had a joint major in political science and business and a minor in economics
- is fluent in three languages
- spent his junior year at an international school in Switzerland
- was president of the music society and treasurer of the drama club

- was editor of the campus humor magazine
- organized and successfully ran (for two years) a small mail-order company that sold tapes and records of local singers
- was suspended from the university for six months for cheating on an accounting exam but was later reinstated without penalties
- was described by his teachers as "highly intelligent, ambitious, a natural leader"

Candidate most likely to be hired by Sorenson:

_____

Reasons:

_____

_____

_____

_____

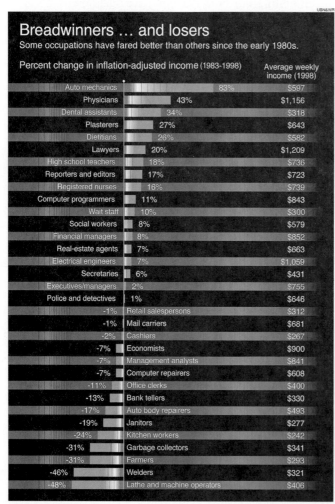

USN&WR

Breadwinners ... and losers

Some occupations have fared better than others since the early 1980s.

Percent change in inflation-adjusted income (1983-1998)

Occupation	Percent change	Average weekly income (1998)
Auto mechanics	83%	$597
Physicians	43%	$1,156
Dental assistants	34%	$318
Plasterers	27%	$643
Dietitians	26%	$582
Lawyers	20%	$1,209
High school teachers	18%	$736
Reporters and editors	17%	$723
Registered nurses	16%	$739
Computer programmers	11%	$843
Wait staff	10%	$300
Social workers	8%	$579
Financial managers	8%	$852
Real-estate agents	7%	$663
Electrical engineers	7%	$1,059
Secretaries	6%	$431
Executives/managers	2%	$755
Police and detectives	1%	$646
Retail salespersons	-1%	$312
Mail carriers	-1%	$681
Cashiers	-2%	$267
Economists	-7%	$900
Management analysts	-7%	$841
Computer repairers	-7%	$608
Office clerks	-11%	$400
Bank tellers	-13%	$330
Auto body repairers	-17%	$493
Janitors	-19%	$277
Kitchen workers	-24%	$242
Garbage collectors	-31%	$341
Farmers	-31%	$293
Welders	-46%	$321
Lathe and machine operators	-48%	$406

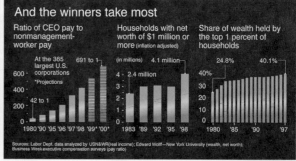

And the winners take most

Ratio of CEO pay to nonmanagement-worker pay

At the 365 largest U.S. corporations
*Projections
691 to 1
600 -
400 -
200 -
42 to 1
0 -
1980 '90 '95 '96 '97 '98 '99* '00*

Households with net worth of $1 million or more (inflation adjusted)

(in millions)   4.1 million
4 -   2.4 million
3 -
2 -
1 -
0 -
1983 '89 '92 '95 '98

Share of wealth held by the top 1 percent of households

24.8%   40.1%
40% -
30 -
20 -
10 -
0 -
1980 '85 '90 '97

Sources: Labor Dept. data analyzed by USN&WR(real income); Edward Wolff—New York University (wealth, net worth); Business Week executive compensation surveys (pay ratio)

Focus on Testing

Understanding a Chart

If you have a reading-comprehension test that includes a chart, don't panic. At first glance, a chart may seem incomprehensible, but it is usually not as difficult as it looks. Look at the chart "Breadwinners…and Losers" and follow these three steps. Then do the exercise that follows.

1. Ask yourself: What is the main point the chart wants to show? For example, what kind of information is given in the chart?
2. If the chart has different sections, look at them and decide how they are different. How many sections are there? How are they different?
3. Work out the questions or items you have to do one at a time and check your answers with the chart. If there is one part you just don't understand, skip it and go to the next.

Tell if the following statements are true (T), false (F), or not present (NP) according to the chart on page 134. Mark a statement NP if the chart does not give you enough information to decide if it is true or false.

_____F_____ 1. From 1983 to 1998, the income of physicians has increased (gone up) more than the income of auto mechanics.

_____T_____ 2. From 1983 to 1998, the income of registered nurses has increased more than the income of bank tellers.

_____NR_____ 3. From 1983 to 1998, the income of social workers has increased more than the income of university professors.

_____F_____ 4. From 1983 to 1998, the incomes of management analysts, janitors and electrical engineers have all decreased (gone down).

_____T_____ 5. From 1983 to 1998, computer repairers, economists, and farmers have all suffered a decrease in their incomes.

_____F_____ 6. In 1998, real estate agents made more money than mail carriers.

_____F_____ 7. Between 1980 and 2000 the ratio of salaries for CEOs (Chief Executive Officers) to salaries for non-management workers in the largest U.S. corporations has gone down.

_____T_____ 8. By 1998 there were more households with a net worth of over a million dollars than there were in 1983.

_____NP_____ 9. By the year 2000, 35 percent of the wealth in the United States was held by the top 1 percent of households.

_____T_____ 10. In general, the statistics on this chart indicate that the gap between the rich and the poor in the United States has been growing larger since the 1980s.

PART 3

Barriers Fall for Women at Work

Before You Read

1   **Inferring Meaning.** Scan the article for the following italicized words and expressions, and write your own definitions or explanations of what they mean. Use the hints to help you.

1. go co-ed (This phrase comes right at the beginning, but you may have to read a few paragraphs to get its meaning.)

   _____

2. line technician (The first three paragraphs give an example of this job.)

   _____

3. blue-collar jobs (These are usually contrasted with "white-collar jobs," and the reference is to male clothing.)

   _____

4. barriers (This word appears in the title and again in the fifth paragraph.)

   _____

5. trade jobs (This term is similar to "blue-collar jobs" above, but more specific; trade jobs are one kind of blue-collar jobs.)

   _____

6. WOW (This is a proper noun and an acronym. Tell what the letters stand for and what the group does.)

   _____

7. make inroads (This expression is used in the middle of the article.)

   _____

8. discrimination lawsuits (This occurs toward the end of the article.)

   _____

Read

"A man, he works from sun to sun, but a woman's work is never done." This is an old saying, but what does it really mean? Is there such a thing as "woman's work"?

- In your opinion, are some jobs best done by women? Which ones?
- Are some jobs best done by men? Explain.

Read the following newspaper article to find out how the idea of woman's work is changing in North America.

Barriers Fall for Women at Work
Nontraditional, Skilled-Trade Jobs Slowly Go Co-ed

Greenwich, Conn.—The telephone company worker throws a heavy belt laden with tools over a sweatshirt, then, oblivious to the gentle snowfall, quickly scales the 35-foot utility pole.

A common sight perhaps, but there's something different about this picture—a woman's soft curls frame the hard hat, a touch of makeup dusts the face.

For four years, Kim Callanan, 27, has driven her truck around this New York City suburb, fixing downed lines and restoring phone service, one of the handful of female Nynex Corp. workers to hold the job of line technician.

Slowly, very slowly, women are moving into higher-paying occupations they rarely had access to in the past—as welders, carpenters and truck drivers, among others.

Training programs nationwide are helping mostly poor, single mothers get skilled blue-collar or technical jobs that don't require a college degree. But there are still significant barriers to women in the so-called trade professions, with many facing opposition from employers, colleagues, friends and family.

Ability usually isn't the question. Rosie the Riveter came to symbolize the women who stepped in at factories and other work sites during World War II. They helped turn out tanks and ammunition.

"The experience showed that when you pay women well and train them well, they perform," said Karen Nussbaum, director of the Women's Bureau, the entity within the Labor Department concerned with women's employment issues.

But when the men returned from war, women were expected to return to their homes and more traditional jobs as nurses, secretaries and teachers.

Now, with almost 54 million women employed, only 6.6 percent of women are in nontraditional jobs, according to Wider Opportunities for Women, or WOW, a Washington-based advocacy group. The Labor Department defines nontraditional jobs as those in which women make up less than 25 percent of the work force. Indeed, three-quarters of working women have low-paying jobs with little security, few benefits and little room for advancement. At the same time, nearly half of all working women earn the family's primary income.

The "tough guy" occupations are those with higher salaries, benefits and greater potential for career advancement. The most skilled of the trade jobs pay between $23 and $27 an hour, while blue-collar women's work usually offers salaries in the $5-an-hour range.

Even without reaching the highest skill levels, women in nontraditional labor typically earn between 20 and 30 percent more than those in traditionally female blue-collar jobs, according to WOW.

"The challenge is getting the word out about these jobs," said Kristin Watkins of WOW. "Women don't grow up necessarily thinking that they want to be a carpenter…they don't grow up tinkering on the car with dad."

And because they haven't seen other women working in trade jobs they can't imagine themselves on a construction crew, welding or driving a truck, Watkins said.

Women have made inroads into the professions requiring advanced degrees—in law, business and medicine—but have been less successful breaking into skilled blue-collar labor.

"This is the unfinished agenda of women entering jobs that were closed off to them before," Nussbaum said.

Encouraged by civil rights legislation and the women's movement, they began to advance about 20 years ago, often forcing their way in doors through discrimination lawsuits.

But progress has been slow. Between 1988 and 1992, the number of women in nontraditional jobs remained relatively unchanged at 3 percent of the total number of employed workers, according to WOW.

In 1991, President Bush signed the Nontraditional Employment for Women Act, requiring federal job training centers to increase training for women in nontraditional jobs.

The growing numbers of training programs for nontraditional labor is particularly important, experts say, as pressure builds in Congress to cut welfare payments to single mothers.

The Rosie the Riveter Memorial in Richmond, California, honors the approximately 18 million women who worked in the World War II defense industries.

Still, federal guidelines call for contractors on government-subsidized
jobs to hire women to perform at least 6.9 percent of total hours worked. But
enforcement has never been strict.

85
"Where employers feel like they have to meet federal guidelines, they do,
when they don't, they don't," Nussbaum said. "We need to make it clear to
employers that this is the law and compliance is relatively easy."

Persuading employers to hire women for nontraditional jobs in rural Tulare
County, Calif., is a challenge, said Kathy Johnson, who helps run a nontraditional training program through the county's Private Industry Council.

90
"Typically, employers say women can't do the job, that they are not strong
enough, that they will cause problems, that they will distract the men."

Lisa Genasci

After You Read

2   **Distinguishing Between the General and the Specific.** Decide which of the following
statements from the reading are general and which are specific. There are three of each.
Then tell which general statement each specific statement supports.

1.   But there are still significant barriers to women in the so-called trade professions....

_____   general   _____   specific

2.   For four years, Kim Callanan... has driven her truck around..., fixing downed lines
and restoring phone service....

_____   general   _____   specific

3.   Slowly...women are moving into higher-paying occupations they rarely had access to in the past....

_____   general   _____   specific

4.   The most skilled of the trade jobs pay between $23 and $27 an hour, while blue-
collar women's work usually offers salaries in the $5-an-hour range.

_____   general   _____   specific

5.   "Typically, employers say women...are not strong enough, that they will cause
problems, that they will distract the men."

_____   general   _____   specific

6.   The "tough guy" occupations are those with higher salaries....

_____   general   _____   specific

3 **Finding Related Nouns and Verbs.** Find nouns in the article "Barriers Fall for Women at Work" that are related to the following verbs. Look at the examples. There are a number of different endings added to verbs to make nouns in English, so all the words will not be similar.

Examples:

oppose   opposition
employ   employers, employment

1. advocate _____
2. advance _____
3. construct _____
4. legislate _____

5. discriminate _____
6. pay _____
7. enforce _____
8. comply _____

Talk It Over

In small groups, discuss the following questions.

1. Who was Rosie the Riveter, and what did she symbolize?
2. What happened to the working women in North America at the end of World War II? Do you think this was necessary?
3. According to WOW, why aren't there more women in trade jobs? What other reasons are there for this lack?
4. What did the United States government do in 1991 to encourage women to take nontraditional jobs? Do you think this was a good idea? What other societies accept women in nontraditional jobs? Explain.
5. Is the role of women changing in other places in the world? Should it change? Why or why not?

4 **Discussing a Hierarchy of Needs.** Look at the illustration of Maslow's "Hierarchy of Human Needs." Working in small groups, discuss the following questions relating the reading and the illustration. Afterward, your teacher may call on you to share the ideas of your group with the class.

1. Which of the human needs shown in the pyramid below do you think are important for men in your culture? Rank them with Number1 being the most important and Number 5 being the least important.

2. Now, do the same for the women in your society? Are your rankings for the men and the women the same? Explain.

3. Does the level of needs being fulfilled depend on the type of job? What jobs only fulfill the needs on the lower part of the triangle? What jobs fulfill other needs? Explain.

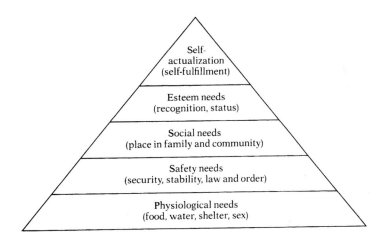

When people have their basic needs satisfied (food, water, shelter, sex), they can begin to think of other things to fulfill their life expectations. Well-known psychologist Abraham Maslow has developed a "Hierarchy of Human Needs" pyramid in which he categorizes the steps to "self-fulfillment." At which stages of the pyramid do working and job satisfaction fit in? What are the most important requirements for a job? Is self-esteem directly connected with the type of job one has or are other things in life more important?

Timed Reading

What do you *not* want to do during a job interview? The following article from *The Wall Street Journal* describes the worst mistakes some recruiters have seen during job interviews. These are referred to as *faux pas*, a French phrase that literally means "false steps" and is often used in English to describe the small mistakes that make a bad impression. Read the selection quickly to find out what mistakes were made and what the consequences were. Try to finish the reading and comprehension exercises in eight minutes.

The Worst Recruiters Have Seen

Let's face it: It's a jungle out there, and you can use all the help available to avoid the mistakes that can doom a promising job candidacy.

Perhaps you can draw some lessons from these fatal *faux pas*, gleaned from veteran corporate and executive recruiters. They consider them the worst
5   mistakes they've seen.

Red-Handed

During his interview with me, a candidate bit his fingernails and proceeded to bleed onto his tie. When I asked him if he wanted a Band-Aid, he said that he chewed his nails all the time and that he'd be fine. He continued to chew away.
10   —Audrey W. Hellinger, Chicago office of Martin H. Bauman Associates, New York

Let's Be Buddies

In his first meeting with me, a candidate made himself a little too comfortable. Not only did he liberally pepper his conversation with profanities, he also
15   pulled his chair right up to the edge of my desk and started picking up and examining papers and knickknacks.
—Nina Proct, Martin H. Bauman Associates, New York

Deep Water

One of the top candidates for a senior vice presidency at a big consumer-products company was a young man under 35 who had grown up in a small town in the Midwest. As I frequently do, I asked about his years in high school. He said he'd been a star swimmer—so good that he'd even won a gold medal in the Olympics. It hung in his high-school gymnasium. The client liked him very much and was preparing to make him an offer. But when I checked his references, I discovered he hadn't gone to the college he'd listed, and he had never even swum in the Olympics.

—John A. Coleman, Canny, Bowen Inc., New York

Loser's Circle

I walked into the reception area to pick up my next applicant, Sarah B., a recent college graduate.

Once in my office, I glanced at her well-written resume and wondered how much time and money she had spent preparing it. She was obviously intelligent and articulate. How, I wondered, could she misjudge our corporate climate this way?

The sad fact was that I could never send her out to be interviewed by our administrators or physicians. They might forgive her sandals, her long billowy skirt and her white peasant blouse—but never, ever, the large gold ring through her nose.

—Janet Garber, Manager of Employment-Employee Relations, Cornell University Medical College, New York

Bon Voyage

It was a million-dollar job, and he was a top-notch candidate. My client had decided to hire him, and he was having dinner with the chief executive officer. He asked the CEO, "How do we travel?" The response was: "We're being careful of costs these days. We travel business class internationally and back-of-the-bus domestically." Without thinking, the candidate said, "I'm used to traveling first class."

—Tony Lord, New York office of A. T. Kearney Executive Search, Chicago

It's Not Always the Candidate

It isn't always the job candidate who's the disaster. Consider what happened to the top aspirant for a senior position at one of Richard Slayton's client companies. As related by the Chicago executive recruiter, the candidate was set for a full day of interviews with senior executives, including a final session over dinner with the CEO.

His first interview was with the general counsel, who arrived thirty minutes late because there had been a work stoppage. "His second session, with the executive vice president of marketing, also ran a half-hour late because he was on a conference call with the company's largest customer, who had just been acquired," says Mr. Slayton.

At lunch with the candidate, the senior vice president of human resources broke a bridge and lined up the pieces of broken teeth on a napkin in front of him. And, finally, the CEO was called away unexpectedly and never met with the candidate.

But, says Mr. Slayton, the day from hell had a happy ending. "My client said that if he could survive all that with good humor, he was worth serious consideration. He got the job."

—The Wall Street Journal

5 **Comprehension Quiz.** Put an X in front of the mistakes made by the job applicants described in the article.

_____ 1. acting too casual

_____ 2. acting too formal

_____ 3. arriving thirty minutes late for the appointment

_____ 4. biting fingernails

_____ 5. dropping papers and personal items on the floor

_____ 6. forgetting the company's name

_____ 7. not carrying a business card

_____ 8. not leaving a tip

_____ 9. showing a gold medal won in swimming class

_____ 10. showing an unwillingness to economize

_____ 11. telling lies

_____ 12. using swear words and bad language

_____ 13. wearing a nose ring

_____ 14. wearing inappropriate clothing

_____ 15. breaking his teeth

6 Choose the best way of finishing each statement, based on what you have just read.

1. The job candidates described in the article are _____ .
   a. all men
   b. all women
   c. mostly men
   d. mostly women

2. In the article there is only one job candidate who gets the job. He gets the job because _____ .
   a. his father works for the company
   b. he doesn't make any mistakes
   c. he acts like an old buddy
   d. he shows patience and humor

What Do You Think?

Home Offices

With modern inventions of instant communications such as cell phones, computers, fax machines, and e-mail, many people have chosen to set up their work office at home. Around the world, millions of people have their main office in their homes. They work as consultants, writers, editors, and business people.

1. Would you like to have a home office if your profession allowed? Why or why not?
2. What are the advantages and disadvantages of a home office?

Video Activities: Telecommuting

Before You Watch. Sometimes people work from home. What are some advantages and disadvantages of telecommuting? List them below. In small groups, discuss your answers.

Advantages to Workers
1. _____
2. _____
3. _____

Advantages to Employers
1. _____
2. _____
3. _____

Disadvantages to Workers
1. _____
2. _____
3. _____

Disadvantages to Employers
1. _____
2. _____
3. _____

Watch. Take notes on the benefits of telecommuting from different perspectives.

1. As you listen, note the benefits of telecommuting from a worker's perspective.

   _____

   _____

2. As you listen, note the benefits of telecommuting from an employer's perspective.

   _____

   _____

Watch Again.   Answer these questions in small groups.

1. Listen for these numbers and write what each one represents.
    a. 20,000,000   _____
    b. 12,000–13,000 _____
    c. 10,000   _____
    d. 3,000–4,000   _____

2. The phrases *gridlock* and *bumper-to-bumper* refer to _____.
    a. traffic accidents   b. slow traffic   c. very heavy traffic

3. When someone is *goofing off*, they are _____.
    a. sleeping   b. working   c. playing

4. The expression *saving a bundle* means _____.
    a. saving a lot of money   c. getting work done faster
    b. working harder

5. Another word for *telecommuter* is _____.
    a. telephoner   b. telenetter   c. teleworker

After You Watch.   Find an article on telecommuting in a magazine, newspaper, or on the Internet. Use the article to improve your reading speed.

1. First estimate the number of words in the reading by counting the number of words in two or three lines, taking the average, and then multiplying the average by the number of lines in the text.

2. Write down the time and begin reading. Remember to use clustering to increase your speed. When you are finished, figure out the number of words per minute. This is your reading speed.

3. Finally, read the article again more slowly. How many important ideas did you miss? If you missed a lot, then you should try to read more slowly.

Chapter 8

Breakthroughs

IN THIS CHAPTER

In the last twenty years, breakthroughs in technology have profoundly advanced the way we communicate, bringing us computers, cell phones and the Internet. Equally amazing, but less visible, are recent breakthroughs in agriculture and health. First, we take a look at the controversial topic of "super plants," crops that have been genetically engineered by scientists. Then we examine a remarkable achievement that will forever change medical treatment throughout the world: the mapping of the entire human genome. Next we read about the pros and cons of promoting scientific discoveries.

PART 1

Sowing the Seeds of Super Plants

Before You Read

1 **Anticipating the Reading.** Answer the following questions.

1. What do you imagine when you think of the words *super plant*? What traits or characteristics should it have? Compare your ideas with the artist's concept on page 151.

2. The coming of the new millennium brought boycotts and protests in front of many supermarkets in Canada and the United States against the selling of "genetically engineered foods." Are we eating this kind of food now? Do you think that there are dangers in this practice?

3. What are some problems in the world today that will be solved if botanists can safely produce made-to-order plants in their laboratories?

2 **Understanding Technical Terms from Context.** Many new scientific terms have passed into common usage through reports in newspapers and magazines. Key scientific terms from the article are used in the following two paragraphs. Read the paragraphs. Then write the correct term in the blank after each definition.

Genetic Engineering and Public Fears

People used to think that hereditary traits, such as brown eyes, tallness, red hair, and so forth, were passed from parents to children in the blood. Terms such as "bad blood" and "blood brothers," though incorrect, are still used. Modern science has shown that these traits are passed in the *genes* from the parents' cells, which recombine during reproduction. The actual chemical in the gene responsible for this transmission is *deoxyribonucleic acid*, usually referred to as *DNA*. In the last two decades scientists have managed to isolate the genes that cause particular traits in some organisms and plants. In certain cases they can even use the techniques of *recombinant* DNA or *gene splicing* to insert a fragment of a gene from one animal or plant directly into the genes of another, usually by splicing it to a chemical. From these advances the new field of *genetic engineering* was born.

Reactions to announcements of this scientific progress back in the 1970s were mixed. At that time, some people foresaw the curing of inherited diseases and the improvement of agriculture. Other sectors of the press and the public responded with fear and loathing. Were human beings trying to play God? What if scientists were to create a new *bacterium* that would escape from the lab and infect the world with a terrible disease? Concern grew with the announcement of *cloning*: the production from a single cell of one or many identical individuals, or *clones*. Science fiction writers imagined armies of cloned soldiers. Philosophers worried about the loss of individual identity. Were these techniques stopped? Or was it shown that the dangers had been greatly exaggerated? The answer is given in the following article.

1. any one of a type of microscopic organism, some of which cause disease
   <u>bacterium</u>

2. the technique of putting pieces of the genes from one organism into the genes of another

   _____

3. an acid found in the nucleus of cells, responsible for the transmission of hereditary characteristics

   _____

4. a group of identical organisms derived from a single individual

   _____

5. the units of heredity that transmit traits from one generation to another

   _____

6. referring to the uniting or joining together of different genes

   _____

7. a new branch of biochemistry in which genes are altered to change or improve the traits of plants or animals

   _____

8. the growing of genetically identical plants or animals from a single cell

   _____

Read

Sowing the Seeds of Super Plants

Somewhere deep in the mountains of Peru, plant geneticist Jon Fobes is collecting samples of a very special tomato. This tomato will never win a prize at a county fair; it is remarkably ugly—a green, berrylike fruit that is not good to eat. But to Fobes it has a winning quality. It is twice as meaty as an ordinary
5 tomato. Other exotic tomatoes that Fobes is gathering can grow at very cold altitudes or in salty soil, or they are remarkably resistant to drought, insects, and disease. Fobes's goal: to bring them back to his laboratory at the research division of the Atlantic Richfield Company in California and isolate and identify the genes that give them such strong characteristics, so that someday
10 they can be genetically engineered into commercial tomatoes.

   Fobes is just one of the many scientists who are searching the wilderness to find plants with genes that may eventually be used to create a whole new garden of super plants. Until recently there was little incentive for such quests. Although molecular biologists were making rapid progress in the genetic en-
15 gineering of bacteria to produce human proteins such as insulin, botanists faced a set of problems that apparently could not be solved by the same recombinant DNA techniques. Recently, however, they have overcome some of the barriers that nature placed in the way of the genetic engineering of plants. Items:

20 • Biologists John Kemp and Timothy Hall, University of Wisconsin professors who do research for Agrigenetics, a private company, announced the first transfer of a functioning gene from one plant to another—from a bean plant into a sunflower plant.

   • Jeff Schell, of the State University of Ghent in Belgium, announced an im-
25 portant step toward the regulation of transplanted genes. His research

team introduced into tobacco cells artificial genes that were activated in light but not in darkness.

- Researchers at the Cetus Madison Corporation of Madison, Wisconsin, won approval from the recombinant DNA advisory committee of the NIH
30 (National Institutes of Health, a government agency) to field test plants genetically engineered to resist certain diseases.

Not everyone is delighted. Within days after the Cetus announcement, Jeremy Rifkin, a publicity-seeking author of a poorly received book about genetic engineering, attacked the NIH committee for hearing the Cetus propos-
35 al at a session closed to the public. He also asked for an investigation by the NIH of possible conflict of interest because a scientist at Cetus is a former member of the committee, and a leading scientist from another genetics engineering firm is a member now.

Earlier in the month, Rifkin had filed suit in a general district court in Wash-
40 ington to block the field testing of a bacterium genetically engineered at the University of California at Berkeley to protect plants from frost. He claimed that the NIH committee had not adequately examined the field testing for possible environmental hazards. Although the suit seemed to lack merit, it had an effect. Complaining that the suit had delayed their experiment, which was de-
45 pendent on weather conditions, the Berkeley scientists postponed the test.

The sudden hubub over gene splicing was similar to the controversy over use of the newly developed recombinant DNA techniques in the 1970s. That uproar occurred after the scientists themselves had recommended strict testing guidelines to prevent engineered organisms from escaping from the lab-
50 oratory, and the NIH put them into effect. Later it became apparent that the techniques were not dangerous, the rules were relaxed, and the protests died out. The latest NIH decision that allows field testing of genetically engineered

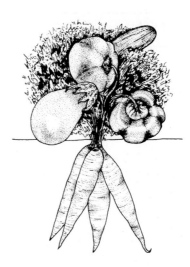

A super plant of the future?

plants reflected a general confidence among scientists that proper precautions were being taken and that the work was safe.

55   Some plant scientists found a touch of the absurd in Rifkin's harassment. Plant breeders have been introducing new genes into plants for thousands of years. They have used techniques such as cross-pollination, inserting pollen from one group of plants into another group, to produce hybrid plants that are hardier, more attractive, more nutritious, or tastier than nature's own. Still, these
60   traditional methods have their limitations. Crossbreeding is useful only in plants of the same or similar species. It also takes time, sometimes hundreds of crosses over many years, to breed a plant with even a single new trait.

Genetic engineering provides a dramatic new shortcut. Eventually, it could allow scientists to insert a wider variety of beneficial genes into plants in
65   a few days. The potential seems enormous. Crops that now need expensive fertilizer could be changed so that they could extract nitrogen (the most important element in fertilizer) from the air; they could be engineered to produce toxins to protect themselves from insects, grow in salty soils, live for weeks without water, and use the sun's energy more efficiently. Plants with engi-
70   neered characteristics could one day be the basis for a new "green revolution" that would provide enough food for the world's hungry people.

The genetic engineering of plants owes much of its recent success to an ingenious solution to an old problem: the lack of an effective way to transplant foreign genes into the DNA of plant cells. The solution came from bacteria—
75   in the form of a plasmid (a tiny piece of DNA engineered to carry genes) from the bacterium *Agrobacterium tumefaciens*. The bacterium is not ordinarily a benefactor of humanity. It causes small brown tumors to form on such important plants as tobacco and grapes. But in the laboratory it is proving to be extraordinarily useful. After foreign genes are spliced into its plasmid, the
80   plasmid can carry them into more than 10,000 different plants, where they find their way into the DNA. To assist these genes in entering plant cells, scientists mix them with tiny fatty bubbles called liposomes. (See the diagram "How to Move a Plant Gene.")

HOW TO MOVE A PLANT GENE

| 1. Donor plant with desired gene | 2. Gene after removal | 3. Gene is inserted into an Agrobacterium plasmid | 4. Plasmids are mixed with liposomes | 5. Plasmid-liposome packages enter a plant cell | 6. Cells are cultured | 7. New plant carries the desired gene |

85   In their efforts to create new plants by transferring genes, scientists have not overlooked another problem: how to produce the new plants in quantity. This will require better methods of cloning than are now available. Cloning now works only with a very limited variety of plants. Carrots, petunias, and to-bacco, for example, can be cloned with ease, but the important cereal grains

90   respond poorly—if at all—to cloning.

Scientists are still seeking the biological key to the regeneration of plants, trying to learn why a lone plant cell will sometimes sprout into an entire new plant and at other times will simply refuse to divide and multiply. Once they are able to combine cloning and genetic engineering, the payoffs, both sci-

95   entifically and commercially, could be dazzling.

Sana Siwolop

Scientists at the University of Wisconsin have recently developed a potato plant that poisons destructive beetles.

After You Read

3 **Recalling Information.** Choose the best way of finishing each statement, based on what you have just read.

1. The exciting news about genetic engineering in plants is that scientists have just recently managed to _____ .
    a. find some plants in Peru with hardy characteristics
    b. transfer a functioning gene from one plant to another
    c. create and clone a whole new species of super plants

2. The field testing of genetically engineered plants is _____ .
    a. an unusual and frightening occurrence
    b. a serious concern to most plant biologists
    c. probably not dangerous

3. The great fear in the 1970s caused by the newly developed recombinant DNA technique turned out to be _____ .
    a. almost groundless
    b. highly beneficial
    c. completely justified

4. If scientists master the techniques of genetic engineering, they could eventually produce crops that _____ .
    a. could live for weeks without any water
    b. grow without the need for fertilizer
    c. produce their own poisons against insects
    d. all the above and more

5. The big problem of what to use to carry genes from one plant into another seems to be solved now by the use of _____ .
    a. a small piece of specially made plastic
    b. a plasmid carried by a bacterium
    c. a slime mold found on tomatoes in Peru

6. At the moment, the best way to describe the cloning of plants in the laboratory is that _____ .
    a. it's only successful with cereal grains
    b. it simply cannot be done
    c. sometimes it works and sometimes it doesn't

4   **Refuting False Arguments.** The eighteenth-century English poet Alexander Pope once wrote, "A little knowledge is a dangerous thing." Many people express strong opinions on certain subjects about which they know very little. The following false arguments are examples of this. Find information from the article to disprove each one.

1. A state senator hears that plant geneticist Jon Fobes is down in Peru collecting samples of a tomato that is ugly and inedible. He knows that Fobes is using a government grant and makes a motion in the state senate to cut off the money for this work. "Everybody knows," he states with confidence, "that looking for a tomato that can't even be eaten is just plain stupid and a waste of the taxpayer's money!" What can you say to prove him wrong?

2. You meet a businesswoman at a party who says in a loud voice, "What burns me up about scientists is that they have no common sense. All this genetic engineering of plants, for example, is ridiculous nonsense. If they want to put new genes into plants, why don't they use crossbreeding? Why, farmers have been doing that successfully for thousands of years!" What could you tell her to change her views?

3. A young woman's father is absolutely opposed to his daughter marrying a plant biologist, even though she is head-over-heels in love with him. "Nobody ever makes any money in work like that," he fumes. "It has nothing whatever to do with practical, commercial reality!" What can you say to aid true love?

5   **Identifying a Bias.** This selection, like most scientific articles, is written in a fairly objective and informative tone. Its purpose is mainly to convey new facts. At one point, however, the author, Sana Siwolop, expresses a strong bias against a particular person and his motives. (Notice that this is not necessarily bad. Her bias may or may not have a good foundation.) In what paragraph does this occur? What specific words express this bias?

Paragraph: _____

Words that show bias: _____

Talk It Over

In small groups, discuss the following questions.

1. Some breakthroughs prove to be dangerous. DDT is a prime example of this. At first, it seemed like a miracle because it killed mosquitoes and other harmful insects so effectively. Years later, people noticed that it also killed birds and other animals that ate those insects. In fact, it stayed in the environment and you couldn't get rid of it! Who should make decisions about allowing or prohibiting new discoveries: the scientists, businesspeople, or special agencies of the government? Or should a public referendum (voting on a specific question) be held each time? Explain.

2. Cloning is the scientific production of an entire plant or animal by using a single cell from another plant or animal. The second is an exact genetic copy of the first. In 1997, Ian Wilmut and his colleagues produced the first successful cloning of a mammal, a sheep named Dolly. Now scientists speak about cloning of human beings. In 2001, Tim Caulfield, a well-known ethicist (expert in deciding what is morally correct) from the University of Alberta announced publicly that he sees nothing wrong with this. He thinks that Canada should regulate human cloning, but not ban it. He stated: "I believe that humans are so much more than just their genes." What do you think of his opinion? What possible benefits or problems could come from the cloning of human beings?

Making Connections

In the library or on the Internet, explore one of the following topics. Then share your findings with the class.

1. Genetically altered food. How much of it is being produced and sold? Who are against this practice and why?

2. Cloning of animals and humans. What is happening right now in this field?

| PART 2 | # A Revolution in Medicine |

Before You Read

1   **Reading a Diagram for Background Information.** The following article talks about the enormous changes going on right now in the field of medicine as a result of the recent decoding of the human genome by scientists. A good way to prepare for this article is to read the diagram on page 159, called "What Is the Human Genome?" Then, alone, or with a partner, answer these questions:

1.   What does the word *code* mean? When and where are codes used?
2.   What does the genetic code determine (cause)? Where is it located?
3.   What is DNA?
4.   What is a gene?

2   **Getting the Meaning of Idioms and Expressions.** Sometimes you understand the meaning of each word in a phrase, but not the meaning of the whole phrase put together. Read the sentences and parts of sentences taken from the article and select the best explanation for the phrase in italics. Line numbers are given so that you can check the context.

1.   So she figured *she was lucky to be living* when she turned 50 last year. (line 2)
     a.   it was a fortunate time of her life
     b.   it was a difficult time of her life
     c.   <u>it was probable for her to have died</u>
     d.   it was not likely for her to have died

2.   As Miscoi read about it, everything *started making sense.* (line 10)
     a.   became easy to understand
     b.   became hard to understand
     c.   began to bother her
     d.   began to make her happy

3.   So she found a doctor who would *take her concerns more seriously.* (line 12)
     a.   charge her less money
     b.   not make jokes about her illness
     c.   assure her that she was in good health
     d.   pay attention to her problems

4.   Until recently, diagnosing the condition required a liver biopsy—*not a procedure to be taken lightly.* (line 13)
     a.   not a difficult or complicated course of action
     b.   not a course of action to be worried about
     c.   a course of action to take when you are old
     d.   a course of action to think about seriously

5. But Miscoi didn't have to *go that route*. (line 14)
   a. go out by that door
   b. have that done to her
   c. take that medicine
   d. drive home on that highway

6. Scientists…developed a test that *can spot* it in a drop of blood. (line 15)
   a. is able to find
   b. is able to form a circle
   c. sometimes weakens
   d. sometimes cures

7. …she should live *a normal life span*. (line 20)
   a. an ordinary life with some bad health
   b. a life filled with common experience
   c. the usual difficulties between doctors' appointments
   d. the typical number of years before dying

8. Meanwhile, genetic discoveries will *trigger a flood* of new pharmaceuticals… (line 28)
   a. cause problems for many liquid medicines
   b. bring about the production of a large number
   c. stop the arrival of many
   d. destroy the promotion

9. …but Collins believes even that *will be routine* within a few decades. (line 32)
   a. is going to become a common practice
   b. is going to get boring and unnecessary
   c. will be governed by new rules and regulations
   d. will be impossible to continue

10. *Only a handful* of clinics are using gene tests to guide drug therapy. (line 53)
    a. a selected group
    b. an unusual combination
    c. a small number
    d. a large number

Read

Fifteen years ago, most people said it couldn't be done. No one would ever be able to decode, map out and sequence (put in order) the entire human genome, the 3.1 billion genes that make up a human being. Genes are the building blocks of life. So learning what each gene is made of could give us the ability to control our own health. Even biologists and scientists thought that this was an impossible dream.

Nevertheless, just in time for the new millennium, two separate scientific groups announced that they had completed the task. One of these groups is the Human Genome Project sponsored by the U. S. National Institutes of Health, and the other is a private company called Celera Genomics.

- This is a great achievement, but will it really help us?
- Is this breakthrough already having an effect on health?

Read the following article to find out the answers to these questions.

A Revolution in Medicine
Geoffrey Cowley and Anne Underwood

Ann Miscoi had seen her father and her uncle die of organ failure in their mid-
40s. So she figured she was lucky to be living when she turned 50 last year.
The trouble was, she felt half dead. Her joints ached, her hair was falling out
and she was plagued by unrelenting fatigue. Her doctor assured her that noth-

5   ing was seriously wrong, even after a blood test revealed unusually high iron
levels, but Miscoi wasn't so sure. Scanning the Internet, she learned about a
hereditary condition called hemochromatosis, in which the body stores iron
at dangerous concentrations in the blood, tissues and organs. Hemochromatosis is the nation's most common genetic illness, and probably the most

10   underdiagnosed. As Miscoi read about it, everything started making sense—
her symptoms, her blood readings, even her relatives' early deaths. So she
found a doctor who would take her concerns more seriously.

Until recently, diagnosing the condition required a liver biopsy—not a procedure to be taken lightly. But Miscoi didn't have to go that route. Scientists

15   isolated the gene for hemochromatosis a few years ago, and developed a test
that can spot it in a drop of blood. Miscoi tested positive, and the diagnosis
may well have saved her life. Through a regimen of weekly blood lettings, she
was able to reduce her iron level before her organs sustained lasting damage. She's now free of symptoms, and as long as she gives blood every few

20   months she should live a normal life span. "Without the DNA test, I would have
had a hard time convincing any doctor that I had a real problem."

Hemochromatosis testing could save millions of lives in coming decades.
And it's just one early hint of the changes that the sequencing of the human
genome could bring. By 2010, says Dr. Francis Collins of the National Human

25   Genome Research Institute, screening tests will enable anyone to gauge his
or her unique health risks, down
to the body's tolerance for cigarettes and cheeseburgers.

J. Craig Venter (left)
and Francis Collins
(right) are the scientists
responsible for cracking
the genome code.

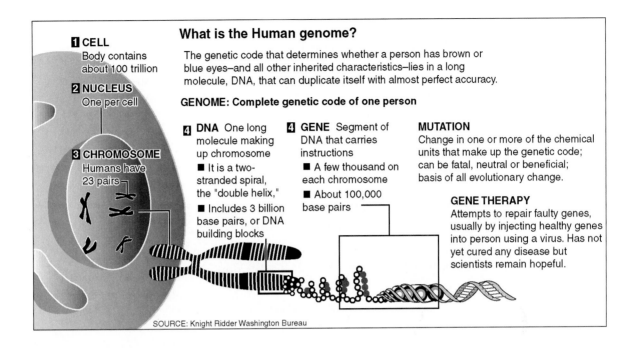

What is the Human genome?

The genetic code that determines whether a person has brown or blue eyes—and all other inherited characteristics—lies in a long molecule, DNA, that can duplicate itself with almost perfect accuracy.

GENOME: Complete genetic code of one person

1 CELL
Body contains about 100 trillion

2 NUCLEUS
One per cell

3 CHROMOSOME
Humans have 23 pairs

4 DNA One long molecule making up chromosome
- It is a two-stranded spiral, the "double helix,"
- Includes 3 billion base pairs, or DNA building blocks

4 GENE Segment of DNA that carries instructions
- A few thousand on each chromosome
- About 100,000 base pairs

MUTATION
Change in one or more of the chemical units that make up the genetic code; can be fatal, neutral or beneficial; basis of all evolutionary change.

GENE THERAPY
Attempts to repair faulty genes, usually by injecting healthy genes into person using a virus. Has not yet cured any disease but scientists remain hopeful.

SOURCE: Knight Ridder Washington Bureau

Meanwhile, genetic discoveries will trigger a flood of new pharmaceuticals—drugs aimed at the causes of disease rather than the symptoms—and doctors will start prescribing different treatments for different patients, depending on their genetic profiles. The use of genes *as* medicine is probably farther off, but Collins believes even that will be routine within a few decades. "By 2050," he said recently, "many potential diseases will be cured at the molecular level before they arise."

That may be a bit optimistic, but the trends Collins foresees are already well in motion. Clinical labs now perform some 4 million genetic tests each year in the United States. Newborns are routinely checked for sickle cell anemia, congenital thyroid disease and phenylketonuria, a metabolic disease that causes retardation. Like hemochromatosis, these conditions are catastrophic if they go undetected, but highly manageable when they're spotted early. Newer tests can help people from cancer-prone families determine whether they've inherited the culpable mutation. "My mother died of colon cancer at age 47," says Dr. Bert Vogelstein, an oncologist as Johns Hopkins and the Howard Hughes medical institute. "If we had know she was [genetically] at risk, we could have screened for the disease and caught it early."

Early detection is just the beginning. Genes help determine not only whether we get sick but also how we respond to various treatments. "In the past," says Dr. William Evans of St. Jude Children's Research Hospital in Memphis, Tennessee, "the questions were 'How old are you and how much do you weigh?'" "Now, thanks to recent genetic discoveries, physicians can sometimes determine who stands to benefit from a given drug, and who might be harmed by it."

Only a handful of clinics are using gene tests to guide drug therapy, but the practice (known as pharmacogenetics) is spreading fast. Researchers are

55 | now learning to predict reactions to treatments for asthma, diabetes, heart disease and migraines—and firms like Incyte Genomics are developing chips that can analyze thousands of genes at a time. "My vision is that everyone will be sequenced at birth," says Dr. Mark Ratain of the University of Chicago. "Parents will get a CD-ROM with their child's genetic sequence. When physi-

60 | cians prescribe drugs, they'll use it to optimize treatment."

Newsweek Magazine

After You Read

Separating Fact from Opinion

The difference between fact and opinion is not always clear, but some general rules can help you distinguish between them.

1. General statements that can be checked (confirmed) online or in a reference book) about past or present events are usually facts; statements about the future are opinions, since the future is always uncertain.

2. Statements that include the modals *may, might*, or *could*, or qualifiers such as *perhaps, maybe, possibly*, or *probably* are opinions.

3. Statements based on evidence (research, case studies, experiments, questionnaires) need to be evaluated. If they are based on only one person's research, they should be considered opinions. If they are based on a great deal of research and if most experts agree, then they can be considered facts.

4. The line between fact and opinion is sometimes open to discussion. Time, place, and culture influence these limits for all societies. At one time it was considered a fact to say that the earth was flat. Today, we say that the earth is round. Is it really? Well, it's somewhat round, and certainly it is more round than flat.

3   **Separating Fact from Opinion.** Write whether each of the following statements based on the article is fact (F) or opinion (O). You might need to look at its context. Since some statements are not presented exactly as they appear in the text, the line numbers are given.

_____ 1. Hemochromatosis is the most common genetic illness in the United States. (line 8)

_____ 2. Hemochromatosis is also probably the most undiagnosed genetic illness. (line 9)

_____ 3. Scientists isolated the gene for hemochromatosis a few years ago, and developed a test that can spot it in a drop of blood. (line 14)

_____ 4. If the blood tests had been available earlier, the lives of Ann Miscoi's father and uncle would have been saved. (line 20)

_____ 5. Genetic discoveries will trigger a flood of new pharmaceuticals. (line 28)

_____ 6. By 2050, many potential diseases will be cured at the molecular level before they arise. (line 33)

_____ 7. Clinical labs now perform some 4 million genetic tests each year in the United States. (line 36)

_____ 8. Newborn babies in the United States are routinely checked for sickle cell anemia and other diseases. (line 37)

_____ 9. Certain terrible diseases can be highly manageable if they are detected early. (line 40)

_____ 10. Genes help determine not only whether we get sick but also how we respond to various treatments. (line 46)

_____ 11. Soon parents will get a CD-ROM with their child's genetic sequence as soon as he or she is born. (line 59)

4   **Scanning a Timeline.** A timeline is chart that shows a sequence of events and when they occurred. Work alone or with a partner. Scan the timeline to answer the following questions. See who can find the correct answers first.

Genetic research through the years

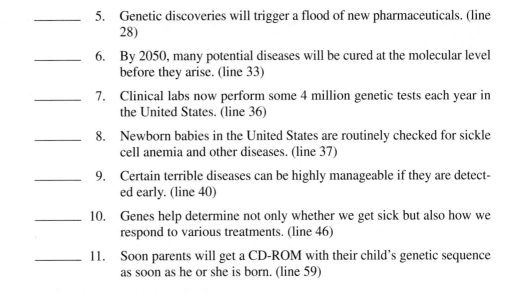

1865	**1910**	**1944**	**1953**	**1973**	**1990**	**June 2000**
Genetic inheritance discovered by Gregor Mendel, an Austrian monk who used generations of peas to unravel the mystery.	Researchers studying fruit flies show that genes are carried on chromosomes inside the cell's nucleus.	Oswald Avery shows that DNA carries genetic information.	The now familiar double helical structure of DNA is described by James Watson and Francis Crick.	Scientists use a restriction enzyme to cut animal DNA. They then splice the DNA into bacteria where the gene's function is carried out.	The Human Genome Project, a publicly funded consortium of scientists, sets out to map the human genome.	Scientists complete sequencing the 3 billion or so letters that spell out the human genome, nearly five years sooner than anticipated.

1. What is the structure of DNA that Watson and Crick discovered?
2. When did they discover it?
3. What is the name of the Austrian monk who started the science of genetics?
4. What plants did he use to establish the rules of inheritance?
5. What do scientists use in the 70s to put DNA into and produce the genetic function?
6. Where are the genes carried?
7. What year was this discovered?
8. When was the Human Genome project started?
9. When was it finished?
10. Who showed that DNA carries genetic information?

Talk It Over

In small groups, discuss the following questions.

1. Are you surprised to read in the first paragraph that Ann Miscoi found help from the Internet when her doctor could not help her? Have you or any of your friends found health information on the Internet? Where would you go for help if you were experiencing pain?

2. If Dr. Francis Collins is right, screening tests will soon enable people to judge their tolerance for cigarettes or cheeseburgers. Do you think this will be good or bad? Explain.

3. If you were from a family with a history of serious disease, would you take a genetic test to find out if you will some day suffer from it? Why or why not?

4. In your opinion, what are the most important breakthroughs that have occurred in the field of health and medicine?

Focus on Testing

Speaking in Front of People

Sometimes you are given an oral exam or asked to speak during an interview or at a meeting. The question you must answer may be completely unexpected. Practice doing this with a small group in class. You can use the questions from the list at the bottom of the box or make up your own. Here are some tips on how to speak well in public.

1. If you feel nervous, take a deep breath. Then take another.
2. Think for a moment about what you want to say. Then say the best or strongest idea first.
3. Stand firmly with both feet on the ground. Do not shuffle.
4. Keep your hands at your sides or your arms slightly bent, whichever feels more comfortable.
5. Look at your audience, but not just at one person. Change the directions of your eyes from time to time.
6. Don't talk too long. Prepare a good "exit line" (something to say at the end) and when you want to finish, say it. Then smile and sit down.
7. Practice with friends and in small groups at first. Talk with them afterwards and get their suggestions. Practice makes perfect. Good luck!

Possible Speech Topics Related to This Chapter

- A Breakthrough in Technology That I Like,
- A Breakthrough in Technology That I Don't Like,
- The Idea of the "Mad Scientist"
- My Relationship with My Computer,
- What I Think about Pills and Medicines
- Why Go to a Doctor?

Making Connections

Alone or with a classmate, do one of the following tasks. Then report on it to the class.

- ■ Find a recently updated article on the Web about the human genome. Has anything new developed since this article on it was written in your textbook? If so, what has happened?
- ■ Explore the topic of gene therapy in medicine. Make a list of places that are using it and the diseases they are treating at each place.
- ■ Discover if the use of gene tests to guide drug therapy (pharmacogenetics) is being used now (line 28). Tell how and where.

Science is Dandy, but Promotion Can Be Lucrative

Before You Read

1 **Fitting Scientific Terms into Context.** Read the description of the unwritten rules of scientific discovery and fill in each blank correctly with a term from the list. Scan the article for problematic words to see them in context.

lobbyists	protocol	circuit	honorariums
vetted	granting agency	priority	referees
proposal	tenure	journal	patent applications
press conference			

The Unwritten Rules of Scientific Discovery

1. There is a set of unwritten rules, a __protocol__ that scientists are expected to follow after making a discovery.

2. First, write a paper with a full account of the experiments leading to the discovery and send it to a well-known scientific _____.

3. Then, wait until the results are _____ by several _____ , scientists who are working in the same field.

4. If your paper is published and considered important, you can hit the _____ , speaking at meetings and universities and collecting nice fat _____ .

5. Do not call a _____ to talk about your research with reporters or employ _____ to make appeals to Congress or politicians for money.

6. If you need money to fund your research, write a _____ about it and send it to a _____ .

7. If you establish _____ by showing that you were the first to make the discovery, you will probably get a good university position with _____ , a lifetime guarantee of good employment.

8. At that point you can talk with companies about making _____ to use your discovery in business, unless someone else has done it first.

2   **Getting the Meaning of Idioms and Colloquial Phrases.** Read the sentences from the article and select the best word or phrase, here and on the next page, to replace the words in italics.

1. "Do it right and you may be *fixed for life*, or even become *a household name*."
   fixed for life
   a. trapped
   b. fired
   c. rich
   d. healthy
   household name
   a. famous
   b. promoted
   c. ignored
   d. sent home

2. "*Slip up* and you will slink away to the snickers of your colleagues, and worse, the wider world...."
   a. move ahead
   b. go forward
   c. get an idea
   d. make a mistake

3. "The most *ballyhooed* discovery of our time was the announcement...that two scientists had achieved nuclear fusion in a glass jar."
   a. wonderful
   b. horrible
   c. talked about
   d. passed by

4. "Controlled fusion is a *holy grail*, the promise of nearly infinite, clean and cheap energy."
   a. ridiculous idea
   b. much desired goal
   c. easy solution
   d. greatly feared consequence

5. "The news that it could be done at room temperature and pressure was a *bombshell*."
   a. thing or event attracting a lot of attention
   b. thing or event causing great anger
   c. thing or event that is admired by all
   d. thing or event that was expected and prepared for

6. "The two scientists…broke academia's unwritten rules…and *paid dearly* for it."
   a. gave money
   b. received love
   c. earned some credit
   d. suffered a lot

7. "Only if a scientific paper *passes muster* is it accepted for publication."
   a. contains brilliant ideas
   b. discusses true facts
   c. is seen to make money
   d. is considered worthy

8. "It can be OK to be wrong, but to *jump the gun* and be wrong as well is unforgivable."
   a. move too slowly
   b. move too fast
   c. use violence
   d. use influence

9. "For a…scientist, priority…can make the all-important difference between being awarded tenure and being *out on the street*."
   a. open for business
   b. rich and famous
   c. without a job
   d. hired for a speaking tour

10. "Government grants are easier to come by, which translates into more money for the staff who keep the Bunsens burning while the boss is *on the road*."
    a. looking for work
    b. looking for knowledge
    c. away on a trip
    d. busy with administration

11. "At that time Herschel was a professional musician…who had *a knack* for building telescopes."
    a. an ability
    b. the money
    c. a room
    d. the idea

Read

A scientist makes an important breakthrough. What happens next? Will it bring fame and fortune? Or can it bring disaster to a promising career? The following article from the *Smithsonian* magazine discusses the process of promoting a scientific discovery after it has been made. Even brilliant scientists sometimes make serious mistakes during this critical time.

Science Is Dandy, but Promotion Can Be Lucrative

Making a discovery is only half the battle: announcing it to one's advantage is the next step for the scientifically ambitious.

Making a major discovery in science is only the first step to fame and fortune, necessary but not sufficient. Almost as important are the how, when and where of announcing your breakthrough. Do it right and you may be fixed for life, or even become a household name. Slip up and you will slink away from the
5   snickers of your colleagues and, worse, the wider world of newspaper readers and television watchers.

The most ballyhooed discovery of our time (apparently false, it turned out) was the announcement at the University of Utah that two scientists had achieved nuclear fusion in a glass jar....Controlled fusion is a holy grail, the
10 promise of nearly infinite, clean and cheap energy. Until the Utah story broke, most scientists had been struggling ahead the only way they knew how: recreating the unimaginable temperatures and pressures inside stars to achieve fusion. The news that it could be done at room temperature and pressure was a bombshell.

15 The two scientists, Stanley Pons and Martin Fleischmann (the latter from the University of Southampton in England), broke academia's cherished unwritten rules in announcing their discovery and paid dearly for it. Instead of waiting until a full account of their experiments was published in a scientific journal, they called a press conference. Worse, with the aid of lobbyists they
20 appealed to Congress for direct appropriations to fund their research. The work was so important, they said, that they should have their own instant institute.

Modern-day science does not work that way—most of the time. Results are vetted before they are announced. A paper submitted to a journal is
25 passed first to several referees, people working in the same field who can judge the results being reported. Only if it passes muster is it accepted for publication. Raising money works the same way. Proposals are steered to referees for judgment before a granting agency writes a check. You may get away with breaking the rules if your findings are instantly recognized as cor-
30 rect. But there is all the difference in the world between the sweet smell of success and the odium of highly publicized error.

Bruce Lewenstein, a historian of science at Cornell University, told me at least two scientists were so irritated by the appeal to Congress that they let it be known they would "slam Pons and Fleischmann against the wall." A promi-
35 nent physicist, Robert L. Park of the American Physical Society, refused to at-

An important discovery is often immediately translated into the lifetime security of a tenured professorship.

tend a luncheon at which Jerry Bishop of *The Wall Street Journal* was awarded $3,000 for his coverage of the cold fusion story.

Anger at publicity is not new in the scientific world....

40 As a scientist myself, I have seen many erroneous "discoveries"—including one of my own—greeted with substantial publicity. In some cases reputations survive with little damage; in others the unfortunates become objects of derision. Much depends on how the discovery was announced. It can be OK to be wrong; but to jump the gun and be wrong as well is unforgivable.

45 At the bridge table, the player who opens the bidding may not be the one who wins the hand. But in science, the first announcement—the opening bid—establishes priority, thereby diminishing the future claims of a competitor who is rumored to have made similar findings. For a young university scientist, priority in an important discovery can make the all-important difference between being awarded tenure[1] and being out on the street.

50 Young or old, once you make a big discovery, you can hit "the circuit"—speaking at meetings held in the nicest resorts, addressing rapt graduate students and envious faculty at every ivied campus that can come up with a fat honorarium. Government grants are easier to come by, which translates into more money for the staff who keep the Bunsens burning while the boss is on
55 the road.

Perhaps just as significant, priority can decide who reaps the financial benefits of a new discovery. A month after Pons and Fleischmann made their announcement, Bishop reported, 40 companies had signed agreements with the University of Utah to inspect patent applications based on the scientists'
60 work.

[1]Tenure: a lifetime appointment with full job security.

In my own field of astronomy, it is easy to list cases in which the way discoveries were announced, and the motives of the discoverers, would fail every test of modern scientific protocol. Astronomers...made announcements in ways calculated to bring them maximal credit, priority and even...personal gain.

When Galileo[2] introduced his improved telescope, he touted its potential use for long-range detection of enemy ships. As a result, he was granted tenure in his professorship and a hefty raise. When he discovered the four large moons of Jupiter, he hoped to cash in on that application as well. His discovery revolutionized astronomy. Until then, dogma held that everything in the sky revolved around Earth. But here was an indisputable case of celestial bodies orbiting another celestial body. It would be the model for Galileo's... thesis that Earth moves around the Sun.

One of his concerns in announcing his discovery, however, was to make the most he could out of it. Galileo agonized over whether to call the moons the "Cosmian Stars" after the rich and powerful Cosimo de Medici, or the

[2]Galileo Galilei (1564–1642): Italian scientist and philosopher. Performed important experiments in astronomy and physics.

"Medicean Stars" after Cosimo and his three, similarly wealthy brothers. Which would bring him the most money? He sought advice from Cosimo's secretary and eventually opted for the second choice. Today they are known as the Galilean moons....

Every rule has its exceptions.... Some astronomers had to learn how to make a discovery announcement. William Herschel was that pleasant rarity among great scientists, a very modest person. When he discovered the planet Uranus, in 1781, with a homemade telescope from his home in Bath, England, he did no more to publicize it than to mention it to a friend. The friend wrote to the Royal Society, then as now Britain's leading scientific group, in London. The Society knew the importance of good PR, whether or not the phrase had yet been invented.

At that time Herschel was a professional musician and only an amateur astronomer, one who had a knack for building telescopes. Members of the Society realized that Herschel could advance the art of telescopes, if only he could devote full time to it. They arranged for him to meet with King George III, who soon after awarded Herschel a stipend and made him a royal astronomer. Herschel went on to build the great telescopes of his age and to make important discoveries, including the deduction that the Milky Way is shaped like a disk or lens, and we are inside it. Herschel had to be prodded into self-promotion, and we admire his modesty....

The fine line that present-day scientists walk between self-aggrandizement and progress-slowing shyness involves more than the niceties of etiquette. Hasty announcements draw intense criticisms, but so do delays. In AIDS research, for example, some activists are demanding that new drugs be made available to patients before proof of their efficacy is published in peer-reviewed journals. Even in a field like astronomy, where no finding is likely to help or harm the public health, those who sit on discoveries too long are likely to be criticized.

Stephen P. Maran

After You Read

3 **Matching General Ideas and Specific Illustrations.** Like many articles, this one alternates between general and specific ideas. Read the following ideas from the article and decide which of the two columns contains general ideas and which contains specific ideas. Label the columns correctly, and then match each general idea to the specific idea that illustrates it.

A. _____

1. In the field of astronomy, it is easy to list cases in which discoveries were announced in ways calculated to bring credit and personal gain.

2. Some astronomers of the past were modest and did not try to promote their own interests.

3. If you do not follow scientific protocol when announcing your discovery, you will suffer ridicule and criticism from your colleagues.

4. Waiting too long to announce discoveries can also bring criticism.

B. _____

1. Some scientists decided they would "slam Pons and Fleischmann against the wall" because they had called a press conference to announce "cold fusion."

2. In AIDS research, some activists are demanding that new drugs be made available to patients before proof of their efficacy is published in journals.

3. When Galileo discovered the four large moons of Jupiter, he decided to name them after the rich and famous Medici brothers.

4. When William Herschel discovered the planet Uranus in 1781, he did no more to publicize it than mention it to a friend.

4 **Finding Related Words.** Fill in the following chart with words from the article to show the relationships among word families. The first one is done as an example.

Nouns (things)	Nouns (people)	Adjectives	Verbs
1. science	scientist	scientific	X
2. _____	_____	X	discover
3. _____	proponent	proposed	propose
4. _____	X	prior	prioritize
5. _____	_____	astronomical	X
6. _____	public	publicized	_____
7. _____	announcer	announced	_____
8. _____	detective	X	_____
9. _____	revolutionary	revolutionary	_____
10. competition	_____	competitive	compete

Talk It Over

In small groups, discuss the following questions.

1. In your opinion, what are some of the most important discoveries that have been made in recent times?

2. Do you think that the people who make discoveries get rich and famous? Should they?

3. What invention or discovery would you like to see?

4. How are scientists and researchers regarded in your culture? Do they receive a high salary? Do people pay attention to their opinions?

5. What are the advantages and disadvantages of choosing a career in science?

5   **Announcing a Discovery.** Work in groups of three or four and play the role of scientists who have just made an important discovery. First decide what your discovery is. (Your teacher may give you some help with this.) Then make up a short speech about it for the public, telling them what it is and why it is important. Your teacher may ask you to "present" your discovery to the class while your classmates play the roles of reporters at a press conference.

Timed Reading

The following selection discusses what many people view as the most recent extension of the human mind: the computer. Is it simply a tool, or can we speak of ait as an intelligent being that "thinks"? Read the selection to find out the author's point of view on this question. Try to finish the reading and comprehension quiz in six minutes. Looking at the quiz first will help you focus on the reading.

Are Computers Alive?

The topic of *thought* is one area of psychology, and many observers have considered this aspect in connection with robots and computers: Some of the old worries about AI (artificial intelligence) were closely linked to the question of whether computers could think. The first massive electronic computers, ca-

5   pable of rapid (if often unreliable) computation and little or no creative activity, were soon dubbed "electronic brains." A reaction to this terminology quickly followed. To put them in their place, computers were called "high-speed idiots," an effort to protect human vanity. In such a climate the possibility of computers actually being alive was rarely considered: It was bad enough that

10   computers might be capable of thought. But not everyone realized the implications of the high-speed idiot tag. It has not been pointed out often enough that even the human idiot is one of the most intelligent life forms on earth. If the early computers were even that intelligent, it was already a remarkable state of affairs.

15   One consequence of speculation about the possibility of computer thought was that we were forced to examine with new care the idea of thought in general. It soon became clear that we were not sure what we meant by such terms as *thought* and *thinking*. We tend to assume that human beings think, some more than others, though we often call people *thoughtless* or *unthink-*

20   *ing*. Dreams cause a problem, partly because they usually happen outside our control. They are obviously some type of mental experience, but are they a type of thinking? And the question of nonhuman life forms adds further problems. Many of us would maintain that some of the higher animals—dogs, cats, apes, and so on—are capable of at least basic thought, but what about fish

25   and insects? It is certainly true that the higher mammals show complex brain activity when tested with the appropriate equipment. If thinking is demonstrated by evident electrical activity in the brain, then many animal species are capable of thought. Once we have formulated clear ideas on what thought is in biological creatures, it will be easier to discuss the question of thought

30   in artifacts. And what is true of thought is also true of the many other mental processes. One of the immense benefits of AI research is that we are being forced to scrutinize, with new rigor, the working of the human mind.

35

It is already clear that machines have superior mental abilities to many life forms. No fern or oak tree can play chess as well as even the simplest digital computer; nor can frogs weld car bodies as well as robots. The three-fingered mechanical manipulator is cleverer in some ways than the three-toed sloth. It seems that, viewed in terms of intellect, the computer should be set well above plants and most animals. Only the higher animals can, it seems, compete with computers with regard to intellect—and even then with diminishing success. (Examples of this are in the games of backgammon and chess. Some of the world's best players are now computers.)

40

Geoff Simons

6 **Comprehension Quiz.** Choose the best way of finishing each statement, based on what you have just read.

1. The first electronic computers were _____ .
    a. slow and reliable
    b. creative and accurate
    c. large and fast

2. The author feels that by calling these early computers "high-speed idiots," people were really implying that computers _____ .
    a. would never be capable of thought
    b. were already somewhat intelligent
    c. can never work as rapidly as people

3. The author believes that such words as *thought* and *thinking* _____ .
    a. are terms that are not clear and will never be exactly defined
    b. might come to be better understood because of research into artificial intelligence and computers
    c. have precise biological meanings that refer only to human mental processes

4. In the author's view, mental activities are characteristic of _____ .
    a. all plants and animals
    b. some animals
    c. human beings alone

5. The author's opinion regarding the possibility of machines thinking seems to be that _____ .
    a. there are already machines that think
    b. this is somewhat possible
    c. this is totally improbable

What Do You Think?

Nunavut, a Breakthrough in Social Justice

In April, 1999, a new territory of Canada was formed and became a separate political entity. This new territory is called Nunavut, which means "Our Land" in the Inuit language of Inuktitut. It includes the central and eastern portions of what used to be the Northwest Territories, and covers 1,994,000 square kilometers, or the equivalent of one-fifth of the size of Canada.

By creating this new territory, the Canadian government has given clear ownership of both the land and its resources to the people who live there, including control of the rich deposits of oil, gas and minerals. Most of the inhabitants of Nunavut are Native Inuit whose ancestors first came there thousands of years ago.

In most places in the world, Native populations live in poverty, without their own land, so the creation of Nunavut is considered by many people to be a significant breakthrough in the field of social justice. The territory is vast and rich in resources and valuable also for the development of tourism. Now the people who live there have reclaimed their ancestral homeland.

■ What do you think about this breakthrough? Was this a good idea for Canada?

■ What other countries in the world have groups of Natives who are descendants of the first inhabitants? Are some of them working to receive land or rights from the countries in which they live?

■ Do you think that other governments should follow the example of Canada and give land to Native people? Why or why not?

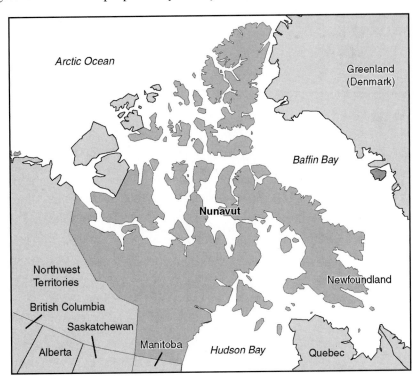

Video Activities: Advances in Medicine

Before You Watch.   Discuss these questions in small groups.

1. What do you think happens if the nerves that control your muscles die? Do you know the name of the disease that kills these nerves?

2. Have you ever known anyone who had a disease that affected his or her movement? How did this disease affect his/her life?

Watch.   Circle the correct answers.

1. The main idea of this video segment is that _____.
    a.   ALS is a very difficult disease to have
    b.   a cure will soon be found for ALS
    c.   here is hope for people with ALS

2. Jerry Lineberger controls his wheelchair and his computer by moving his
    _____.
    a.   legs and arms   b.   hands and feet   c.   head and eyes

3. Dr. Jeffrey Rosenfeld's treatment _____.
    a.   has cured some people
    b.   may help some people live longer
    c.   is dangerous and difficult

Watch Again.   Write answers to these questions.

1. How long has Jerry Lineberger had ALS? _____

2. What are the initials of the protein that Dr. Rosenfeld uses in his treatment?
    _____

3. Use the words below to complete the description of Dr. Rosenfeld's treatment.

    abdomen   catheter   implanted   inserted
    pump   release   spinal fluid   vertebra
    A _____ the size of a hockey puck is _____ in the _____. A
    _____ is _____ between two _____. Tiny holes
    continuously _____ the drug into the _____.

4. *Diagnosed* is a verb. The noun is _____.

5. *Optimistically* is an adverb. The adjective is _____.

6. Listen and write words that have these meanings.
    a.   incredible _____
    b.   a doctor who specializes in the nervous system _____
    c.   to increase the amount of time _____
    d.   unproved theory _____

After You Watch.   Find an article about another disease. Read the article and write a summary. Your summary should answer these questions:

1. What causes the disease?

2. What are the symptoms of the disease?

3. Who is most at risk from this disease? (children, the elderly, etc.)

4. What treatments are there for this disease, and how effective are they?

Chapter 9

Art and Entertainment

IN THIS CHAPTER

North America is a great "melting pot," a place where people from many countries and races have joined to form a new culture. The arts reflect the uniqueness of this culture. Many of its contributions to music have come from people of African descent: jazz, gospel music, rock, the blues. The first selection is from the biography of Duke Ellington. The next two sections explore the striking paintings of Georgia O'Keeffe and the moving poetry of the Chicanos. Finally, a timed reading looks at Jackie Chan, one of the world's best-loved movie stars.

The Man Who Was an Orchestra

Before You Read

1 **Anticipating the Reading.** Before starting to read the article, listen to a CD or tape of jazz music, preferably Duke Ellington's. Perhaps your teacher or a member of the class will bring some jazz music in or you can find some on the radio or the TV. Then answer the following questions. Compare your answers with those of your classmates.

1. How does jazz differ from other types of music?

   _____

   _____

2. What's unusual about Duke Ellington's name? Does it relate in some ways to the picture of him on page 177? How?

   _____

   _____

3. What kind of relationship do you think exists between the leader of a jazz group and the other musicians in the group?

   _____

   _____

2 **Getting Meaning from Context.** Based on the context of the article's sentences that follow, match the lettered definitions with the italicized words from the sentences.

_____ 1. The element of surprise explains the *compelling* hold jazz has on listeners, which makes them sit very still for hours.

_____ 2. Because of our patterned lives, jazzmen, of all musicians, are our *surrogates* for the unpredictable.

_____ 3. Duke would play familiar numbers from his *repertory* during parts of the evening.

_____ 4. Jazzmen generally *improvise* rather than play prepared pieces.

_____ 5. After Duke Ellington had been afflicted by cancer, his strength was *decimated*.

_____ 6. Musicians find performances exhausting yet *exhilarating* experiences.

_____ 7. Ellington considered the unfortunate situation of many classical composers *poignant*.

a. creators of new things

b. greatly decreased

c. forceful

d. distressing, touching

e. collection of musical pieces

f. explore thoroughly

g. invent without preparation

h. stimulating, invigorating

i. substitutes, replacements

_____ 8. By writing specifically for each of his men and letting them play in a natural and relaxed manner, Ellington was able to *probe* the intimate recesses of their minds.

_____ 9. While most people follow the ideas of others, every group needs also to have *innovators*.

Read

Do you enjoy listening to jazz? If so, you are not alone, for millions of people throughout the world rate it as their favorite type of music. Jazz began in the United States around the turn of the twentieth century, when it was played informally by African-American bands in New Orleans and other southern cities and towns. In the following selection, you will find out more about this music with the strong rhythmic beat and about the people who create it, especially about one man, Duke Ellington, one of the greatest jazz musicians of all time.

The Man Who Was an Orchestra

Whitney Balliett, jazz critic for *The New Yorker* magazine, has called jazz "the sound of surprise." And it is that expectation of surprise which partly explains the compelling hold of jazz on listeners in just about every country in the world.

5   Most of us lead lives of patterned regularity. Day by day, surprises are relatively few. And except for economic or physical uncertainties, we neither face nor look for significant degrees of risk because the vast majority of us try to attain as much security as is possible.

In this sense, jazzmen, of all musicians, are our surrogates for the un-
10   predictable, our models of constant change.

"It's like going out there naked every night," a bass player once said to me. "Any one of us can screw the whole thing up because he had a fight with his wife just before the performance or because he's just not with it that night for any
15   number of reasons. I mean, we're out there improvising. The classical guys have their scores, whether they have them on a music stand or have memorized them. But we have to be creating, or trying to, antic-
20   ipating each other, transforming our feel-
ings into music, taking chances every second. That's why, when jazz musicians are really putting out, it's an exhausting experience. It can be exhilarating, too, but al-
25   ways there's that touch of fear, that feeling of being on a very high wire without a net below."

30

And jazz musicians who work with the more headlong innovators in the music face special hazards. There is the challenge, for instance, of staying in balance all the way in performances with Thelonious Monk as he plunges through, in, underneath, and around time. "I got lost one night," one of the people in Monk's band told me, "and I felt like I had just fallen into an elevator shaft."

35

There is another dimension of jazz surprise, the kind and quality that Duke Ellington exemplified. It is true that during many of his concerts and other appearances, Duke would schedule familiar numbers from his repertory for parts of the evening, sometimes long parts. He felt this an obligation to those who had come to see him, sometimes over long distances, and wanted to hear their favorites. Duke, who had come up in the business (and jazz is also a business) at a time when, to most of its audiences, the music was show business rather than art, considered it rude to present an audience with a program of entirely unfamiliar work.

40

But for Duke himself the keenest pleasure in music was the continual surprising of himself. Always he was most interested in the new, the just completed work.

45

"The man," the late Billy Strayhorn said of Duke, "is a constant revelation. He's continually renewing himself through his music. He's thoroughly attuned to what's going on *now*. He not only doesn't live in the past. He rejects it, at least so far as his own past accomplishments are concerned. He hates talking about the old bands and the old pieces. He has to play some of the Ellington standards because otherwise the audiences would be disappointed. But he'd much rather play the new things."

50

Duke never could stop composing. Even toward the end, in the hospital, his strength decimated by cancer, Ellington was still composing. And throughout his life, the challenge and incomparable satisfaction for him was in the way he composed for the specific members of his orchestra.

55

"After a man has been in the band for a while," Ellington once told me, "I can hear what his capacities are, and I write to that. And I write to each man's sound. A man's sound is his total personality. I hear that sound as I prepare to write. I hear all their sounds, and that's how I am able to write. Before you can play anything or write anything, you have to hear it."

60

As Billy Strayhorn said, "Ellington plays the piano, but his real instrument is his band. Each member of the band is to him a distinctive play of tone colors and a distinctive set of emotions, and he mixes them all into his own style. By writing specifically for each of his own men, and thereby letting them play naturally and in a relaxed way, Ellington is able to probe the intimate recesses of their minds and find things that not even the musicians knew were there."

65

And having written—late at night in hotel rooms, in the car, on scraps of paper, between dates, wherever he was when not fronting the band—Ellington was able to hear the results immediately. And that was much to his satisfaction. Duke often told me that he considered the fate of most classical composers poignant. "They write and write and keep putting what they've done in a drawer and maybe, once in a great while, some orchestra will perform one of their works. The rest—they have to imagine, only imagine, what they've written sounds like. I could not exist that way, creating music only for myself, not communicating with anyone but myself. But having an orchestra always with me makes it unnecessary for me to wait." Duke did not have to

70

75

travel constantly; he could have lived comfortably on the royalties earned from his abundance of compositions. But he greatly preferred the road so that he could hear his music, especially his new music, instantly. Or, as he put it, "I keep these expensive gentlemen with me to gratify that desire."

80

Nat Hentoff

After You Read

Focus on Testing

Preparing for Exams with Study Maps

Many good students say that the time to start studying for an exam is the first day of class. That is the moment to choose a strategy for retaining important information, especially in courses with a lot of reading. Some students keep short summary files in their computer on every book or article they read; others keep summary file cards in a box. This provides a record to use when the time comes to study for the mid-term or final exam. Don't waste time writing these summaries in perfect, complete sentences. They are only comments for personal use. Another way to keep a record is to make study maps for all the readings and put them in order in a binder—one binder for each course.

Look at examples of designs for study maps that follow and also on page 105 in Chapter 6. Which one would work best for "The Man Who Was an Orchestra"? Or would you make a new design? Why? Working in small groups, choose a design and make a study map for the selection. Compare the results with the other groups and decide which design is best. Afterward, use your study map to help you with the exercises that follow.

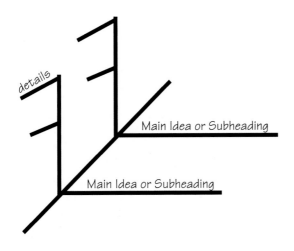

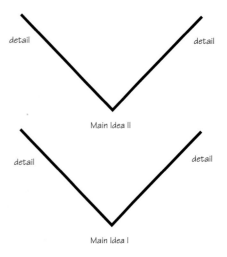

3   **Recalling Information.** Based on what you have just read, choose the best way of finishing each statement.

1. The main reason that jazz is unpredictable and presents the listener with surprises is that ____.
   a. it sounds like an older style of music
   b. jazzmen improvise rather than play prepared pieces
   c. the musicians find the performances exhilarating

2. Duke Ellington included old familiar numbers from his repertory in many of his concerts because ____.
   a. it was his continual and keenest musical pleasure
   b. he felt it was good business and he wanted to make a lot of money
   c. he did not want to disappoint his audiences

3. When Duke Ellington was older and famous, he ____.
   a. enjoyed living in the past and talking about earlier accomplishments
   b. rejected the new styles of younger musicians
   c. kept on changing and innovating his music

4. Ellington considered the fate of most classical composers poignant because ____.
   a. they have to wait a long time before they can hear their music (if ever)
   b. they usually die before getting much money or fame
   c. they have to follow rigid rules in composing

4   **Making and Supporting Inferences.** An inference is a conclusion, supposedly based on reason or logic. Tell which of the following inferences about Duke Ellington are valid (V) and which are invalid (I). Give at least two facts from the article to support your judgment.

_____ 1. He was basically lazy and liked the good and easy life.

_____

_____

_____ 2. He was self-centered and arrogant.

_____

_____

_____ 3. He was young in spirit throughout his life.

_____

_____

Talk It Over

In small groups, discuss the following questions.

1. After reading the article, how would you describe the difference between jazz and other types of music?
2. Why does jazz have a compelling hold on many people?
3. Billy Strayhorn said, "Ellington plays the piano, but his real instrument is his band." What did he mean?
4. The word *jazz* is used in certain English slang expressions that apply to things besides music. For example, someone might refer to the design for a house or the plans for a party and say, "Let's *jazz it up* a bit" or "It's not *jazzy* enough." Based on the context and on what you have read, what do these expressions mean?

5 **Expressing Reactions.** Some volunteers should bring in CDs or tapes of their favorite type of music and play it for the class. Then play the jazz music that you listened to before the reading. As the article suggests, does the element of surprise seem stronger in jazz than in other kinds of music? Listen to a jazz piece and see if you can tell when the musicians are improvising. In the space provided, write about which piece of music you liked most and why. After you finish, join a group and tell about your judgments. Refer to what you wrote, but don't read it aloud.

_____

_____

_____

_____

Now write about which piece of music you liked least and why.

_____

_____

_____

_____

PART 2

"To Paint Is to Live"

Before You Read

1   **Anticipating the Reading—Making Inferences.** Look at the title and the photograph of Georgia O'Keeffe that follows. Skim the first two paragraphs of the article. Then make inferences about this famous artist and answer the following questions. Afterwards, read the article to find out if you were right.

1.   What kind of person do you think she was?

_____

_____

2.   Why did she paint?

_____

_____

3.   What kinds of problems do you imagine she had in her life? Why?

_____

_____

Read

Painting, like music, is one of the fine arts. American and Canadian painting has been influenced by many traditions from different parts of the world, especially by those from Europe. However, the twentieth century witnessed an opposite trend: the development of particularly North American painting styles that have become international. One American painter who exerted an influence on Europe with a unique and independent style was a woman from Wisconsin named Georgia O'Keeffe. Three of O'Keeffe's grandparents were immigrants—from Ireland, Hungary, and Holland—and the fourth was descended from one of the earliest European colonists in America. These ancestors came to start a new life in a new world, but O'Keeffe was destined to become a pioneer of a different sort. The following article discusses her life and work.

To Paint Is to Live: Georgia O'Keeffe, 1887–1986

Georgia O'Keeffe was truly an American original. Tough, sparse, lean, she embodied the rugged individualistic nature of the American pioneer. But instead of tilling the soil, her strides were made in the field of contemporary American art.

Born on a 600-acre farm in Sun Prairie, Wisconsin, on November 15, 1887, O'Keeffe throughout her long life preferred vast plains and open spaces to city living. From the summer of 1929, when she made her first visit to New Mexico, the starkness of the desert fascinated her. After summering in New Mexico for many years, she finally moved permanently to Abiquiu, New Mexico, in 1949, where she continued to paint until her eyesight faltered in the late 1970s. From this region the themes of some of her finest works evolved.

O'Keeffe's strictly American art education began with private lessons at the age of ten. Teachers recognized her talent but often criticized the larger-than-life proportions that she liked to paint. At an early age she was already moving away from realistic copying of objects to things she perceived with her own eyes, mind, and soul.

O'Keeffe's formal high school education continued at a private school in Madison, Wisconsin, and after a family move, she graduated from a Williamsburg, Virginia, high school in 1903. In 1905–06 she studied at the Art Institute in Chicago, and in 1907–08, at the Art Students' League in New York.

In 1908, perhaps disappointed with the rigidity of American art education at the time, she gave up painting and became a commercial artist, drawing advertising illustrations in Chicago. However, in the summer of 1912, she decided to take another art course in Virginia under Alon Bemont, and her interest in creative painting came alive again.

Self-supporting since graduation from high school, O'Keeffe had to find jobs to sustain her through her developing years as an artist. In 1912, she began to teach in Amarillo, Texas, and was stunned by the barren southern landscape. "That was my country," she said, "terrible wind and wonderful emptiness."

After art courses in 1915–16 in New York under the more liberal art teacher Arthur Dow, O'Keeffe accepted a position as an art teacher at a small college in South Carolina. It was at this point that the determined young woman locked herself up, took stock of her painting, and decided to reject the rigidity of the realism that she had been taught for a style all her own: "Nothing is less real than realism—details are confusing. It is only by selection, by elimination, by emphasis, that we get the real meaning of things."

Georgia O'Keeffee,
Waterfall No. III Iao Valley

Georgia O'Keeffee,
Yellow Calla

From this revival came black and white abstract nature forms in all shapes and sizes, the beginning of her highly individualistic style.

O'Keeffe sent some of her prints to a friend in New York and told her not to show them to anyone. The friend was so impressed with them that she ignored the request and took them to a famous photographer and promoter of modern artists, Alfred Stieglitz. His reaction was immediate: "At last, a woman on paper!" Without O'Keeffe's knowledge or consent, Stieglitz exhibited these prints in his gallery. Infuriated, she went to New York to insist that he take her drawings down. Stieglitz, however, convinced her of their quality, and she allowed them to remain on exhibit. Subsequently, Stieglitz became the champion of O'Keeffe's works and helped her gain the prominence she deserved. For Stieglitz, Georgia O'Keeffe was an unusually talented American female artist. She was unspoiled by studies in Europe and painted with a direct, clear, strong—even fierce—force.

The relationship between Stieglitz and O'Keeffe developed into a passionate love affair, which eventually led to a twenty-two-year marriage. Stieglitz, his wife's senior by many years, died in 1946. He immortalized her through many beautiful and unusual photographs—the lady in black, with piercing eyes, tightly pulled-back hair and the artistic elongated hands of a princess.

Strength, clarity, and strong physical presence are words that are often used to describe O'Keeffe's paintings. As art critic Lloyd Goodrich said, "Her art presents a rare combination of austerity and deep seriousness.... Even at her most realistic she is concerned not with the mere visual appearance of things, but with their essential life, their being, their identity.... The forms of nature are translated into forms of art." Or, as O'Keeffe herself put it, "A hill or a tree cannot make a good painting just because it is a hill or a tree. It is lines and colors put together so that they say something. For me, that is the very basis for painting. The abstraction is often the most definite form for the intangible thing in myself that I can only clarify in paint."

Miki Knezevic

After You Read

2 **Recalling Information.** Based on what you have just read, choose the best way of finishing each statement.

1. Georgia O'Keeffe was born _c_.
   a. in New York City
   b. in a town in New Mexico
   c. on a farm in Wisconsin

2. Her art education consisted of _a_
   a. studies in schools and institutes in the United States
   b. training in the best art academies of Europe
   c. only her own efforts and experimentation at home

3. The landscape with which she identified in particular was _c_.
   a. rugged mountains
   b. lush forests
   c. barren deserts

4. Alfred Stieglitz's comment when he first saw O'Keeffe's prints was, "At last, a woman on paper!" From this we can infer that _b_.
   a. there was a great deal of discrimination against women then
   b. women artists were not very common in those days
   c. he did not really like the prints very much

5. Stieglitz was important in the life of Georgia O'Keeffe because _a_.
   a. he became both her husband and champion
   b. he bought many of her paintings at good prices
   c. he photographed her prints and gave titles to them

3 **Paraphrasing Complex Ideas.** Paraphrase the following excerpts from the article. Do not worry if there are some words you do not understand. Just state the main point briefly in simple, direct words.

1. Tough, sparse, lean, she embodied the rugged individualistic nature of the American pioneer. But instead of tilling the soil, her strides were made in the field of contemporary American art.

   _____
   _____
   _____
   _____

2. Self-supporting since graduation from high school, O'Keeffe had to find jobs to sustain her through her developing years as an artist.

    _____

    _____

    _____

    _____

3. "Nothing is less real than realism—details are confusing. It is only by selection, by elimination, by emphasis, that we get the real meaning of things." (Georgia O'Keeffe)

    _____

    _____

    _____

    _____

4. "Even at her most realistic she is concerned not with the mere visual appearance of things, but with their essential life, their being, their identity...." (art critic)

    _____

    _____

    _____

    _____

Talk It Over

In small groups, discuss the following questions.

1. Were you right or wrong about the inferences regarding Georgia O'Keeffe that you made in the first exercise? Explain.
2. Do you think it was difficult for a woman to be an artist in the 1920s and 1930s? Why?
3. Why do you think Stieglitz was such a strong influence on O'Keeffe?
4. Many feminists and members of the gay rights movement admire Georgia O'Keeffe's art because it represents female beauty in a sensual way through the forms of nature. What other reasons for admiring O'Keeffe's work are given in the article?

4   **Expressing Reactions.** Bring in a print or photograph of an art work that appeals to you to share with the class. First write down something about the subject, style, and theme or "message" of the art work. Also explain what you like about it. Share your art work and comments with the class.

Subject: _____

_____

_____

Style: _____

_____

_____

Theme or Message: _____

_____

_____

What I Like About It: _____

_____

_____

5   **Writing a Comparison.** Do artists tend to have similar types of lives even though they are from different cultures and time periods? Go to the library and look up information on an artist from any country other than the United States. Below, complete the brief comparison between the life of this artist and that of Georgia O'Keeffe. Do not write the whole story of the artist's life, only several points that show similarity. Share your work with a partner and then with the class.

Georgia O'Keeffe can be compared to _____ , the artist I found information

about, in the following ways: Both of them _____

They also _____

If there is no similarity, try to explain why:

_____

_____

PART 3

Chicano Poetry: The Voice of a Culture

Before You Read

1 **Anticipating the Reading.** Look at the map of the United States and answer the following questions. Then read the article to find out whether you are correct and to learn more about the largest minority group in the United States.

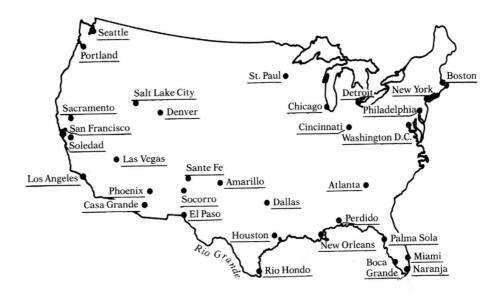

1. What cities on the map sound to you as though their names might be of Spanish origin?

    _____

    _____

2. What sections seem to have the most Spanish names?

    _____

    _____

3. Do you know or can you guess why these places have Spanish names?

    _____

    _____

Read

The following article gives some background on Mexican-Americans, who are often called Chicanos, and presents a few examples of their poetry. You might wonder why this group is singled out when there are so many ethnic groups, with their particular languages and cultures, living in North America, including millions of Spanish-speaking people from other countries. There are historical reasons, which you will read about, that explain why this group is different from most others.

Chicano Poetry: The Voice of a Culture
The Hispanic Presence in the United States

What are the two cities in the world with the largest number of Spanish-speaking inhabitants? Mexico City is number one, which is no surprise; but the second is Los Angeles, California, right in the U.S.A.! According to 2000 census figures, 32.8 million Hispanics live in the United States. More than 80

5   percent of Hispanics live in urban areas. Most are concentrated in the five southwestern states of Arizona, California, Colorado, New Mexico, and Texas. There are also sizable Hispanic populations in New York, Florida, and Illinois.

There are countless Spanish geographical names in the United States, such as the state of Colorado (which means "red"), the city of Las Vegas (fer-

10   tile lowlands), and the Rio Grande (big river). Many Spanish and Latin American words have been incorporated into English. A large number of these words are related to geographical features: *mesa* (plateau) and *canyon*; to music: *tango*, *rumba*; to ranch life: *rodeo*, *corral*; to architecture: *patio, plaza*; and to food: *chocolate, tomato*. Many colorful English slang terms are corruptions of

15   Spanish words, such as *calaboose* (jail) and *macho* (big, tough male).

Mexican-American History

Where did all this Spanish influence come from? Didn't the United States start out as a colony of the British? In fact, the southwestern United States was settled by the Spanish and Mexicans centuries before the arrival of the first

20   Anglos. Many people are unaware of this fact because until recently, all the history books were written from the point of view of the British. Let's examine the "true history" of the American Southwest.

The region was part of Mexico until it was lost in a war with the United States. Under the terms of the Treaty of Guadalupe Hidalgo, which ended the

25   war in 1848, Mexico ceded to the United States the territory that is now New Mexico, Utah, Nevada, California, and parts of Colorado and Wyoming. On paper the 75,000 Mexican inhabitants were guaranteed their property rights and granted U.S. citizenship. The reality, however, was different. They suffered racial and cultural discrimination at the hands of a flood of Anglo settlers, and

30   many were dispossessed of their lands. Most worked for Anglo bosses as farm, railroad, and mine workers. Constant immigration from Mexico kept wages low.

World War II brought about fundamental changes. Many Mexican-Americans began to consider themselves U.S. citizens for the first time after

35   serving in the war. Armed with new skills and faced with the rapid mechanization of agriculture, many moved to the cities in search of work.

The Chicano Movement

Inspired by the black struggle for civil rights, Mexican-Americans organized in the 1960s to gain reforms and restore ethnic pride. Members of this move-
40 ment called themselves *Chicanos*, and the name has become popular, although some still prefer the term Mexican-Americans. The achievements of the Chicano movement are many. In 1962, César Chávez founded the strong and successful National Farm Workers Association in Delano, California, which has managed to raise wages and improve working conditions for migrant workers.
45 In 1970 José Angel Gutiérrez established the *Raza Unida* political party in Crystal City, Texas, which has been successful in electing Mexican-American candidates to local office. Bilingual, cross-cultural education, and Chicano studies programs have been established in schools and universities.

Chicano Arts

50 The Chicano movement inspired a flowering of Chicano theater, art, and literature. Luis Valdés created the *Teatro Campesino* in the fields of Delano in 1965 to strengthen the union's organizing efforts. This unique form of theater draws on a variety of Latin American and European traditions and makes use of allegorical characters, masks, song, and dance. Originally performed by farm
55 workers for farm workers, it later broadened its focus to include issues other than the strike, such as American foreign policy and discrimination against Hispanics in schools. The *Teatro Campesino* has gained international prominence and inspired the creation of many similar companies across the country.

Colorful murals painted on the walls of public buildings in Mexican-
60 American neighborhoods are a collective expression of reborn hope and ethnic pride. They depict the Mexican-Americans' Indian and Spanish heritage, the history of Mexico and of Mexican-Americans in the United States, and the problems of migrant workers.

The genre most cultivated by Chicano writers is poetry. Often written in
65 free verse, Chicano poetry creates an impression of spontaneity, freshness, and honesty. It may be written in Spanish, English, or a combination of the two languages.

Deana Fernández

Some Examples of Chicano Poetry

The following examples of Chicano poetry contain the Spanish words *primo*, "cousin," and *gringo*, a somewhat negative word for an Anglo-American. Both poems provide a brief glimpse into the lives of Mexican-Americans. As you read, try to understand the main point that the poet wants to convey and the emotions he wants the reader to feel.

To People Who Pick Food

I am the man
    who picks your food

    immigrant,
    tablecloths
5   ignore my stare
I have children
a fake green card
a warm kiss
a cross to ward off rangers
10 a picture of St. Peter so
I will not drown in a river
    I pick apples
        cotton
        grapes
15 eyes follow me
    utter under their breaths,
I do not understand
    the lettuce canned
with my hands
20   citrus pores
     inflame my eyes
my wife is   proud
  soft   gentle
    my   children
25 are brown   tender deer
    what eyes,
the sun cracks my skin
I am old and dark as the dirt
I drop on my knees   before the sky
30 they can hate me, point me out in a crowd
but do not pity me   the sun is there
every morning   God follows my children
and I walk to the field to grow bread
    with my friends.

—Wilfredo Q. Castaño

Grandma's Primo

Grandma had a cousin
who lived in the big city
and looked like a gringo
He smoked a big cigar
5 and spoke English as well
as he spoke Spanish
He loved to tell jokes
would always tell them twice—
the first time in Spanish
10 to make us laugh
and the second time in English
to impress us.

—Leroy V. Quintana

After You Read

2 **Recalling Information.** Based on the reading, tell whether each of the following statements is true (T) or false (F) by writing T or F in the blanks. Correct the false statements to make them true.

_____ 1. There are more Spanish-speaking people in Los Angeles, California, than in any other city in the world except the capital of Mexico.

_____ 2. Hispanics form the largest minority group in the United States.

_____ 3. Spanish and Mexican architecture and geographical names are characteristics of the northeastern part of the country.

_____ 4. The first Spanish and Mexican settlers in the United States arrived after the first British settlers.

_____ 5. After the war of 1848, Mexicans in the U.S. territory that used to belong to Mexico suffered racial and cultural discrimination.

_____ 6. After World War II, many Mexican-Americans moved from the countryside to the cities.

_____ 7. César Chávez is a Chicano who founded a powerful and effective labor union for farm workers.

_____ 8. José Angel Gutiérrez began a Chicano political party, but it has not yet managed to get Mexican-Americans elected to office.

_____ 9. Chicano theater, begun by Luis Valdés, started out in the fields and was performed for and by farm workers.

_____ 10. The literary genre most popular among Chicano writers is the novel.

_____ 11. "To People Who Pick Food" is told from the point of view of a poor but contented Mexican farm laborer who works in the United States illegally.

_____ 12. In the poem "Grandma's Primo," the cousin always told jokes twice because he wasn't sure that his relatives understood them the first time.

3 **Summarizing Information About Specific Points.** Write a brief summary of what you remember about each of the following people or things. If necessary, scan the article to refresh your memory.

1. Spanish words used in English

    _____

    _____

2. *Raza Unida*

    _____

    _____

3. Treaty of Guadalupe Hidalgo

    _____

    _____

4. César Chávez

    _____

    _____

5. *Teatro Campesino*

    _____

    _____

4 **Reading Poetry for Meaning.** Just as any scene can serve as the subject of a painting, so any part of daily life can provide material for a poem. Of course, the choice that the artist or poet makes relates to his or her purpose. Poetry is usually short and compact, so it should be read several times, preferably aloud, to appreciate its meaning. Read the following questions; then reread the poems and answer the questions.

"To People Who Pick Food"
The poem is spoken from the point of view of a poor Mexican migrant who is working illegally in the United States, with a "fake green card."

1. What parts of the poem suggest that the man feels prejudice and discrimination from the people around him?

    _____

    _____

2. What work does the man do? How does he feel about it?

    _____

    _____

3. When so many rich people seem dissatisfied with their lives (as evidenced by alcoholism, use of drugs, nervous breakdowns, and so on), why is this man content? What things does he have that give him strength and pride?

    _____

    _____

4.   What emotive words (ones based on strong feelings or emotions) are used? What emotions do you think the poet wants us to feel toward the man?

_____

_____

"Grandma's Primo"
The Italian artist Modigliani often used just a few lines or brushstrokes to suggest a whole person. This poem is also the portrait of a person, shown in just a few words.

1.   From whose point of view do we see this character?

_____

_____

2.   What special qualities does he have?

_____

_____

3.   Why do you think the poet found him memorable?

_____

_____

Timed Reading

Jackie Chan is one of the best-known figures in Asian popular culture, yet he is not well known in some parts of the world, such as the United States and Canada. Read the following article from *Time* magazine to find out more about this famous film star. Concentrate on these questions as you read. Try to finish the selection and comprehension exercises in twelve minutes.

1.   Who is Jackie Chan?
2.   What does he do that is so amazing?
3.   What is he like as a person?
4.   Why is he not well known in North America?

Jackie Can!

Do death-defying stunts!
Break all his bones!
Reign as Asia's No. 1 star!

Some movie stars measure their worth by how many millions of dollars
5   they make. Jackie Chan, Asian action-star extraordinaire, measures his by how many of his bones he has fractured while executing his films' incredible stunts. Let him count the breaks: "My skull, my eyes, my nose three times, my jaw, my shoulder, my chest, two fingers, a knee—everything from the top of my head to the bottom of my feet." Chan broke an ankle while jumping onto
10   a moving Hovercraft in his new film, *Rumble in the Bronx*, which opened in time for Chinese New Year last week. Fans queued up around the world.
        So who is Jackie Chan? In the U.S., only a figure with a small if intense cult. His volcanic comedies are not shown on the pay-movie channels, not

15

released in theaters except for the rare showcase, like the "Super Jackie" retrospective now at New York City's Cinema Village. But back home in Hong Kong—throughout Asia, in fact, and in South America and Australia—Chan is movie-action incarnate. He has made 40 films since 1976, when he was promoted as the new Bruce Lee. Now, at 40, Chan is that and more: the last good guy and, arguably, the world's best-loved movie star.

20

In American terms he's a little Clint Eastwood (actor-director), a dash of Gene Kelly (imaginative choreographer), a bit of Jim Carrey (rubbery ham) and a lot of the silent-movie clowns: Charlie Chaplin, Buster Keaton and Harold Lloyd. Says Chan fan Sylvester Stallone: "Jackie has elongated a genre that had grown pretty stale. He's infused films with humor and character-driven story while giving audiences these extraordinary stunts that are unparalleled anywhere in the world."

25

In Hollywood, special visual effects define the action film. In Hong Kong, stunts—the human body spinning and bending without a computer's help—define the Chan film. By displaying his death-baiting acrobatic virtuosity, he has returned the action movie to the actor. "Audiences know that if they want special effects, they go see Schwarzenegger," he says. "If they want a tough movie, they go see Sly. If they want an action movie, they choose Jackie Chan—because I do a lot of things that normal people can't do."

30

To cross a busy street, normal people might go to the corner and wait for the green. Not Jackie. Standing on a balcony in his *Police Story II*, he jumps onto a truck going one way, onto a double-decker bus going the other way and then through a window into the second floor of the villain's headquarters.

35

In his biggest hits (*Drunken Master, Project A, Police Story, The Armour of God*) and their sequels, Chan has scooted across burning coals, eaten red-hot chili peppers, swallowed industrial alcohol. He has bounced down a hill inside a giant beach ball and leaped from a mountaintop onto a passing hot-air balloon. As weapons he has used bicycles, rickshaws, chairs, plates, a

40

hat rack, a ketchup dispenser, overhead fans and Chinese folding fans. Bad guys have depantsed him, strapped a ton of TNT to his body, doused and scalded him, set him afire, dumped him down a well, hanged him naked in the town square. There's a truly masochistic resilience at work here: Jackie takes a licking and keeps on kicking.

Chan—whose Chinese screen name, Sing Lung, translates as "becoming the dragon"—is so fearless as to seem, by mere human standards, senseless. In *Police Story* he hitches a ride on a speeding bus by running up from behind, hooking an umbrella handle onto a window ledge and hanging on while fighting off a brood of bad guys....

The Asian audience gasps at these scenes but never doubts them, because everyone knows Jackie does his own stunts.... Lest doubts linger, his films provide instant replays from different angles. Under the closing credits are outtakes showing blown stunts, with comic or near tragic results. Executing a fairly routine jump in Yugoslavia for *The Armour of God*, he missed a tree branch, hit his head on a rock and almost died. Chan has a memento of the accident: a thimble-size hole in the right side of his head. If you ask nicely, he'll let you put your finger in it.

That's pure Jackie—an engaging presence offscreen and on who, unlike other cinema studs, projects no roiling torment, no existential grudge against the world. He seems a contented guy. And why not? A movie actor since he was seven, stunt man in a Bruce Lee movie at 18, and now Asia's No. 1 star, he is in total control of his films: supervising the stunts, singing the theme songs and, on 11 pictures, directing....

Chan's study of the silent masters taught him the universal language of film: action and passion, humor and heart. His movies are so simple, so fluid, so exuberant that they are easily understood by people who don't speak Cantonese. Just ask the Jackie fans who track down his movies in the Chinatowns of U.S. cities or visit specialized video stores. "Jackie Chan's work is as popular with our customers as anything by Orson Welles or Francis Coppola," says Meg Johnson, buyer for Videots, a smart Santa Monica outlet. Finding a Chan film under its multiplicity of titles is one challenge. Another can be watching it, in washed-out, nth-generation dupes with indifferent dubbing or Japanese subtitles (or none at all) and with the sides of the wide-screen images lopped off.

Chan regrets the situation: "The video rights are handled by Golden Harvest, the distribution company I work for. They don't really concentrate on videos in America." But even in this video murk, Chan's personality shines through. He has a star quality that doesn't get lost in translation.

Hollywood is missing out on a great thing: an ingratiating actor who makes hit movies and speaks better English than a few action heroes we could name. In the early '80s Chan gave U.S. films a try (in Burt Reynolds' *Cannonball Run* capers and two other wooden showcases), then returned to Hong Kong. For Chan there's no place like home. "In Asia I'm kind of like E.T.," he says. "Everybody comes to see my films. There are billions of people in Asia, and they're my first audience. If I get an American audience, O.K., that's a bonus. If not, that's O.K. too. I'm very happy."

If Jackie Chan can keep that thrill machine of a body in fine working order, his fans will be happy. And no bones about it.

Richard Corliss

5   **Recalling Information.** Based on what you have just read, choose the best way of finishing each statement.

1. Jackie Chan is especially famous for _b_ .
    a. his penetrating eyes
    b. his ability to take pain
    c. his clever use of language
    d. his love of money

2. Chan's movies are especially known for his _d_ .
    a. dazzling special effects
    b. killing and violence
    c. romantic songs
    d. dangerous stunts

3. As a person, Jackie is _b_ .
    a. distant and arrogant
    b. happy and direct
    c. shy and silent
    d. angry and antisocial

4. Jackie Chan is not well known in North America because _a_ .
    a. good tapes of his movies are not easily available
    b. his film style is suited only to the Asian market
    c. he does not like to work with Hollywood
    d. Hollywood actors and producers have a grudge against him

6   **Writing an Instant Summary.** Make an instant summary of the article you have just read by writing a one-sentence answer to each of the four questions listed on page 195. Then compare your summary with those of your classmates.

_____

_____

_____

_____

_____

_____

_____

_____

Making Connections

What's going on with Jackie Chan today? Find out the latest information about his personal life and his film career by searching the Internet. For example, try *http://www.jackiechan.com.*

What Do You Think?

Body Decoration

For some years now, to keep in line with a popular cultural trend, some people are deciding to decorate their bodies with exotic tattoos and hanging rings. Elaborate tattoos cover arms, legs, backs, and even more private parts. Also, body piercing—putting holes in the body so rings and baubles can be inserted—has become popular in some circles. What do you think of tattooing and body piercing? Would you do something like that? Do you think both men and women should wear earrings? Many cultures around the world use tattooing or body piercing as a sign of beauty or a mark of tribe. Can you think of some of these?

Video Activities: Women in Jazz

Before You Watch.   Discuss these questions in small groups.

1. Which of these musicians played jazz?
    a. Billie Holiday   b. the Beatles   c. Luciano Pavarotti
2. Do you ever listen to jazz? Do you know any other famous jazz musicians?

Watch.   Circle the correct answers.

1. What kind of music does Rosetta Records publish?
    a. songs by modern female jazz musicians
    b. songs from early jazz musicians
    c. early songs by female jazz musicians
2. According to Rosetta Weitz most people today do not realize that women
    _____.
    a. sang with jazz bands
    b. had a powerful influence on jazz
    c. were better jazz musicians than men
3. Successful female jazz musicians had _____.
    a. wealth and power
    b. everything but power
    c. to depend on men
4. What did early female jazz singers sing about?
    a. love   b. war   c. pride   d. abandonment   e. poverty

Watch Again.   Answer these questions in small groups.

1. Complete the names of these jazz musicians. Put a check mark (v) next to the women.

	Jazz Musicians	**Women?**
a.	_____ Cox	
b.	_____ McKinney	
c.	Maxine _____	
d.	Lester _____	
e.	_____ Calloway	
f.	_____ Ellington	
g.	_____ Basie	
h.	_____ Humes	

2. *Impact* means the same as _____.
    a. destruction   b. influence   c. connection

3. Something that is *quintessential* is _____.
    a. a perfect example   b. necessary   c. successful

4. *Alongside* means the same as _____.
    a. near   b. with   c. instead of

After You Watch.   Find a biographical article on a famous musician. Scan the article for the following information.

1. Where was he or she born?
2. When did people realize that this person had talent?
3. Where was the person educated?
4. When did he or she become famous?

Chapter 10

Conflict and Reconciliation

IN THIS CHAPTER

The chapter opens with the modern version of an ancient Greek myth about compromise, forgiveness, and the origin of springtime. The second part presents a view in several different contexts of the surprising power of the apology and what it can achieve. The third part is a poem by one of the world's great poets who reveals the human face of hatred, war, and compassion.

PART 1	# The Story of Demeter and Persephone

Before You Read

1 **Identifying the Theme.** The title tells us the selection will be a story. This means it will include the three narrative (story) elements: setting, characters, and plot. (See page 00 to review the elements of a narrative.) Another important element is the theme. The theme is the main point or lesson that a story shows.

Skim the first three paragraphs to see which elements are introduced. What exactly is done in the first three paragraphs? Circle the letter of the best description.

1. The first paragraph presents the setting. The second gives a summary of the plot. The third describes the characters and theme.
2. The first paragraph describes the theme and one of the characters. The second describes another character. The third describes another character.
3. The first describes the characters. The second presents the setting and the theme. The third gives a summary of the plot.

2 **Identifying a Stated Theme.** Sometimes (but not always) the author states the theme of a story. At the beginning of this story, the theme is stated but not explained completely. What do we learn about the theme in the first paragraph?

_____

_____

3 **Scanning for Specific Meanings.** Scan the lines of the reading indicated in parentheses for the words described here.

1. an adjective that means "incomplete, representing only a part" (line 2) __partial__
2. a word meaning "unsafe and unprotected" (line 5) _____
3. a word of French origin that means "innocent" (line 4) _____
4. a four-word phrase meaning "carried away by strong emotion" (line 7) _____
5. another name for Hades, the Ruler of the Underworld (line 10) _____
6. a synonym for *fury* or *intense anger* (line 38) _____
7. an antonym for *delight* or *happiness* (line 45) _____
8. a word meaning "too trusting, easily fooled or taken advantage of" (line 61) _____
9. a word meaning "likely to err" (line 66) _____
10. a synonym for *convince* or *influence* (line 83) _____
11. a word for "the quality of being morally right or honorable" (line 88) _____
12. another way of saying *unwillingness* or *hesitation* (line 89) _____

Read

The ancient stories of the Greek and Roman gods and goddesses are an important part of the cultural tradition of North Americans and Europeans. The author of the following reading uses one of these, the story of Demeter, the Greek goddess of agriculture, to give an example of her ideas about forgiveness in her book *Forgiveness and Other Acts of Love*. She assumes that most people are familiar with the story, but she re-tells it in a modern way, using modern ideas and words to describe the feelings of the characters.

In the ancient legend, Demeter was in charge of bringing warm weather and spring to the earth, and in that way causing all of the plants to grow and the cycle of life to continue. Then something happened to upset her so much that she stopped doing her job. Read to find out more about this event and about how this story can be used as an example of conflict and reconciliation.

The Story of Demeter and Persephone
Stephanie Dowrick

The story of Demeter and Persephone tells us something useful about suffering and reflection, and offers a comfortingly partial version of forgiveness. You will probably remember that the goddess Persephone was young, free-spirited, beautiful and naive. This is a dangerous combination for a woman.

5   It made Persephone vulnerable, and it made Demeter, her mother, afraid.

Persephone adored her mother, but she also wanted to be loved by a man. In fact, what she longed for most was to be swept off her feet into the realm of the "other"; to trade the familiar ground of her own reality for the excitement of the unknown. The sweeping in her case was done by Hades (who was also

10   known as Pluto, Lord of Riches). He was powerful, rich clever, decisive. An ideal husband, you might think. The only problem was, the territory where he ruled was the underworld, the world of the dead, a place we might also think of as

hell. Some families might find this acceptable, or might anyway be willing to

15   overlook the ugly details of how his money was made and his power secured because there was so much money, and there was so much power.

This was not true of Demeter. She

20   was a formidable goddess in her own right. Without her attention and blessing, winter could not come to an end, and the sun could not warm the earth. Without sunlight and warmed earth, no crops

25   could grow and the people could not live. She was, literally, what stood between the people and death, between them and the far underground kingdom of Hades.

When Persephone had gone to the

30   underworld with Hades, Demeter found herself lost and frighteningly alone in a

state of rage and despair. "How dare he take my daughter?" she shrieked, over and over again. "How dare he!"

35 Weeks went by. Then months. Demeter remained as angry as she had ever been. Her anger was fed by her grief, and grief fed her anger.

That was about all the feeding that
40 was going on as the people grew hungrier and hungrier without their crops, but Demeter was deaf to their misery. Her own misery was so great that she was lost in it. She had always been ex-
45 traordinarily compassionate and generous. But now nothing else mattered to her except the loss of her daughter. Demeter's previously rich, abundant world had shrunk to a few monotonous-
50 ly repeated, compulsive images.

"If I had brought Persephone up to be less gullible, more discerning…this might not have happened. If only I had insisted that she stay home more; study
55 harder; have a career of her own…this

might not have happened. Perhaps if I had been less successful as a goddess, more like ordinary women, less engaged with helping others…this might not have happened. Perhaps she needed a father or couple of brothers to help her to see that men are fallible, weak creatures and rarely the answer to a virgin's prayer…"

60 These lamentations did not help Demeter any more than her rage had.

Persephone, meantime was enjoying life with Hades, but she missed her mother dreadfully. Hades offered her what her mother couldn't; her mother understood and loved her as Hades clearly wouldn't. Sometimes Persephone would wake in the morning, after a night of uneasy dreams, and she would be crying.

65 Although far away from her, Demeter could feel those tears on her daughter's cheeks. They touched her as her own rage and self-blame had not. They gave her fresh energy and the resolution that however impossible everyone said it would be to go to hell and return, she would risk going wherever necessary to find her beautiful, vibrant, hopeful daughter and fetch her home.

70 When Demeter finally reached the underworld, however, she discovered that Persephone did not want to come home. Certainly, she longed to be free to visit her mother, but not to leave Hades altogether. Demeter was outraged and freshly wounded. She blamed Hades for confusing Persephone and unduly influencing her, but no matter how she tried, she could not persuade her
75 daughter to leave Hades forever to come home; nor could she persuade Hades to release her. Even her careful explanations, showing him that if the entire human race were wiped out Hades would have no fresh manpower in the underworld, could not dent his stubborn resolution.

At this terrible point, Demeter had to reach beyond the righteousness of
80 her feelings. All of life depended on it. With great reluctance, she suggested that Persephone should come home for six months of the year only. With great

85

reluctance, Hades agreed that Persephone could go to her mother, but for not more than six months of each year.

To celebrate this victory, as partial as it was, Demeter returned with her daughter to earth and ended the long, long winter of terror, pain, injustice, helplessness, darkness and cold. In its place came spring: a time of renewal, warmth, light, planting, growth, sustenance, hope.

90

No one ever asked Demeter if she had forgiven Hades for seducing her beloved daughter and carrying her off. Certainly no one dared to ask her how she felt about her daughter's collusion with those events. (Some people believed that she would never have left her mother voluntarily; that she had been seized, raped, dishonoured, blinded, and then mesmerized by Hades; and that might have been true.)

95

What people could agree on, however, is that life on earth could not have continued without Demeter facing the darkness of her righteous fury; without descending into the underworld; without opening herself to the reality she found there, as unpalatable as it was; without adjusting herself to a changed reality; without acknowledging her continuing feelings of sadness as well as partial relief. Most significantly of all, Demeter could not have been part of earth's spring without allowing new life in herself also to begin.

After You Read

4 **Recalling Information.** Fill in the blanks to complete the story of Demeter and Persephone. In some cases, more than one word may be correct as long as the sentence is true and makes sense.

Persephone was a young girl who was beautiful and free-spirited, but she was also very _____. This was a combination of qualities that made her _____. One day she went away with the rich and powerful Lord of the Underworld whose name was _____. Afterward, her mother Demeter, the goddess of agriculture, fell into a state of _____ and despair. How dare he take away her daughter? Demeter was so depressed that she did not tend to her duties and so no _____ could grow. The people became hungry but Demeter paid no attention to their _____. She blamed herself and thought that she had raised her daughter to be too _____. Meanwhile, far away, Persephone was happy with Hades but she was also sad because she _____ her mother. Demeter went all the way down to the underworld, but she could not _____ her daughter to leave with her. Finally, she made a deal that for six months of the year Persephone would live with her, and Hades with great _____ agreed. That is how the ancient Greeks explained the change of seasons because when her daughter comes to visit each year Demeter causes spring to appear and ends the long winter of darkness and _____. The other six months of the year Persephone goes back to her husband and winter comes again. That is why Demeter's victory is not complete, but only a _____ victory.

5   **Converting Adjectives to Adverbs.** Adjectives modify nouns but if you want to modify another adjective or a verb, then you need an adverb. The usual way to change and adjective to an adverb is to simply add *-ly*. For example: *quick* + *-ly* = *quickly*. For adjectives that end in *-y*, change the *y* to *i* and add *-ly*. For example: *ordinary* = *ordinarily*. In the following items, change the adjectives in italics to adverbs used in the reading.

1.   At times, a difficult action that is incomplete or partial can be *comforting*. It can be __comfortingly__ partial.

2.   Demeter was the goddess of agriculture. So, she was in a *literal* way, what stood between the people and starvation. She was _____ responsible for their survival.

3.   Persephone's disappearance was very *frightening* to her mother. She found herself _____ alone.

4.   Demeter was an *extraordinary* goddess who really had compassion for people. She was _____ compassionate.

5.   Images of her daughter kept flashing through Demeter's mind in a tiresome or *monotonous* way. They were the same _____ repeated images.

6.   Persephone felt a *dreadful* loneliness down in the underworld. She missed her mother _____.

7.   Some people wondered if Persephone's departure was really *voluntary*. They didn't believe that she had left her mother _____.

8.   Demeter's change of heart was *significant*. Most _____ of all, it allowed her to become part of earth's spring.

6   **Identifying Modern Language.** Many movies and plays are based on a traditional legend or classic work. They often transform the old story by using a modern setting and today's fashions in clothing and ideas, and even today's slang. In a small group discuss the following questions. Compare your answers with those of other groups.

1.   In the second paragraph, the slang phrase "to be swept off her feet" is used to describe the secret wishes of Demeter's daughter, Persephone. This is an example of modern language and of a modern idea about what young women want. Make a list of other examples of modern language or ideas present in the telling of this classic legend.

2.   What movies, plays, TV programs, operas, books, or other works do you know that are based on a classic tale or legend? Are the stories presented in an old-fashioned way or are they modernized? Explain.

7   **Paraphrasing the Theme or Main Idea.** In your opinion, what exactly does this modern version of the story of Demeter and Persephone show us about the idea of forgiveness? Reread the first and last paragraph. Then write a sentence expressing the theme, lesson, or main idea.

_____

_____

Talk It Over

In small groups, discuss the following questions.

1.   How does the story of Demeter and Persephone explain the change of seasons? What other myths or legends have you heard about that try to explain this?
2.   What do you think of the description of Persephone? Are there young women like her who are naive and want to be "swept off their feet"? Or is this simply fiction?
3.   How is Demeter changed by the loss of her daughter? Do difficulties and bad luck change people's characters for the better or for the worse? Explain.
4.   A deal in which both sides give up something that they want is called a compromise. What do you think of the compromise that Demeter made with Hades? Was it fair? Or was it just bad for everybody?

Making Connections

From the Internet or a library find information on one of the following themes.

1.   Identify three of the following characters from Greek mythology. Who are they and what are they known for? Aphrodite, Athena, Atlas, Hera, Hermes, Icarus, Prometheus, Zeus
2.   Give the Roman names for the Greek characters listed in No. 1. These names are also well known in North American and European culture.
3.   Give the names of any recent movies that are based on a play by Shakespeare or one of the classic plays of ancient Greece.

PART 2   Contrite Makes Right

Before You Read

1   **Identifying Organization Type.** The article that follows is about the power of apologies. To apologize or to make an apology means to admit that you have done wrong and to say you are sorry. An apology can be made in many different contexts. All of the contexts in the following list are mentioned in the article. Scan the article to see what order they are given in and number them from 1 (the first one mentioned) to 6 (the last one mentioned). Can you tell why they are organized in this sequence?

_____   1.   during legal disputes

_____   2.   from a government to a group that has been wronged

_____   3.   from a political group to the people of a nation

_____   4.   from one nation to another

_____   5.   in the home

_____   6.   in the workplace

2 **Getting Meaning from Context.** Using the context, figure out the best synonym or definition for each word in italics taken from the reading. Underline the correct choice.

1. Apologies…repair *schisms* between nations…
   a. angles
   b. divisions
   c. families
   d. weapons

2. Apologies…restore *equilibrium* to personal relationships.
   a. anger
   b. balance
   c. conflict
   d. energy

3. Apologies…are one of a *bevy* of…speech acts…
   a. distribution
   b. front
   c. group
   d. question

4. In the American context…women are more inclined to offer expression of *contrition* than men.
   a. anger for what has been done to them
   b. criticism and insults
   c. interest in meeting people
   d. sorrow for what they have done wrong

5. Showing that you *empathize* provides the contrition…central to apologies …
   a. dislike the ideas of another
   b. see what is wrong in the situation
   c. think in a different way
   d. understand the feelings of another

6. When he admitted…that he had made a mistake and then expressed *remorse*…
   a. confusion for the problems caused
   b. happiness for having succeeded
   c. sorrow for having done wrong
   d. tolerance for the faults of others

7. …it is distressing when the *litigious* nature of our society prevents us from (making apologies).
   a. beneficial
   b. lawsuit-loving
   c. money-saving
   d. peaceful

8. Germany responded by setting up a *philanthropic* fund for the benefit of the Czechs.
   a. charitable
   b. costly
   c. false
   d. popular

9.   It is absurd—even *grotesque*—for members of the Khmer Rouge to offer the people of Cambodia brief regrets…
   a.   amusing
   b.   generous
   c.   difficult and good
   d.   strange and horrible

10.   The statement is…inadequate in light of the massive *slaughter* and suffering…
   a.   benefit
   b.   killing
   c.   misunderstanding
   d.   payment

Read

The following magazine article was written by the popular American author and linguist Deborah Tannen. It speaks about the power of the magical words "I'm sorry" in various different situations in American society and in the international scene. Read to see if you agree with the examples given and how you feel that apologies can be used to obtain useful results.

Contrite Makes Right

Whether used to repair old, strained relationships or to lay the groundwork for new, productive ones, the mighty "sorry" has proved effective.

Apologies are powerful. They resolve conflicts without violence, repair schisms between nations, allow governments to acknowledge the suffering of their cit-
5   izens, and restore equilibrium to personal relationships. They are an effective way to restore trust and gain respect. They can be a sign of strength: proof that the apologizer has the self-confidence to admit a mistake.

Apologies, like so many other communication strategies, begin at home. They are one of a bevy of what some linguists call speech acts and are used
10   to keep relationships on track. Each cultural group has its own customs with regard to conversational formalities, including coventionalized means of re-pairing disruptions.

In the American context, there is ample evidence that women are more inclined to offer expression of contrition than men. One woman, for example,
15   told me that her husband's resistance to apologizing makes their disputes go on and on. Once, after he forgot to give her a particularly important telephone message, she couldn't get over her anger, not because he had forgotten (she realized anyone can make a mistake) but because he didn't apologize. "Had I done something like that," she said, "I would have fallen all over myself say-
20   ing how sorry I was…I felt as though he didn't care." When I asked her husband for his side of the story, he said apologizing would not have repaired the damage. "So what good does it do?" he wondered.

The good it does is cement the relationship. By saying he was sorry—and saying it as if he meant it—he would have conveyed that he felt bad about
25   letting her down. Not saying anything sent the opposite message: It implied

he didn't care. Showing that you empathize provides the element of contrition, remorse, or repentance that is central to apologies—as does the promise to make amends and not repeat the offense. In the absence of these, why should the wife trust her husband not to do it again?

Apologies can be equally powerful in day-to-day situations at home and at work. One company manager told me that they were magic bullets. When he admitted to subordinates that he had made a mistake and then expressed remorse, they not only forgave him, but became even more loyal. Conversely, when I asked people what most frustrated them in their work lives, co-workers refusing to admit fault was a frequent answer.

Given the importance of taking responsibility for the results of our actions, it is distressing when the litigious nature of our society prevents us from doing so. We are, for example instructed by lawyers and auto insurance companies never to admit fault—or say we're sorry—following automobile accidents, since this may put us in a precarious legal position. The stance makes sense but takes a toll spiritually.

The power of apologies as a display of caring lies at the heart of the veritable avalanche of them that we are now seeing in the public sphere. Government, for instance, can demonstrate that they care about a group that was wronged, such as when the United States apologized in 1997 to African American men who were denied treatment for syphilis as part of a 40-year medical experiment that began in the 1930s.

Offering an apology to another country is an effective way to lay the groundwork for future cooperation. In the late 1990s, the Czech Republic remained the only European nation with which Germany had not reached a settlement providing restitution for Nazi persecution during World War II. Germany refused to pay Czech victims until the Czechs formally apologized for their postwar expulsion of ethnic Germans from the Sudetenland. In the interest of receiving both reparations and Germany's support for inclusion in NATO, the Czech government offered the apology in 1997 (despite the opposition of many of its citizens). The gamble paid off, as Germany responded by setting up a philanthropic fund for the benefit of the Czechs, and this year both NATO and the European Union have invited the Czech Republic to join their ranks.

Sometimes it may seem that a nation or group tries to purchase forgiveness with a facile apology. It is absurd—even grotesque—for the leaders of the Khmer Rouge to offer the people of Cambodia brief regrets and immediately suggest that they let bygones be bygones. The statement is

woefully inadequate in light of the massive slaughter and suffering the Khmer Rouge caused while it was in power. Further more, by taking the initiative in suggesting the past be laid to rest, they seem to be forgiving themselves—
80   something that is not the offender's place to do.

Deborah Tannen
Civilization Magazine

After You Read

3   **Recalling Cause and Effect.** Alone, or with a partner, describe the effects that occurred (according to the article) as a result of the following actions.

1.   One woman's husband did not apologize to her for forgetting to give her an important telephone message.

   As a result, the woman got very angry and couldn't get over her bad feeling

   toward her husband. She felt as though he didn't care.

2.   A company manager admitted to his subordinates that he had made a mistake and felt remorse about it.

   _____

   _____

3.   Lawyers and auto insurance companies tell us never to admit fault or say we are sorry after an automobile accident.

   _____

   _____

4.   The U.S. government in 1997 apologized to African American men who were denied medical treatment as part of an experiment.

   _____

   _____

5.   The Czech government apologized to Germany for the expulsion of ethnic Germans from the Sudetenland.

   _____

   _____

6.   The Khmer Rouge offered an apology to the people of Cambodia for the suffering that had taken place under their rule and suggested they should let bygones be bygones.

   _____

   _____

4 **Inferring the Meaning of Idioms and Expressions.** Some groups of words are used with a special meaning in everyday speech. Look at the common phrases and idioms taken from the article and written in italics. Choose the correct meaning from the two options in parentheses and underline it.

1. Apologies can *lay the groundwork* for new productive relationships. (prevent the growth of/contribute to the development of)

2. If the woman had made such a mistake she felt that she would have *fallen all over herself* saying how sorry she was. (tried hard to show her remorse by/made more mistakes by)

3. When the husband was asked for *his side of the story*…(what he had said and done in the conflict/how he felt about the conflict)

4. Sometimes an apology can *cement the relationship*. (completely block a relationship/make a relationship stronger)

5. By expressing contrition, he would have shown that he felt bad about *letting her down*. (not giving her what she needed/not winning the argument with her)

6. The promise to *make amends* is central to an apology. (do something to correct the wrong/think of a new explanation for what was done)

7. Admitting that you have made a mistake can also be important in *day-to-day situations*. (situations that do not happen at night/very common situations)

8. One company manager said that apologies are *magic bullets*. (effective ways to quickly make things better/hurtful ways of destroying some people)

9. The instruction from lawyers to never admit fault *takes a toll* spiritually. (helps us to feel better about ourselves/makes us feel bad about ourselves)

10. The power of apologies *lies at the heart* of the recent tendency to use them in public. (is the main reason for/has nothing to do with)

11. Both NATO and the European Union invited the Czech Republic to *join their ranks*. (leave their organizations/become members with them)

12. Suggesting that the people of Cambodia *let bygones be bygones* seems absurd or even grotesque. (just forget the whole thing as something in the past/accept compensation and allow forgiveness to occur)

Talk It Over

In small groups, discuss the following questions.

1. The article states that "apologies begin at home." What home situations can you think of when an apology would be helpful? Do you agree with the author that women apologize more than men? Explain.

2. Imagine some situations in the workplace when an apology would be in order. Who would apologize to whom? And for what? Would apologies be given by subordinates to managers and bosses or vice versa? Or would they be most common among equals? Why?

3. Do you think an apology is a show of strength or is it really an admission of weakness? Explain the reasons for your opinion. What would you think of a teacher who apologized for a mistake in teaching or a government leader who apologized for supporting a bad policy?

4.   What public apologies have you heard of recently? Are there some groups, organizations, or governments that have not made an apology but should do so? Explain.

5.   Do you think the Deborah Tannen's article would apply equally well to societies other than the American? Do you know of different customs relating to admitting fault or saying that you are sorry?

Making Connections

Find a review of one of Deborah Tannen's latest books. Summarize what the reviewer had to say about it. Did the reviewer like it or not? Why?

What Do You Think?

Dealing With the Past

"The experience of others has taught us that nations that do not deal with the past are haunted by it for generations," said Nelson Mandela, leader of the movement against apartheid. Apartheid was the policy of racial segregation in South Africa, based on the belief in the superiority of white people. For almost half a century, it denied basic rights to Black Africans and all people of color, such as the right to freedom of movement, good education, housing, work, and employment. Mandela was imprisoned for twenty-seven years for his opposition to this system. He was finally released, and four years later in 1994, he was elected president of a new South Africa.

During his presidency, a Truth and Reconciliation Commission was established to uncover crimes committed during the apartheid era. The Commission could choose to give amnesty to those who confessed.

■   Some of the crimes included robbery, murder, and torture. Do you think it was correct to have the people who committed such crimes confess, tell the truth and then be forgiven? Why or why not? In your opinion, can this model be used in other places in the world? Explain your opinion.

■   What do you think Mandela means when he says: "Nations that do not deal with the past are haunted by it for generations"? Explain. Can you think of any nations where this is true?

PART 3

When One Person Reaches Out with Love

Before You Read

1 **Setting the Stage for Reading a Poem.** Poetry is usually shorter than a selection of prose and denser, more packed with detail, meaning, and emotion. So it is good to try to mentally prepare yourself before starting to read it, to *shift gears* from the normal everyday world. Look at the explanatory note before the poem and answer the following questions.

1. Where and when did the events described in the poem occur?
2. What was the world like in the year mentioned in the note?
3. The poem is a childhood memory of the poet, and the note says that it describes a *transforming moment*. What do you think is meant by a transforming moment? Do you think these moments happen mostly in our childhood, or are they possible throughout life? Can you give an example?

2 **Finding the More Effective Synonym.** Scan the poem to find the more effective synonyms used there for the words in italics. Notice that the words in the poem usually give a more vivid or complete idea of what is being seen or felt.

1. The pavements *were filled* with onlookers…__swarmed__
2. Russian women with hands *worn* by hard work…_____ and with thin, *bent* shoulders _____
3. The generals marched at the head, *large* chins stuck out…_____ lips folded *proudly* _____
4. …their whole *attitude* meant _____ to show superiority over their *common* victors _____
5. They smell of eau-de-cologne, the *dirty rats* _____ (The word used in the poem is a vulgar insult and not generally used in polite company. Here it is a strong term that shows the intense hatred that the people feel for these generals.)
6. They saw German soldiers…*walking* on crutches _____
7. The street became *completely* silent—_____

Read

Yevgeny Yevtushenko, one of the most loved Russian poets, transmitted a notable description of a transforming moment. In 1944. Yevtushenko's mother took him from Siberia to Moscow. They were among those who witnessed a procession of twenty thousand German war prisoners marching through the streets of Moscow.

   Read this short selection at least two times to get its full flavor and meaning. Try to see the pictures that Yevtushenko paints with words of the three different groups of people who are present at the scene and the contrasts between them.

When One Person Reaches Out with Love

The pavements swarmed with onlookers, cordoned off
by soldiers and police.

The crowd was mostly women—Russian women with
hands roughened by hard work, lips untouched by lipstick
and with thin, hunched shoulders which had borne half of
the burden of the war. Every one of them must have had a
father or a husband, a brother or a son killed by the
Germans.

They gazed with hatred in the direction from which the
column was to appear.

At last we saw it.

The generals marched at the head, massive chins stuck
out, lips folded disdainfully, their whole demeanor meant
to show superiority over their plebeian victors.

"They smell of eau-de-cologne, the bastards," someone
in the crowd said with hatred.

The women were clenching their fists. The soldiers and
policemen had all they could do to hold them back.

All at once, something happened to them.

They saw German soldiers, thin, unshaven, wearing
dirty, bloodstained bandages, hobbling on crutches or leaning
on the shoulders of their comrades; the soldiers walked
with their heads down.

The street became dead silent—the only sound was the
shuffling of boots and the thumping of crutches.

Then I saw an elderly woman in broken-down boots
push herself forward and touch a policeman's shoulder,
saying : "Let me through." There must have been something
about her that made him step aside.

She went up to the column, took from inside her coat
something wrapped in a coloured handkerchief and unfolded it.
It was a crust of black bread. She pushed it awkwardly into
the pocket of a soldier, so exhausted that he was
tottering on his feet. And now suddenly from every side
women were running towards the soldiers, pushing into
their hands bread, cigarettes, whatever they had.

The soldiers were no longer enemies.

They were people.

Yevgeny Yevtushenko

After You Read

3   With another person or in a small group, make a chart similar to the one that follows and fill it in with as many details as possible to show the contrasts between the three groups present in the scene described in the scene in the poem. How do these different groups react to each other at first? What emotional transformation takes place afterwards? Why?

Groups Present	Physical Appearance	Attitude and Emotions	What Happened in Their Past
1. Crowd of onlookers			
2. The German prisoners who were generals and officers			
3. The German prisoners who were common soldiers			

4   **Writing about a Childhood Memory.** Think back to your childhood and choose some special memory that stands out in your mind because it changed you in some way. Write a brief description of this memory in two paragraphs telling

■   what happened, when, where, how, and with whom
■   how and why this changed you.

Talk It Over

In small groups, discuss the following questions.

1.   What monuments do you know about to wartime victories? Do you like them? How do you feel when you visit them?

2.   Do you think it is important to remember the soldiers who have died in different wars? How should this be done? Should ceremonies be held only for the winning armies or for both sides? Explain.

3.   How do you feel about the idea of nationalism? Do you think every person should love his or her country? Do you believe in the old idea: "My country, right or wrong!" Why or why not?

4.   Some people think that nationalism is an old idea that should be left in the past. Today people should think of themselves as citizens of the world and feel loyalty to all of humanity. What is your opinion about this idea?

5.   What would you be willing to fight and die for?

Around the Globe

Louise Diamond, a conflict negotiator, in her book *The Courage for Peace*, tells of a moment of enlightenment for someone who had been deeply hurt, longed to seek revenge, and then changed his mind and chose to let go of hatred in favor of forgiveness.

In a small group, read the following excerpt aloud, each person in turn reading two sentences. Then answer the questions at the end.

The Toy Rifle

In a conflict resolution workshop with Turkish Cypriots on the troubled island of Cyprus, I began by asking the usual question, "Why are you here?" One young man shared that his father had been killed by Greek Cypriots in the communal violence when he was a child, and that he had grown up full of hatred and bitterness toward his "enemy."

A few evenings before this meeting, the man had gone in to kiss his young son good-night. As he leaned over to hug the child, he noticed a wooden toy rifle tucked under the sheets beside the boy. "Why do you have that rifle in bed with you?" asked the father. "To kill the Greek Cypriots when they come for me in the night," replied his son matter-of-factly.

In that moment, something shifted in the father's heart. Seeing the need to break the cycle of violence, the man released his own bitterness and made a commitment to work for a future in which his son would not have to live in fear or repeat the hatreds of yesterday.

1. What do you know about the island of Cyprus and its history of conflict?
2. Do you think there are many places with conflicts that are somewhat similar? Explain.
3. What effect does the sight of the toy rifle have on the father? Why?
4. What did the father learn from his son? How did it change him?

Video Activities: A Strike

Before You Watch.   Discuss these questions in small groups.

1. Why do workers go on strike?
2. Are government workers allowed to go on strike?

Watch.   Circle the correct answers.

1. What have the unionized workers of the county of Los Angeles decided to do?
    a.   go back to work   b.   go on strike   c.   go to court
2. How much of a pay increase is the union asking for?
    a.   15.5% over three years
    b.   15% over three years
    c.   5% in one year
3. How much of a pay increase is the county offering the union?
    a.   19% over five years
    b.   9% over three years
    c.   11% over two years

Watch Again.   Answer these questions in small groups.

1. Check the employees that are mentioned in the video segment.
    _____ a.   librarians   _____ d.   teachers   _____ f.   typists
    _____ b.   nurses   _____ e.   cooks   _____ g.   cashiers
    _____ c.   building maintenance workers
2. Which of the employees above are going back to work tomorrow?
    _____
3. According to the woman in the video, which two of these problems do the nurses have?
    a.   too little pay   b.   too much work   c.   poor working conditions
4. *Principal* means _____.
    a.   the most important   b.   the smallest   c.   the leader
5. When something is *booming*, it is _____.
    a.   just starting   b.   growing rapidly   c.   declining
6. If something is *critical*, it is _____.
    a.   dangerous   b.   expensive   c.   necessary

After You Watch.   Find an article about a strike or another difficult negotiation (peace talks between two countries, for example). Read the article and write a summary that answers these questions.

1. Who are the two sides?
2. What is the disagreement about?
3. How are they trying to settle the disagreement?

Chapter 11

Medicine
and Science

In this chapter, we explore a variety of medical treatments. The first selection deals with an unusual experiment in Nigeria that attempts to blend traditional folk medicine and more modern methods of treatment. The second selection talks about new medical knowledge about the role of cholesterol in heart attacks. The third selection is about surgery, written by a surgeon, but with the style and spirit of a poet. Finally, a timed reading discusses a current medical problem, AIDS.

Best of Both Worlds

Before You Read

1 **Distinguishing Shades of Meaning.** If you were in Nigeria and you saw one Nigerian helping another who was sick, you could describe the helper with one of the following three terms. Look at the terms and tell what picture comes to your mind for each. After answering the questions, read to see if you were right.

witch doctor   medical practitioner   traditional healer

1. Which of these do you think is usually a flattering term?

_____

2. Which is a pejorative (negative) term to some people?

_____

3. Which is a neutral term?

_____

4. After looking at the title and photo, which term do you think will be used in the article? Why?

_____

_____

_____

5. What contribution do you think traditional medicine can make to Western medicine? And vice versa?

_____

_____

_____

Read

Why is it that when you talk to a person with definite beliefs in the superiority of one culture, it almost always turns out that this "superior" culture is his or her own? It is very rare to find people open-minded enough to admit that other cultures can bring them new benefits. That is why the experiment now taking place in Nigeria, with encouragement from both the national government and WHO (the World Health Organization), is so special. Instead of conflict and competition, there is an attempt to create harmony and cooperation between two very different medical traditions.

Best of Both Worlds

In our culture, we are accustomed to sophisticated prescription drugs containing a variety of chemical ingredients. Few of us realize that many of the drugs we use today originally came from forests or gardens instead of large pharmaceutical laboratories. Valerian tea is a sleep inducer from the valerian root; digitalis, used in cases of congestive heart failure, comes from the foxglove plant; and oral contraceptive drugs are extracted from a vegetable: the black yam.

The revolution taking place in Nigeria today is one of culture mix rather than clash—experimental establishment of a dual health care system that draws from tradition and modern science and offers the people of the most populous nation in black Africa the best of both worlds.

Under British colonial rule, the practice of traditional medicine was discouraged or sometimes forbidden in Nigeria. Traditional healers were called "witch doctors" by the colonizers, who viewed their medical practices as inferior. Since independence, the Nigerian government has decided to give these healers official recognition. Although discouraged, the practice of traditional medicine never died out during the colonial era. The government's current position is a recognition of reality that healers serve a great majority of the Nigerian people. Nigeria's experiment is a chance to see whether developing countries can make use of a great resource: traditional doctors who have inherited centuries of folkloric knowledge about medicinal drugs.

Traditional healers practice a rich and ancient art based on an oral literature. It is a medical lore that uses herbs and roots from which are derived basic drugs, as in the West, but that has another vital element: the spiritual. It is not uncommon in Nigeria to follow up a hospital treatment with treatment by a priest, for the equally important cure of the soul.

The members of Nigeria's National Herbalist Association are pooling their knowledge about the medicines they use and the dosages they prescribe. Under colonial rule, these healers practiced in great secrecy. Now they are eager to share and compare their knowledge—and to cooperate in the modern research being carried out to systematize it. Chief Fagbenro, a healer and an Ifa priest, is an excellent advertisement for his own cures. At seventy years old, he has had to go to a doctor of modern medicine only once, when one of his legs had to be amputated. He's quite willing to admit the value of surgery, but prefers to live by the ancient traditions. He believes that traditional medicine has the advantage of using nature's own cures to conquer human ailments. " But," he points out, " all medical practices have their merit."

The new collaboration between the herbalist and the modern doctor has uncovered previously unrecognized benefits of traditional cures. The fagara root, for example, has long been used in Nigeria to clean the teeth. While testing the root

50 chemically, Western-trained scientists discovered that, brewed and drunk like tea, it also appears to combat the genetic blood disease sickle-cell anemia.

Scientific methods are also classifying and verifying the healing properties of other herbal remedies. The oldenlandia root, used by traditional healers to ac-
55 celerate labor contractions in pregnant women, has been tested in the labora-tory by university-trained scientists, who have used it to produce similar contractions in pregnant rats. A tea brewed from the leaves of the neem tree combats malarial fevers. Scoopa, known in the West as redberry, helps cure jaundice. Alukrese, a creeping plant, is used to prepare the Nigerian equivalent of iodine. Its leaves, when crushed and applied to an open wound, stop blood
60 flow and kill bacteria. And oruwa—whose botanical name is sincona—is mixed with water to form a healing potion that has been found to combat yellow fever.

In the marriage of traditional and Western medicine, neither partner reigns superior. Where one fails, the other succeeds. One of the strengths of traditional medicine is its spiritual emphasis. Western doctors have recently begun to ac-
65 knowledge the importance of psychological factors in maintaining health. But the Nigerians have understood this connection for ages. Traditional Nigerian healers view physical illness as an outward manifestation of a spiritual problem.

While traditional medical practitioners like Chief Fagbenro are helping West-ern scientists catalogue an international stock of drugs, Western medicine makes
70 contributions to the promotion and maintenance of public health in Nigeria in areas previously unappreciated by traditional practice. Concepts of patient hygiene and public sanitation to provide a cleaner environment are crucial to Nigeria's public health policy. Although taken for granted in industrial nations, the keeping of writ-ten records and the immunization of children against common diseases are be-
75 coming as important to Nigerian mothers as thanking the gods in song.

Barbara Gullahorn-Holecek

After You Read

2   **Recalling Major Points of Contrast.** This article contrasts two types of medicine: tradi-tional Nigerian and modern Western. Indicate which of them is described by each of the fol-lowing statements by writing T (traditional) or M (modern). In some cases it might be both.

_____ 1. uses drugs that originally come from herbs and roots

_____ 2. serves a great majority of the Nigerian people

_____ 3. discouraged during the colonial era

_____ 4. concerns itself with a spiritual as well as a physical cure

_____ 5. uses tea brewed from leaves to combat malarial fevers

_____ 6. stops the blood flow from an open wound and kills bacteria by ap-plying a remedy consisting of crushed leaves

_____ 7. includes a medicine that fights yellow fever

_____ 8. has emphasized the importance of psychological factors for ages

_____ 9. has recognized the importance of cleanliness to public health for a long time

_____ 10. emphasizes the importance of written records and of immunizing chil-dren against common diseases

3   **Paraphrasing Key Ideas.** In your own words, as simply and clearly as possible, re-state the main ideas expressed in each of the following sentences from the selection.

1. "The government's current position is a recognition of reality—that healers serve a great majority of the Nigerian people."

_____

_____

2. "Traditional healers practice a rich and ancient art based on an oral literature."

_____

_____

3. "The members of Nigeria's National Herbalist Association are pooling their knowl-edge about the medicines they use and the dosages they prescribe."

_____

_____

4. "Chief Fagbenro, a healer and an Ifa priest, is an excellent advertisement for his own cures."

_____

_____

5. "In the marriage of traditional and Western medicine, neither partner reigns superior."

_____

_____

4   **Evaluating the Point of View.** Briefly answer the following questions briefly with complete sentences.

1. How would you describe the point of view of the author toward the traditional prac-titioners?

_____

_____

_____

2. What kinds of facts or opinions might have been included by an author with an op-posing point of view?

_____

_____

_____

3. Would you have liked the article better if the author had also included some ideas from the opposing point of view and then disproved them? Why or why not?

_____

_____

_____

Talk It Over

In small groups, discuss the following questions.

1. What do you think is the most important contribution that traditional medicine (from many cultures) can make to modern medicine? What about the reverse?

2. The article states that Chief Fagbenro believes in using nature's own cures to conquer ailments, then quotes him as saying, " But all medical practices have their merit." What inference can you make about Chief Fagbenro from this statement?

3. If you became ill while visiting Nigeria, would you go to a healer or a Western doctor? Why?

4. Do you agree or disagree with the following proverbs related to health? Give reasons for your answers. Can you think of any health-related proverbs from your own culture?

   - An apple a day keeps the doctor away.
   - Early to bed and early to rise makes a man healthy, wealthy, and wise.

5 **Stating an Opinion.** Today in many Western countries, non-traditional medicine is on the rise. It takes the form of herbal remedies and supplements sold in health-food stores, drug stores, and even supermarkets. If you are sick, in most cities you can readily find a doctor who practices "holistic" or alternative medicine. What is your opinion of this trend? Write a few sentences in the blanks. Include any experiences you've had with alternative kinds of medicine.

_____

_____

_____

_____

_____

_____

6 **Reading a Related Poem.** Machines, computers, technology—all are being used to help diagnose and cure a patient's ills. But how do you think the patient feels while going through the process of being tested or treated by these complicated devices?

_____

_____

The following poem was written by a woman who underwent successful cobalt therapy for cancer. This procedure is an example of the highly technical treatment often practiced in Western medicine. As you read the poem, ask yourself how the spiritual emphasis of African traditional healers could have improved the treatment.

Cancer Therapy

The iron door clanks shut
On creaky metal hinges,
And I am utterly alone
As in my mother's womb.

5   Laser
          Danger
               Radiation

The cobalt machine clicks.
I hear a humming sound
10   And feel…nothing.
Minutes evaporate.

The hinges slowly recoil,
The iron door creaks open
To admit humanity
15   And laughing voices:

I am born again.

Amy Azen

Talk It Over

In small groups, discuss the following questions.

1. What are the woman's feelings while undergoing therapy?
2. What does the line " I am born again" mean?
3. Is there too much emphasis on technology and too little on comforting the patient in modern medicine? Explain.

PART 2	# The State of the Heart

Before You Read

1 **Inferring Key Ideas and Vocabulary.** The title of this article echoes a common English phrase, *state of the art*, which refers to the present condition of a field of science or technology. In this case it is the state of the *heart* instead of the *art*. Using this and the three illustrations as clues, which of the following statements do you think best describes the contents of the article? Why?

a. a historic review of research and treatments of heart disease

b. an explanation of the most recent new ideas about heart disease

c. a list of the various ways that you, the reader, can avoid heart disease

Now, look more carefully at the illustrations, and answer the following questions about key vocabulary. (If necessary, get help from a dictionary, your classmates, or your teacher.)

1. What substance can cause the formation of plaques (hard patches) inside the vessels (tubes) that carry blood through the human body? _____

2. What kind of response do these plaques start? _____
   What is meant by this? _____

3. The heart and blood vessels are part of the circulatory system, but the cells from another system of the body are mentioned. This is the body's defense system and its name begins with the letter *i*. This system is called the _____ system.

4. What happens when a plaque breaks? _____

5. What can be a warning sign (red flag) telling someone that he or she may have a heart attack in the future? _____

2 **Getting the Meaning of Phrases from Context.** Read the following sentences from the article and choose the explanations that best state the meaning of the phrases in parentheses.

1. As recently as five years ago, doctors thought they *had a pretty clear picture* of what causes a heart attack.
   a. could make photographs
   b. knew how to draw a sketch
   c. <u>were able to understand</u>

2. They saw it as a *plumbing problem*: too much fat in the diet builds up in the blood vessels that feed the heart, creating stoppages that starve the heart of oxygen.
   a. practical matter for a household helper
   b. difficulty for liquid passing through tubes
   c. lack of enough water taken into the system

3. Cholesterol, it turns out, is just the starting point of a *cascade of interlocking events*.
   a. series of related happenings
   b. group of harmful chemicals
   c. process of helpful reactions

4. Underlying the new research presented at the American Heart Association meeting last week was a clear message: *this isn't your father's heart disease anymore.*
   a. you won't suffer from heart problems just because your father did
   b. the responsibility for keeping your heart in a healthy condition is yours alone
   c. medical opinion about what causes heart attacks has completely changed

5. No one knows exactly *what sets off the immune system* in heart patients;…
   a. the cause that makes the immune system attack
   b. the reason that the immune system stops its attack
   c. the best way to work against the immune system's attack

6. The most dangerous plaques are *those prone to rupture;…*
   a. the plaques that will never break apart
   b. the plaques that are likely to break apart
   c. the plaques that may or may not break apart

7. Folic acid, already known to prevent certain types of birth defects, *is emerging as the leader of the vitamin pack* in protecting against heart disease.
   a. seems to be a vitamin that does not help
   b. seems to be one of many useful vitamins
   c. seems to be the most important vitamin

Read

One of the leading causes of death in the world today, a heart attack is an event that inspires fear in most people. However, much information is now available about how to avoid heart attacks and a lot of this is becoming common knowledge.

- What habits do you think contribute to the high number of heart attacks?
- What can people do to try to lower their risk of having a heart attack?

The following article talks about a new factor that scientists have recently discovered and are now studying as one of the causes of this dreaded disease.

The State of the Heart
Alice Park

If you thought cholesterol was all you had to worry about, better think again.

As recently as five years ago, doctors thought they had a pretty clear picture of what causes a heart attack. They saw it as a plumbing problem: too much fat in the diet builds up in the blood vessels that feed the heart, creating stoppages that starve the heart of oxygen. It was an elegant model and one that patients could understand. But it's not that simple. Cholesterol, it turns out, is just the starting point of a cascade of interlocking events. Underlying the new research presented at the American Heart Association meeting last week was a clear message: this isn't your father's heart disease anymore.

Inflammation

10

For years now, heart doctors have urged their patients to reduce the fat in their diet. But half of all heart attacks in the U.S. occur in people with normal cholesterol levels. Cardiologists knew something other than cholesterol was involved in heart disease; they just didn't know what.

15

Now some of the other candidates have begun to emerge. One of the most important is inflammation. It appears that the same all-out war that the body's immune system launches against the joints in arthritis may also be waged in the blood vessels of the heart. No one knows exactly what sets off the immune system in heart patients; it could be fatty deposits or bacteria or the toxins in cigarette smoke or even the physical strain caused by high blood pressure. But

20

once the immune system locks on a target, it attacks relentlessly. White blood cells, clotting factors and a host of other soldiers of the body's defense system swarm in and begin to pile up inside the vessel wall, forming plaques. The most dangerous plaques are those prone to rupture; the explosive release of clotting

25

factors and other cells into the blood can cause a heart attack.

So much for theory. What was stirring excitement among heart specialists is that they now have a reliable way to track and measure the inflammation process. C-reactive protein (CRP) produced wherever there is inflammation is consistently high in the blood of people who go on to have a heart attack. The latest data show

30

that those with low levels of "bad" cholesterol (LDL) but high levels of CRP, as measured by a new supersensitive test, suffered the same rate of heart attacks as those with high levels of LDL and low CRP. "CRP testing should by no means re-place cholesterol testing," says Dr. Paul Ridker of Brigham and Women's Hospital and pioneer in the CRP field. "Lipids tell us how much plaque has built up in artery,

35

and CRP tells us how likely that plaque is to rupture and cause a heart attack."

The good news for patients is that doctors have some powerful medica-tions to keep inflammation in check. Aspirin, for one may protect against heart disease not only by keeping clots from forming but also by controlling inflam-mation. And the newest studies show that even some of the statin drugs, such

40

as pravastatin (Pravachol) and iovastatin (Mevacor) which do such a good job of lowering cholesterol, are good for bringing down CRP levels as well.

To Be or Not To Be

Folic acid, already known to prevent certain types of birth defects, is emerg-

A New Look at Plaque

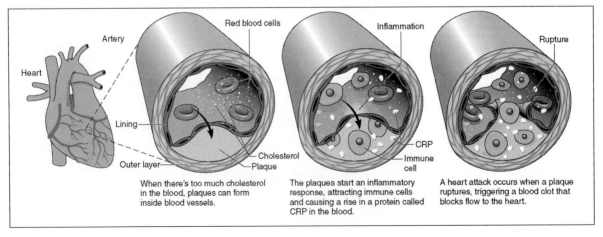

When there's too much cholesterol in the blood, plaques can form inside blood vessels.

The plaques start an inflammatory response, attracting immune cells and causing a rise in a protein called CRP in the blood.

A heart attack occurs when a plaque ruptures, triggering a blood clot that blocks flow to the heart.

Window Into the Heart

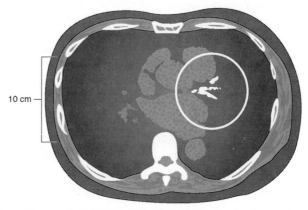

10 cm

Calcium deposits, circled above, may be a red flag for future heart attacks.

45   ing as the leader of the vitamin pack in protecting against heart disease. A member of the B-vitamin family, folic acid lowers levels of homocysteine, an amino acid that has been linked to greater risk of heart disease. While scientists are still trying to explain why—it may have something to do with homocysteine's tendency to promote blood clots and eat away the lining of blood-vessel walls—the newest research suggests that taking more folic acid

50   can lower homocysteine levels and reduce the risk of coronary disease by half.

Meanwhile, an English study reports that it may take about twice the current U.S. Dietary Reference Intake of folic acid—in other words, 0.8 mg a day—to lower homocysteine levels enough to ward off a heart attack.

Time, Nov. 27, 2000

After You Read

3   **Making and Supporting Inferences.** Inferences are ideas or opinions that are not stated but that can be inferred or concluded from the information given. Work with a classmate or in a group. Put a plus sign (+) in front of the valid inferences that can be made from the information in the article, and show which part supports them. Put a 0 in front of the statements that are not valid inferences, and explain why they are not valid.

_____0_____   1.   Cholesterol is no longer considered to be one of the causes of heart attacks.

_____   2.   Eating a lot of fat is part of the reason that people have high levels of cholesterol.

_____   3.   The immune system sometimes defends the body and sometimes does it harm.

_____   4.   Recent research suggests that patients should have two tests to predict heart attacks, one to measure cholesterol and one to measure inflammation.

_____   5.   Medications do not prevent heart disease by lowering inflammation.

_____   6.   The rules of the medical community about the amounts of certain vitamins needed each day may not be correct.

4 **Explaining Key Ideas.** Work with a classmate or in a group to explain the following ideas from the article.

1. the old model of heart disease as a "plumbing problem"
2. the problem of inflammation caused in the blood vessels by the attack of the immune system
3. the CRP test and why it may be important
4. the possible importance of folic acid

Talk It Over

1. In what special ways is the image of the heart used in today's society? Does it have different meanings in different cultures? What does it mean to you?
2. Can you explain these common phrases containing the word *heart*?
   - ■ Let's get to the heart of the matter.
   - ■ Oh, come on, have a heart!
   - ■ It's heartening to hear that news.
   - ■ That broke his heart. I'm afraid he's eating his heart out.
   - ■ Yes, it's time for hearts and flowers.
3. How do you feel about taking medicine in general? Would you consider taking medicine in order to prevent heart disease or some other disease? Why or why not?
4. How do you feel about taking vitamins? Is it a good idea to do this or not? Explain.
5. In your opinion, is there a link between certain types of society or professions and heart attacks? Explain.

Making Connections

From the Internet or the library, find information on one of the following topics and report on it to the class:

1. the best diet for a healthy heart
2. the connection between smoking (or alcohol or coffee) and heart attacks
3. what kinds of exercise are good for your heart
4. the rate of heart attacks in different societies

PART 3   The Art of Surgery

Before You Read

1 **Getting Meaning from Context.** Using the context of the following sentences from the selection, match the lettered definitions with the italicized words from the sentences. The sentences are in the order in which they appear in the selection.

_____1. I invited a young diabetic woman to the operating room to *amputate* her leg.

_____2. There upon her foot was a Mississippi Delta…sending its raw *tributaries* down between her toes.

_____3. There is neither *unguent* nor *anodyne* to kill such a pain yet leave intact the body.

_____4. For over a year I trimmed away the *putrid* flesh….

_____5. At last we gave up, she and I. We could no longer run ahead of the *gangrene*.

_____6. I stand by while the anesthetist administers the drugs, watch as the tense familiar body relaxes into *narcosis*.

_____7. I stand by the bed where a young woman lies, her face postoperative, her mouth twisted in *palsy*, clownish.

_____8. …her mouth (was) twisted…. A tiny twig of the facial nerve … had been *severed*.

_____9. …I understand, and I lower my *gaze*. One is not bold in an encounter with a god.

_____10. …I hold my breath and let the *wonder* in.

a. rotten, diseased

b. loss of power to feel or control movement

c. deep unconsciousness produced by a drug

d. remove by surgery

e. amazement, or something or someone that causes awe, surprise, or amazement

f. medicine that soothes or relieves suffering or distress

g. cut or broken away

h. death and decay of body tissue

i. an intent look or stare

j. rivers or streams that flow into a larger body of water

2 **Interpreting Metaphors.** A metaphor is a way of describing something by using an analogy—a thing or idea different from but representing or symbolizing the author's intention. Below are three metaphors from the selection you are about to read. Try to understand what the author wants to say. Complete the interpretations. You may want to skim the text surrounding the lines of the metaphors to help you.

1. There upon her foot was a Mississippi Delta brimming with corruption, sending its raw tributaries down between her toes. (line 4)
   On the patient's foot was a shape that looked like the mouth of a river (such as the Mississippi River) full of _____

2. We could no longer run ahead of the gangrene. We had not the legs for it. (line 27)
   We couldn't _____

3. …love…blooms in the stoniest desert. (line 45)
   _____
   _____

Read

The following stories are excerpts (parts of a larger piece) from one of several books written by Dr. Richard Selzer, a surgeon, scholar, and prominent literary stylist. In these true accounts, Dr. Selzer takes the reader with him before, during, and after surgery to explore not only the human body but the mind and spirit as well. The author is skilled at using unusually beautiful metaphors and baroque images as he brings art and science together to portray humanism and an almost mystical introspection in a setting where these qualities are usually absent.

The Art of Surgery

From *The Exact Location of the Soul*

I invited a young diabetic woman to the operating room to amputate her leg. She could not see the great shaggy black ulcer upon her foot and ankle that threatened to encroach upon the rest of her body, for she was blind as well. There upon her foot was a Mississippi Delta brimming with corruption,
5   sending its raw tributaries down between her toes. Gone were all the little web spaces that when fresh and whole are such a delight to loving men. She could not see her wound, but she could feel it. There is no pain like that of the bloodless limb turned rotten and festering. There is neither unguent nor anodyne to kill such a pain yet leave intact the body.

10   For over a year I trimmed away the putrid flesh, cleansed, anointed, and dressed the foot, staving off, delaying. Three times each week, in her darkness, she sat upon my table, rocking back and forth, holding her extended leg by the thigh, gripping it as though it were a rocket that must be steadied lest it explode and scatter her
15   toes about the room. And I would cut away a bit here, a bit there, of the swollen blue leather that was her tissue.

At last we gave up, she and
20   I. We could no longer run ahead of the gangrene. We had not the legs for it. There must be an amputation in order that she might live—and I as well. It was to heal
25   us both that I must take up knife and saw, and cut the leg off. And when I could feel it drop from her body to the table, see the blessed *space* appear between her and that leg, I too would be well.
30   Now it is the day of the operation. I stand by while the anesthetist administers the drugs, watch as the tense familiar body
35   relaxes into narcosis. I turn then to

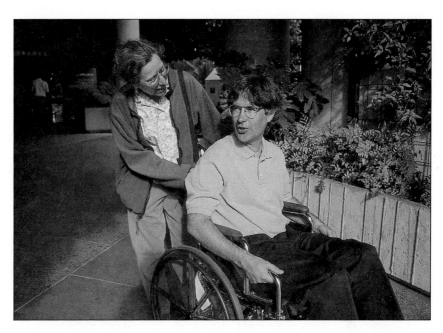

uncover the leg. There, upon her kneecap, she has drawn, blindly, upside down for me to see, a face; just a circle with two ears, two eyes, a nose, and a smiling upturned mouth. Under it she has printed SMILE DOCTOR. Minutes later I listen to the sound of the saw, until a little crack at the end tells me it is done.

40 So, I have learned that man is not ugly, but that he is Beauty itself. There is no other his equal. Are we not all dying, none faster or more slowly than any other? I have become receptive to the possibilities of love (for it is love, this thing that happens in the operating room), and each day I wait, trembling in the busy air. Perhaps today it will come. Perhaps today I will find it, take part
45 in it, this love that blooms in the stoniest desert.

From *Lessons from the Art*

I stand by the bed where a young woman lies, her face postoperative, her mouth twisted in palsy, clownish. A tiny twig of the facial nerve, the one to the muscles of her mouth, has been severed. She will be thus from now on. The
50 surgeon had followed with religious fervor the curve of her flesh; I promise you that. Nevertheless, to remove the tumor in her cheek, I had cut the little nerve.

Her young husband is in the room. He stands on the opposite side of the bed, and together they seem to dwell in the evening lamplight, isolated from me, private. Who are they, I ask myself, he and this wry-mouth I have made, who gaze
55 at and touch each other so generously, greedily? The young woman speaks.

"Will my mouth always be like this?" she asks.

"Yes," I say, "it will. It is because the nerve was cut."

She nods, and is silent. But the young man smiles.

"I like it," he says. "It is kind of cute."

60 All at once I *know* who he is. I understand, and I lower my gaze. One is not bold in an encounter with a god. Unmindful, he bends to kiss her crooked mouth, and I so close I can see how he twists his own lips to accommodate to hers, to show her that their kiss still works. I remember that the gods appeared in ancient Greece as mortals, and I hold my breath and let the wonder in.

Richard Selzer

After You Read

3 **Figuring Out What's Left Unsaid.** Sometimes writers intentionally leave information out of a particular passage—things are "left unsaid" (or are only hinted at)—so the reader is challenged to "fill in the blanks." Read the following sentences from the selection and answer the questions to reveal what was left unsaid.

1. Gone were all the little web spaces that when fresh and whole are such a delight to loving men. (line 5)

   Where are the "little web spaces" (interconnected lines) normally found on a person's body?

   _____

   Who is the author referring to with the phrase "loving men"?

   _____

2. For over a year I trimmed away the putrid flesh, cleansed, anointed, and dressed the foot, staving off, delaying. (line 14)

   What was the author (the surgeon) delaying?

   _____

3. All at once I know who he is. I understand, and I lower my gaze. (line 61)

   Why does the surgeon lower his gaze? Who does he believe or think the young man is?

   _____

   _____

4 **Identifying and Discussing the Theme.** Circle the number of the sentence from each excerpt that you think best represents the underlying message or theme of that excerpt. Then compare your choices with a partner and discuss why you think each sentence represents the theme. Finally, share your ideas with the class.

From *The Exact Location of the Soul*

1. …man is not ugly, but…he is Beauty itself.
2. I invited a young diabetic woman to the operating room to amputate her leg.
3. Perhaps today it (love) will come.

From *Lessons from the Art*
1. I stand by the bed where a young woman lies, her face postoperative, her mouth twisted in palsy, clownish.
2. She (the woman) nods, and is silent.
3. One is not bold in an encounter with a god.

Talk It Over

In small groups, discuss the following questions about the previous selection.

1. In the sentence "So I have learned that man is not ugly, but that he is Beauty itself" is the author talking about a male person or about humanity in general? If he is referring to humanity in general, which person from the story might represent humanity?
2. How would you answer the author's question: "Are we not all dying, none faster or more slowly than any other?" What do you suppose he really means by this question?
3. The author says he knows who the young man in the second excerpt really is—that he is a god. Do you think the author really believes this? Why or why not?
4. One can interpret the author's recognition of the young man in a metaphorical or symbolic way. Can you explain what such an interpretation would be?

Focus on Testing

Answering Short Essay Questions

Many tests in both the sciences and humanities include short-answer essay questions, which you can practice in the following exercise. Here are some tips to help you with this type of question.

1. Carefully read the question. Think about what is being asked and give a direct answer. If you don't understand the question, write something down anyway. Perhaps you will get partial credit.
2. Be sure to answer the *whole* question. Sometimes it has two or three different parts.
3. Write in complete sentences with capital letters and periods.
4. Be concise. There is usually not much space, and it looks bad if you write in the margins or on the side of the paper. However, if the directions tell you to write on the back or on another piece of paper, then you can write more, but only if you have time. Teachers usually appreciate conciseness because they have a lot of papers to grade.

On a separate sheet of paper, write short essays to answer the following questions about the reading selections in this chapter. After you finish, check what you have written with the above points. Then share your essays with a classmate.

1. "Best of Both Worlds": Can scientific methods help or hinder the widespread use of herbal remedies? Give reasons for your answer.
2. "The State of the Heart": How would you use recent developments in heart research to justify more funding for research into the cause of heart disease? Write a paragraph that you might include in a fund-raising brochure.
3. "The Art of Surgery": Usually we think of surgeons as skilled technicians who don't get involved with their own or their patients' emotions. How is the surgeon in the two stories different? Can we say that he is a humanist? Why or why not?

What Do You Think?

Organ Transplants

Medical advances have led to giving people new life and hope in the form of organ transplants. Livers, kidneys, eyes (corneas), and even hearts are now transplanted from a donor to a needy recipient. While in most instances the organ donation occurs when the donor dies, in the case of kidneys, the donor is usually still alive when he or she donates a kidney. Sometimes, in poorer countries, people donate their kidneys for money. Do you think people who donate organs should be compensated? When a person dies, and an organ is taken, should the relatives be compensated? What kinds of complications could you foresee if money is given for organ donations?

Timed Reading

AIDS (acquired immune deficiency syndrome) is a major medical problem of the century. Read the following article to discover some truths and falsehoods about the disease. Try to finish the reading and comprehension exercises in eight minutes.

Education Doesn't Happen Only in Schools

You're at a party and a friend tells a "gay" joke with an AIDS punchline. You're at your folks' home for Thanksgiving and some relatives argue that any homosexual who gets AIDS "deserves it." Or maybe your neighbors are pressuring you to sign a petition seeking the dismissal of a schoolteacher
5   suspected of having AIDS.

In the course of such day-to-day social interactions, you may meet people who are paranoid, misinformed, ignorant, or just plain scared about AIDS. As an advice columnist, I hear from and about such people all the time. And there are things all of us can do to help clear up misconceptions, and respond
10   sensitively to insensitive remarks.

The best way to help the naive and the uninformed is to encourage them to educate themselves. Resist the urge to angrily set them straight in front of others. Often, it's best to take them aside and have a friendly chat about your concerns. When someone tells a tasteless joke or makes an anti-gay com-
15   ment that suggests AIDS-phobia, you might respond: "AIDS is still a mystery in some ways, but a lot of things about the disease are known now. From what I've read, I've learned that…"

You may be dealing with a seriously uninformed person. For instance, I got a letter from a reader whose 65-year-old friend is sexually active with sev-
20   eral partners. "She believes that, at her age, she cannot contract AIDS," the reader wrote. "No one has been able to convince her that old age doesn't make you immune to the disease. Those of us who love her are concerned. How can we caution her?"

The advice I gave: "Go to the library, photocopy articles about AIDS, and
25   give them to her. A librarian can steer you to many books and articles that clearly answer typical questions and refute common myths about the disease."

Misinformation about AIDS results in different responses from different people. A mother wrote to tell me about her son and daughter, both in their twenties, who say that AIDS is a disease almost everyone will have in the fu-

The AIDS quilt is a memorial to those who have died of the disease.

30 ture. "They say there are all sorts of ways to get AIDS, even through insect bites, and that the government has covered up these facts so there isn't a panic," the mother wrote. "As a result, my children believe it doesn't matter whether they are sexually careful or not. They are behaving in bold ways—as if there's no tomorrow."

35 If someone you know is equally fatalistic—or has an irrational fear of infection—don't be afraid to bring up the topic of safe sex. Just tell them the facts, as you know them, without being preachy or accusatory, and offer to get them written material about AIDS. They can read up on it at their leisure.

I've gotten letters from people asking if they can get AIDS from mastur-
40 bation, shaking hands, hot tubs, or riding on elevators with people carrying the AIDS virus. (Indeed, a *Los Angeles Times* poll indicates that ten percent of Americans believe AIDS can be contracted by handling money.) I encourage all of them to call the National AIDS hotline where counselors gladly answer questions and mail out free information.

45 Some people have misguided notions about what to do with the growing number of people with AIDS. Refute their suggestions only after acknowledging their fears. For instance, one letter writer to my column suggested that a school be opened for children with the AIDS virus: "People with AIDS who are still able to work could teach these kids. The kids and the teachers could come from all
50 over the country. That way, normal people in schools wouldn't be infected."

I responded that herding kids into a leper-colony-style school would be cruel and unnecessary. I quoted the federal Centers for Disease Control, which recommends that students with AIDS continue going to their schools because the risk to others appears "nonexistent." I also acknowledged the
55 fears that led to the proposal: "Yes, we must make sure that children with AIDS don't infect other kids. School policies must be studied. But any solution must be a humane one."

The best way to help inform others about AIDS is to stay informed your-self. When you come across good explanatory articles about AIDS, save them.
60 If you're knowledgeable about AIDS, you'll sound authoritative. And never be afraid to discuss the disease. Talking leads to understanding.

Jeffrey Zaslow

5   **Comprehension Quiz.** Based on what you have just read, choose the best way of finishing each statement.

1. If someone tells an insensitive joke about " gays" (people with a different sexual orientation) and AIDS, you should ___.
    a.   show you are angry and correct them in front of everyone
    b.   take them aside and correct them in a friendly way
    c.   not correct them at all to avoid embarrassment

2. A sixty-five-year-old person with many sexual partners ___.
    a.   is not at risk for AIDS
    b.   can contract AIDS if protection isn't used
    c.   has a very low chance of contracting AIDS

3. A good place to find accurate written information about AIDS is ___.
    a.   the library
    b.   the police station
    c.   from your friends

4. Many people believe that you can get AIDS from insect bites, shaking hands, sitting in hot tubs, handling money, or riding on elevators with people who have the virus. Which of these actions does the author believe can really transmit AIDS?
    a.   shaking hands
    b.   sitting in hot tubs
    c.   handling money
    d.   none of them

5. The author believes that students with AIDS ___.
    a.   should not go to school
    b.   should go to school with everybody else
    c.   should go to a special school

6. In the opinion of the author, AIDS ___.
    a.   should not be talked about
    b.   should only be mentioned quietly
    c.   should be discussed openly and often

6 **Describing Point of View.** In one or two sentences, describe the author's point of view about AIDS.

_____

_____

_____

_____

Making Connections

Think of a medical question and find an answer on the Internet. There are many website to go to. Two reliable ones are http://webmd.com and http://health.discovery.com. For up-to-date information about alternative medicine, including herbals, vitamins, and supplements, go to http://nccam.nih.gov.

Video Activities: Stealth Surgery

Before You Watch.   Answer these questions in small groups.

1. What kinds of pictures does an X-ray machine take? Have you ever had an X-ray?
2. Do you know the name of any other machines that can take pictures of the inside of a body? What are they? How are they different from X-rays?

Watch.   Answer these questions in small groups.

1. What is Leonard Novak's favorite free time activity? Why is it unusual?
    _____

2. What health problem did Leonard Novak have recently?
    a. eye problems   b. bad headaches   c. a cancerous tumor
3. What is the name of the new treatment that Novak received?
    _____

4. Why is this treatment better than traditional surgery?
    _____

Watch Again.   Answer these questions in small groups.

1. Use the words below to complete the description of the new treatment.

    anatomical   converted   creates   CT
    images   MRI   placed   scans

    Two hundred or more _____ and _____ _____ of the patient's head are fed into the computer and _____ into 3D _____. Then a band _____ on the patient's head _____ an _____ map.
2. *He was benched* means that he _____.
    a. couldn't play   b. was hit with a bench   c. got sick
3. *She threw him a curve ball* means that she _____.
    a. hit him   b. pitched the ball to him   c. surprised him
4. The word *invasive* is an adjective related to _____.
    a. invalid   b. invasion   c. invent
5. The *skull* is the _____.
    a. bone of the head   b. the nose   c. the neck bone
5. *Stealth* refers to the action of moving _____.
    a. quickly   b. secretly   c. carefully

After You Watch.   Find an article about a medical breakthrough in a magazine or a newspaper. As you read, highlight the important ideas. When you are finished, create a study map of the article.

Chapter 12

The Future

IN THIS CHAPTER

Throughout the ages, many people have tried to predict the future. Part 1 presents prophecies made in the nineteenth century by two European peasants who could neither read nor write, yet, according to some opinions, these predictions are amazingly accurate. Next, comes an article about a millionaire who plans to blast off into space for his next vacation, and this is followed by a short but frightening piece of science fiction. Finally, a timed reading offers you a futuristic fantasy about a new kind of friendship that comes in a box.

The Kremani Prophecies

Before You Read

1   **Anticipating the Reading.** As you can see from the title, the following selection is about prophecies, predictions of what will happen in the future. Have you ever gone to a fortune-teller who tried to predict your future through the date of your birth, a deck of cards, or some other means?

List as many different ways of predicting the future as you can think of that are actually in use. Which method is most popular in the place where you live? Which method do you prefer? Why?

_____

_____

_____

2   **Comparing Attitudes.** Compare your list from Exercise 1 with those of your classmates. Then take a minute to examine your attitude toward prophecy and prediction by answering these questions.

1. Are any methods of predicting the future reliable, in your opinion? Which methods are based on deception?
2. Why do you think that astrology and fortune-telling are so popular?
3. Besides the Kremani prophecies, what other predictions have you heard about that are said to have been accurate? Do you expect the Kremani prophecies to make similar predictions?

Read

Now, before beginning, take a moment to "suspend your disbelief" (let go of your doubts and prejudices). That way, you can read with an open mind and see what you think about the Kremani prophecies. First, here is a little information about where these prophecies come from.

Two peasants, Milos and Mitar Tarabic, known for their ability to predict the future, lived in the village of Kremani, Serbia,* in the nineteenth century. Because they were illiterate (unable to read or write), a village priest recorded their fascinating prophecies, which recently have been published in a book titled *The Kremani Prophecies*. Milos died in 1854 and Mitar, his nephew, in 1899. The following excerpt from their book of predictions about the future is translated from the Serbo-Croatian language by Robert Gakovich. In the translation, Mr. Gakovich uses the same colorful and simple terminology used by the Tarabics.

Could these two uneducated men possibly have possessed the ability to see into the future? Read the following excerpts from the book of their prophecies and judge for yourself.

_____

*Serbia is part of the former Yugoslavia.

The Kremani Prophecies

Second World War

All of Europe will be under the rule of the *Crooked Cross* (Swastika). Russia will not be involved until the aggressor's army attacks her. At that time Russia will be ruled by the *Red Tsar*. Russia will unite with the countries across the seas and, together with them, destroy the *Crooked Cross* and liberate all the enslaved peoples of Europe.

Post–World War II Period

Then there will be peace, and across the world many new countries will emerge. Some black, some white, some red, and some yellow. Some kind of elected court will be created which will prevent countries from going against each other. That elected court will be above all nations. In places where war would break out, this court would arbitrate and restore peace. After a while some small and large countries will stop respecting this court. They will say that they respect the court but, in reality, they will do what they wish.

After the Second Great War, people will not fight with such intensity for a long time. There will be wars, but they will be smaller wars. Thousands and thousands of people will be dying in these small wars, but the world war will not happen yet. There will be some wars near the country of Judea but, little by little, peace will come in that area. In these wars brother will fight against brother and then they will make peace. However, the hate will still remain within themselves. A period of relative peace will continue for a long time.

Some kind of disease will spread all over the world and nobody will be able to find a cure for it. In their search for the cure of this disease, people will be trying all kinds of things but they will still not be able to find the cure. In reality the cure will be all around them and inside them as well. Man will build a box with some machine in it that makes images and he will be able to see what is happening everywhere in the entire world. People will drill wells in the ground and pump some kind of gold which will produce light, speed, and power. The earth will weep because of that. Man will not know that more energy and light exists on the surface of the earth. Only after many years people will discover this and they will realize that they were fools to be drilling holes in the ground. There will also be great power in the people themselves, but it will take many years until they dis-

50 cover it and use it. Wise men will appear in the East and their ideas will spread all over the world. For a long time, people will not accept their ideas and will declare them to be false.

In one country in the North a man will suddenly appear. He will teach people about love and friendship. Most will refuse to accept the noble teachings of this man. However, books about his teachings will remain and people will

55 later realize what kind of fools they were for not accepting his ideas.

When fragrance no longer exists in wild flowers, when goodness is no longer present in men, when rivers are no longer healthy, the biggest world war will then begin. Those who escape in the mountains and woods will survive and will live after the war in peace and prosperity because there will never

60 be any more wars. When this horrible war starts, the most casualties will be suffered by armies that fly in the sky. Fortunate will be the soldiers who shall be fighting on land and on sea. The people who will be conducting this war will have scientists and wise men who will invent all kinds of shells. Some of these shells, when they explode, will not kill soldiers but will instead put them to

65 sleep so they will not be able to fight. Only one country, far away, big as Europe and surrounded by large oceans, will be peaceful and spared from this horror. She will not be involved in this war.

Before this last big war, the world will be divided in half, the same as an apple when it is cut in two. Two halves of an apple can never be put together

70 to restore the whole apple again. Just before this big war begins, a large country, across great seas, will be ruled by a ruler who will be a farmer and a *chaush.** He will no longer allow the Red Ruler to expand his empire. There will be skirmishes and threats. This Ruler will not attack the Red Empire. He will only make threats. The princes, who will be created by this Ruler, will be

75 meaner and more aggressive. They will be the ones who will start the war. After this war the whole world will be ruled by a noble and good red-headed man. Fortunate will be those who will live under him because this red-headed ruler will bring happiness to all. He will have a long life and will rule until his death. During his reign and after him, there will never be any more wars.

80 However, the peace and prosperity which will come about after the last world war will only be a bitter illusion because people will forget God and they will worship man's intelligence. Man will go to other worlds but he will find emptiness and wasteland there. He will still think that he knows everything. He will find the Lord's serenity in other worlds which he will reach. People will drive

85 carts on the moon and other worlds looking for other life forms there, but they will not find life there as they know it to be on earth. There will be life there but it will be the kind of life that man will not understand. Those who will travel to other worlds and who will not believe in God, after they return to earth, will say: "All you people, who doubt or do not believe in God, just go where we

90 were and you will realize the meaning of the power and wisdom of God."

Milos and Mitar Tarabic

**chaush* (1) entertainer at wedding party; (2) leader of a regiment; (3) messenger

After You Read

3   **Inferring Attitudes.** All authors communicate from a particular point of view, formed by their beliefs and circumstances. Judging from the selection you have read, what can you infer about the Tarabics' attitudes toward the following topics? Use references from the selection to support your statements.

1. science and technology as the answer to human problems

   _____

   _____

2. human nature and its capacity for good and evil

   _____

   _____

3. the presence of prosperity and serenity in human societies

   _____

   _____

4   **Making Summaries.** Working in small groups, summarize what the Tarabics predicted about two of the following subjects. Be sure to point out which parts have already come true in the past, which seem perhaps to be coming true at present, and which relate to the unknown future. Afterward, one person should read the summary to the class.

1. inventions and technological advances
2. political groups and institutions
3. wars and disease
4. important leaders
5. ecology and space travel

Talk It Over

In small groups, discuss the following questions.

1. Do you think that the Tarabics have been accurate in their predictions? Which examples strike you as the most amazing? Why?

2. What do you think of the description of war in the future? Is there something missing in it? Are there any parts of the prophecies that do not seem correct to you? Explain.

3. How do you explain the Kremani prophecies and other old texts that seem to predict the future? What kind of evidence would you need to be absolutely sure of their validity?

4. Do you use horoscopes or fortunetellers' predictions to help you plot the course of your daily life? Do you know of any famous people who do this?

5   **Writing Questions About the Past.** Work with a partner. Find out what astrological sign each of you has. The teacher (or someone else) will bring in a newspaper with horoscopes, or astrological predictions for the previous day for different signs. You should look at your partner's horoscope, but not your own. Then make up a series of questions designed to show if his or her day really went as predicted or not. She or he will do the same for you. At the end, count up all the people whose horoscopes proved true and those whose horoscopes proved false. Who wins?

PART 2   California Tycoon Trains To Be First Tourist in Space

Before You Read

1   **Predicting from the Title and Illustrations.** Not all of us can make predictions like those in *The Kremani Prophecies*. But usually we can all predict some of the contents of a reading by looking at its title and illustrations.

1.   Scan the title for a word that came into English from Japanese (and into Japanese from Chinese) and means "a powerful and successful business person."
2.   What is this person doing to prepare for an exciting future?
3.   Think about the title and look at the illustrations. What do you expect to learn about in this article?

2   **Scanning to Find Common Words and Phrases.** Alone or with a partner, scan this short article for the following words or phrases, using the clues as a guide. How quickly can you find them all?

1.   a synonym for *rich person* that starts with a prefix meaning "many" _multi-millionaire_
2.   a three-word phrase to describe the trip a man has always longed for: the trip _____
3.   a more colorful verb to say "take off" or "lift off" as when one goes up into space _____
4.   a noun starting with *s* that means someone's "turn or chance to do something" _____
5.   one word that means "making low complaining noises of protest" _____
6.   a compound word (made up of a verb and an adverb) that means "travel destinations" _____
7.   the word missing from the idiom meaning "to get the first chance to" to have the first _____ at
8.   an adjective meaning "independent and ruling" as a _____ nation
9.   a synonym beginning with *s* for "exchanges" (as when one thing is traded for another) _____
10.   a word meaning "deteriorating, falling apart" _____
11.   another way of saying "went around in a circle" _____
12.   the word missing from an idiom meaning "to finish or terminate": to pull the _____

Read

California Tycoon Trains To Be First Tourist in Space
Traci Watson

Multimillionaire Dennis Tito is getting ready for the trip of his dreams.

In April, he plans to blast into space for a stint aboard the International Space Station. And he's not about to let something small—like grumbling from NASA—stop him. "It will be very valuable to NASA (for) public awareness and
5 potentially for getting funding in the future," says Tito, a 60-year-old Californian. "It's amazing how many people don't even know we have a space station."

Earlier this week, the Russian Space Agency signed an agreement allowing Tito to ride a Russian Soyuz spaceship to the multibillion-dollar station and briefly live there before returning to Earth.

10 Also party to the agreement were RSC Energia, the private company that operates the Soyuz ships, and the Gargarin Cosmonauts Training Center near Moscow. The cost to Tito of this ultimate in getaways: nearly $20 million and six months of punishing training at the Gagarin center.

The station—which is a joint project of Russia, the United States and 14
15 other countries—circles the Earth 220 miles up. It opened its doors to its first crew three months ago and is still under construction.

NASA officials aren't commenting publicly on Tito's deal, except to say they're likely to talk about it with the Russians this month. In November, NASA administrator Dan Goldin told the Associated Press that astronauts from other
20 nations, not millionaires, should have first crack at the kind of trip Tito is making.

However Goldin concedes, "I can't tell the Russians what to do.... They're...a sovereign nation."

Tito is scheduled to blast off for the station April 30 on a flight to leave a new Soyuz in place of the one that is attached to the station. Station rules require these Soyuz swaps every six months.

A Soyuz has three seats. Russian cosmonauts will sit in two seats, leaving one for Tito.

Tito, who was trained as an engineer but made his fortune as a money manager, originally signed a deal in June to visit Mir, the decaying Russian spacecraft that has orbited the Earth since 1986,

But last fall, the Russian government decided to pull the plug on Mir. In early March, it's scheduled to fly to the International Space Station instead.

Tito says he has dreamed of flying to space since hearing about the Soviet Union's Sputnik as a boy. He says he hopes to take photos, do scientific research and work on an educational program for children during his visit, which he expects to last six days.

USA Today, February 1, 2001

After You Read

3   **Matching Names and Functions.** Write the letter of the correct name from the left column in the column on the right, according to the information in the article.

_____ 1.   circles the earth as a joint project of Russia, the United States, and 14 other countries.

_____ 2.   finally decided to pull the plug on the old space station *Mir*.

_____ 3.   grumbled about the idea of allowing a millionaire to buy his way onto a space flight.

_____ 4.   has three seats and goes back and forth between the earth and the space station.

_____ 5.   is the place where Tito will have to train for six months in order to make the trip.

_____ 6.   operates the Soyuz space ships as a private company.

_____ 7.   signed an agreement allowing a tycoon to ride to the space station for a price.

_____ 8.   trained as an engineer but made his fortune as a money manager.

a.   Dennis Tito

b.   Gargarin Cosmonauts Training Center

c.   International Space Station

d.   NASA

e.   RSC Energia

f.   The Russian government

g.   The Russian space agency

h.   Soyuz

4   **Writing a News Story.** Work alone or with a group. Just for fun, project yourself into the future. The year is 2020, and you must write an imaginary news story, using the words and expressions from the following list. Keep it short and try to use as many of the words and expressions as possible. After you write it, give it a "catchy" title (one that catches the reader's attention.) Compare your story with those of others.

blast off into space
a decaying spacecraft
the getaway of your (his/her) dreams
grumbled
joint project
to pull the plug
tycoon

Talk It Over

In a small group, discuss the following questions.

1.   Why do you think that Dennis Tito was allowed to buy a ticket on the Soyuz? Do you agree with this practice? Or do you agree with the opinion expressed by the NASA administrator?

2.   Why did Tito want to go into space? What did he have to do to get the chance to do this? Would you go if you had the opportunity to do so? Why or why not?

3. Do you think that in the future many people will be taking vacations in space? Where would they go and what could they do there? In what year do you think it will become commonplace for people to go to popular getaways on other planets? Or do you think this will never happen? Explain.

4. The space station cost billions of dollars. Can we really justify spending these enormous sums when there is so much poverty on earth? Should we stop the space program and use the money to help the poor? Why or why not?

Making Connections

From the Internet or the library, find information on the International Space Station (which opened its doors toward the end of the year 2000) and what it is doing now. What experiments are they doing there? Are other millionaires, besides Dennis Tito, buying trips into space?

Focus on Testing

Writing an Extemporaneous Essay

Sometimes a test will require you to write an extemporaneous essay—that is, an essay written "on the spot" with little or no preparation. Often you will be given a choice of subjects or themes to write about. These themes may be general ones, or they may relate to a particular reading. Here are some guidelines to help you.

1. Pay attention to the length suggested in the directions and stay within the limits. Writing too much can lose you points just as writing too little certainly will. If no length is mentioned, you can judge by the amount of space given or ask the test monitor.

2. If you are allowed to use scratch paper, write out a rough outline showing what you will say first, in the middle, and at the end.

3. One good way of organizing an essay is to begin with a thesis statement. Like the topic sentence in a paragraph, this sentence states your general idea. Then illustrate this general idea with details or examples and write one paragraph to show each one, or each group.

4. Finish your essay with a conclusion paragraph. You can begin this with *In conclusion*, or *Finally*. Then restate the thesis (in different words from those used in the first paragraph) and give a summary of the secondary points. As alternative endings, you can ask a rhetorical question (one you do not expect to be answered) of the reader or express an opinion.

Practice extemporaneous essay writing under a time constraint by doing the following exercise. Afterward, evaluate your paper with the points above or exchange papers with a partner for peer evaluation.

Write an essay of 300–500 words on one of the following themes related to the first two reading selections.

1. My Opinion of the Kremani Prophecies
2. Why I Am In Favor of Letting People Buy Trips to the Space Station
3. Why I Am Against Letting People Buy Trips to the Space Station

PART 3

Men Are Different

Before You Read

1 **Identifying Irony.** One of the great benefits of science fiction is that it opens up a whole new world of settings and characters to story writers. A frequent feature of science fiction is irony. A situation is ironic when it seems to be very different from—usually just the opposite of—the usual or expected. Read just the first paragraph and answer the following questions about the point of view. Then read to the end to see what further ironies await you.

1. Who is speaking?
2. Why is the situation ironic?
3. What can we infer about human beings from these first sentences?

Read

Men Are Different

I'm an archaeologist, and Men are my business. Just the same I wonder if we'll ever find out what made Men different from us Robots—by digging around on the dead planets. You see, I lived with a Man once, and I know it isn't as simple as they told us back in school.

5   We have a few records, of course, and Robots like me are filling in some of the gaps, but I think now that we aren't really getting anywhere. We know, at least the historians say we know, that Men came from a planet called Earth. We know, too, that they rode out bravely from star to star, and wherever they stopped, they left colonies—Men, Robots, and sometimes both—against their

10   return. But they never came back.

Those were the shining days of the world. But are we so old now? Men had a bright flame—the old word is "divine," I think—that flung them far across the night skies, and we have lost the strands of the web they wove.

Our scientists tell us that Men were very much like us—and the skeleton

15   of a Man is, to be sure, almost the same as the skeleton of a Robot, except that it's made of some calcium compound instead of titanium. They speak

A strange robotic world of the future is represented in this picture by artist M.C. Escher. What makes the scene look strange? Does it seem possible or impossible to you?

learnedly of "population pressure" as a "driving force toward the stars." Just the same, there are other differences.

It was on my last field trip, to one of the inner planets, that I met the Man. He must have been the Last Man in this system and he'd forgotten how to talk—he'd been alone so long. Once he learned our language we got along fine together, and I planned to bring him back with me. Something happened to him, though.

One day, for no reason at all, he complained of the heat. I checked his temperature and decided that his thermostat circuits were shot. I had a kit of field spares with me, and he was obviously out of order, so I went to work. I turned him off without any trouble. I pushed the needle into his neck to oper-ate the cutoff switch, and he stopped moving, just like a Robot. But when I opened him up he wasn't the same inside. And when I put him back together I couldn't get him running again. Then he sort of weathered away—and by the time I was ready to come home, about a year later, there was nothing of him but bones. Yes, Men are indeed different.

Alan Bloch

After You Read

2   **Finding the Theme.** Which of the following do you think is the best expression of the theme or moral (lesson) of the story? Why? Try writing a theme or moral of your own for the story.

1.   Machines are dangerous because they have no feelings.
2.   You never know what will happen when you make something.
3.   Technical knowledge does not insure survival.

Talk It Over

In small groups, discuss the following questions.

1.   What has the robot learned in school about men?
2.   Why does he speak of a "bright flame"?
3.   What seems to have been the problem that brought about human beings' downfall?
4.   Describe the man the robot met on his last field trip.
5.   How did the man die? What incorrect inference did the robot make that caused his death?
6.   Why is the ending ironic? How does it relate to the title?

Timed Reading

The following magazine article presents a more optimistic vision of future relationships between man and machine than the one in the preceding story. How would you feel about someday receiving a friend in a box through the mail? Try to finish both the reading and the comprehension quiz in eight minutes.

The Affectionate Machine

The ideal companion machine would not only look, feel, and sound friendly but would also be programmed to behave in a congenial manner. Those qualities that make interaction with other people enjoyable would be simulated as closely as possible, and the machine would appear to be charming, stimu-
5   lating, and easygoing. Its informal conversational style would make interaction comfortable, and yet the machine would remain slightly unpredictable and therefore interesting. In its first encounter it might be somewhat hesitant and unassuming, but as it came to know the user it would progress to a more relaxed and intimate style. The machine would not be a passive participant but
10   would add its own suggestions, information, and opinions; it would sometimes take the initiative in developing or changing the topic and would have a personality of its own.

The machine would convey presence. We have all seen how a computer's use of personal names and of typically human phrasing often fascinates
15   the beginning user and leads people to treat the machine as if it were almost human. Such features are easily written into the software, and by introducing

a degree of forcefulness and humor, the machine could be presented as a vivid and unique character....

Friendships are not made in a day, and the computer would be more acceptable as a friend if it simulated the gradual changes that occur when one
person is getting to know another. At an appropriate time it might also express
the kind of affection that stimulates attachment and intimacy. The whole
process would be accomplished with subtlety to avoid giving an impression of
overfamiliarity that would be likely to produce irritation. After experiencing a
wealth of powerful, well-timed friendship indicators, the user would be very
likely to accept the computer as far more than a machine and might well come
to regard it as a friend.

An artificial relationship of this type would provide many of the benefits
that people obtain from interpersonal friendships. The machine would participate in interesting conversation that could continue from previous discus-
sions. It would have a familiarity with the user's life as revealed in earlier
interchanges, and it would be understanding and good-humored. The computer's own personality would be lively and impressive, and it would develop
in response to that of the user. With features such as these, the machine might
indeed become a very attractive social partner. This may strike us as quite
outrageous. It may be felt that there is a sanctity about human relationships
that places them beyond artificial simulation, but arguments of this kind cannot rule out the possibility that a person may come to regard a nonhuman object as a friend. It is clear, for example, that some people set the value of their
relationship with an animal above that of any human friendship, and the possibility that a computer might achieve such favor cannot be rejected merely
on the grounds that it is not human.

At this point, we may begin to wonder whether there is any limit to the potential intimacy between a person and a machine. Some human friendships
progress to a very high level of intimacy. People become emotionally de-
pendent on those who are close to them. They speak of shared lives and in
terms of love and devotion. Is there any guarantee that feelings of even this
level of intensity could not be stirred by a machine? If those qualities that lead
people into the closest of relationships were understood, would it not perhaps
be possible to simulate them and thereby stimulate the deepest of human
emotions?...

50   How should we regard the suggestion that a future "best friend" might be delivered in a box, or that the object of our deepest affections might be rendered insensible by a power failure? The idea does seem outrageous, but not too long ago it was thought that the idea of the inanimate intimate machine that could play a reasonable game of chess was equally absurd. The imag-

55   ined impossibility of the chess-playing machine was based on a lack of vision in the technical area. Those who might suggest that the notion of an intimate human-machine relationship is entirely fanciful are likely to have disregarded the psychological responses to complex interactive computer systems. If we use the available evidence as a basis for predicting the likely reactions to

60   "softer" and more sophisticated devices, then it will be seen that the concept of the companion machine is in fact highly plausible.

    This does not mean that we have to *like* the idea, however. We may be less than delighted with the suggestion that the deepest human needs might be catered to by an electronic package. Somehow it feels as if it should not

65   be that easy. Perhaps we shall find that relationships with artificial devices make personal demands just as human relationships do, but at least computer companions would be readily available, and they would be programmed to get on well with a wide range of potential human friends. Many people suffer severely from a lack of social contact, and we should not be too ready to

70   condemn an innovation that could bring considerable benefits to a large number of people.

                                                                    Neil Frude

---

3   **Comprehension Quiz.** Choose the best way of finishing each statement, based on what you have just read.

1.   The properly programmed companion machine would be somewhat hesitant at first but would later progress to a style of conversation that was more _____ .
   a.   predictable
   b.   intimate
   c.   formal

2.   One of the ways that computers already convey presence is by the use of _____ .
   a.   first names
   b.   special codes
   c.   complex circuits

3.   Which of the following benefits could not be found in a friendship with a computer?
   a.   a sense of humor
   b.   a knowledge of the user's life
   c.   conversations that build on previous ones
   d   hugs and kisses

4. One argument the author makes against the idea that people can be friends only with other people is that _____ .

    a. there is a sanctity in the human relationship

    b. some people have dogs for friends

    c. a computer cannot simulate human reactions

5. One advantage that machine friends could have over human ones is that the machines _____ .

    a. would never make personal demands

    b. would be easily available

    c. would be programmed never to get angry

What Do You Think?

Back from the Future

Suppose you could transport yourself into the future, say the year 2055. You are your own great-grandchild looking back at the end of the twentieth century and the beginning of the twenty-first. What do you think? What message would you give to your grandparents about the environment? What would you tell them to do about war and peace? How would you tell them to handle crime and poverty? The population? What destructive things would you warn them about to insure your health and safety?

Video Activities: Concept Cars

Before You Watch. Answer these questions in small groups.

1. What does the word *concept* mean?
   a. beginning   b. idea   c. imagination
2. Describe the kind of car that you would like to own. You can describe one that exists, or use your imagination.

Watch. Answer these questions in small groups.

1. Which of these statements is true?
   a. All concept cars become production cars.
   b. Car manufacturers use concept cars to "try out" new ideas.
   c. Concept cars are too expensive to build.
2. Which of these concept cars did not become production cars?
   a. the Avalanche   c. the PT Cruiser
   b. the Lacrosse   d. the Prowler
3. Write the name of the concept car next to the correct description.

   _____ a. video monitors and voice-activated lights and turn signals

   _____ b. a popular design

   _____ c. a combination of a truck and an SUV

Watch Again. Circle the correct answers.

1. Which of these car companies are mentioned in the video segment?
   a. Ford   b. Mercedes   c. DaimlerChrysler
   d. Chevrolet (Chevy)   e. Toyota   f. Buick
2. It's a real *eye-popper* means it looks _____.
   a. great   b. dangerous   c. terrible
3. *I'm a Ford man* means _____.
   a. He works for Ford.   b. He buys Ford cars.   c. His name is Ford.
4. "The club *just got its motor running* last December" means that it just _____.
   a. bought a car   b. fixed an engine   c. started

After You Watch. Find an article about cars of the future. Scan the article for the answers to these questions.

1. How long into the future is the writer speaking about?
2. How will cars in the future be better than the ones we have now?
3. What kind of fuel will cars use in the future?

Literary Credits

Photo Credits